QUOTATIONS FOR A
LIFETIME
LIFE'S GREAT TRUTHS

QUOTATIONS FOR A
LIFETIME
LIFE'S GREAT TRUTHS

BY
LARRY JOHN PHILLIPS

Progressive
RISING PHOENIX PRESS ®

Published 2025 by Progressive Rising Phoenix Press, LLC
www.progressiverisingphoenix.com

ISBN: 978-1-958640-83-8

Printed in the U.S.A.

Cover Illustration: "Old books, feather pen and ink bottle, old scroll with red wax seal, vintage compass." by Davydenko Yuliia. ShutterStock ID: 367036259, used under license from ShutterStock.com.

Book Layout by Kalpart.
Visit www.kalpart.com

TABLE OF CONTENTS

ACTION

An ounce of action is worth a ton of theory.
FRIEDRICH ENGELS

Twenty years from now you will be more disappointed by the things that you didn't do than by the ones you did do. So throw off the bowlines. Sail away from the safe harbor. Catch the trade winds in your sails. Explore. Dream. Discover.
H. JACKSON BROWN JR.

The test of any man lies in action.
PINDAR

People who know how to act are never preachers.
RALPH WALDO EMERSON

A thought which does not result in an action is nothing much, and an action which does not proceed from a thought is nothing at all.
GEORGES BERNANOS

In the arena of human life the honours and rewards fall to those who show their good qualities in action.
ARISTOTLE

We know what a person thinks not when he tells us what he thinks, but by his actions.
ISAAC SINGER

Who reflects too much will accomplish little.
FRIEDRICH SCHILLER

Think before you act.
PYTHAGORAS

I have always thought the actions of men the best interpreters of their thoughts.
JOHN LOCKE

He who desires but acts not, breeds pestilence.
WILLIAM BLAKE

The best way to make your dreams come true is to wake up.
PAUL VALE'RY

Not all of us can do great things. But we can do small things with great love.
MOTHER TERESA

Never confuse movement with action.
ERNEST HEMINGWAY

Every man feels instinctively that all the beautiful sentiments in the world weigh less than a single lovely action.
JAMES RUSSELL LOWELL

The shortest answer is action.
ENGLISH PROVERB

Strong reasons make strong actions.
WILLIAM SHAKESPEARE

Thought is the seed of action.
RALPH WALDO EMERSON

Action makes more fortunes than caution.
VAUVENARGUES

TSZE-KUNG asked what constituted a superior man. The Master said, "He acts before he speaks, and afterwards speaks according to his actions."
CONFUCIUS

If I rest, I rust.
ALDOUS HUXLEY

All worthwhile men have good thoughts, good ideas and good intentions – but precious few of them ever translate those into action.
J. H. FIELD

Take time to deliberate; but when the time for action arrives, stop thinking and go in.
ANDREW JACKSON

THY actions and thy actions alone, determine thy worth.
FICHTE

I like things to happen; and if they don't happen, I like to make them happen.
WINSTON CHURCHILL

Reward of an act is to have done it.
RALPH WALDO EMERSON

Actions will be judged according to intentions.
MUHAMMAD

For us is the life of action, of strenuous performance of duty, let us live in the harness, striving mightily; let us rather run the risk of wearing out than rusting out.
THEODORE ROOSEVELT

No being can be what he is unless he is putting his essence into action in his field.
ARNOLD J. TOYNBEE

Drastic action may be costly, but it can be less expensive than continuing inaction.
RICHARD E. NEUSTADT

No sooner said than done, so acts your man of worth.
ENNIUS

Great Talkers, little Doers.
BENJAMIN FRANKLIN

Well done is better than well said.
BENJAMIN FRANKLIN

Content yourself with doing, leave the talking to others.
BALTASAR GRACIAN

Watch what we do, not what we say.
JOHN N. MITCHELL

Some things are easier said than done.
TITUS M. PLAUTUS

After all is said and done, more is said than done.
ANONYMOUS

Action speaks louder than words.
ENGLISH SAYING

Thought is sad without action, and action is sad without thought.
HENRI FREDERICK AMIEL

Act quickly, think slowly.
GREEK SAYING

It's wonderful what we can do if we're always doing.
GEORGE WASHINGTON

The way to get started is to quit talking and begin doing.
WALT DISNEY

What you do speaks so loudly that I cannot hear what you say.
RALPH WALDO EMERSON

Leave nothing for tomorrow which can be done today.
ABRAHAM LINCOLN

It is well to think well; it is divine to act well.
HORACE MANN

Most men had rather say a smart thing than do a good one.
JOSH BILLINGS

Sayings remain meaningless until they are embodied in actions.
KAHIL GIBRAN

The great end of life is not knowledge but action.
THOMAS HUXLEY

You'll never plough a field by turning it over in your mind.
IRISH PROVERB

Act decidedly and take the consequences. No good is ever done by hesitation.
THOMAS HUXLEY

If you want to do something, do it!
TITUS M. PLAUTUS

Delay not to seize the hour!
AESCHYLUS

The rewards in business go to the man who does something with an idea.
WILLIAM BENTON

The important thing is somehow to begin.
HENRY MOORE

As long as you can start, you are all right. The juice will come.
ERNEST HEMINGWAY

The way to get ahead is to start now.
WILLIAM FEATHER

Even if you are on the right track, you'll get run over if you just sit there.
WILL ROGERS

The man who removes a mountain begins by carrying away small stones.
CHINESE PROVERB

Knowing is not enough, we must apply. Willing is not enough, we must do.
JOHANN WOLFGANG VON GOETHE

This is a world of action, and not for moping and droning in.
CHARLES DICKENS

Honors and awards fall to those who show their good qualities in action.
ARISTOTLE

There are risks and costs to a program of action. But they are far less than the long-range risks and costs of comfortable inaction.
JOHN F. KENNEDY

Above all, try something.
FRANKLIN D. ROOSEVELT

Words are mere bubbles of water, but deeds are drops of gold.
CHINESE PROVERB

A man of words and not of deeds is like a garden full of weeds.
ANONYMOUS

Talking is easy, action difficult.
SPANISH PROVERB

Men are alike in their promises. It is only in their deeds that they differ.
MOLIERE

Get good counsel before you begin; and when you have decided, act promptly.
SALLUST

Our chief defect is that we are more given to talking about things than to doing them.
JAWAHARIAL NEHRU

To think is easy. To act is difficult. To act as one thinks is the most difficult of all.
JOHANN WOLFGANG VON GOETHE

Unless a capacity for thinking be accompanied by a capacity for action, a superior mind exists in torture.
BENEDETTO CROSE

We must not waste life in devising means. It is better to plan less and do more.
WILLIAM ELLERY CHANNING

Everyone must row with the oars he has.
ENGLISH PROVERB

By his deeds we know a man.
AFRICAN PROVERB

To do is to be.
SOCRATES

Having the world's best idea will do you no good unless you act on it. People who want milk shouldn't sit on a stool in the middle of a field in hopes that a cow will back up to them.
CURTIS GRANT

The only measure of what you believe is what you do. If you want to know what people believe, don't read what they write, don't ask them what they believe, just observe what they do.

ASHLEY MONTAGU

The superior man is modest in his speech, but excels in his actions.

CONFUCIUS

Trust in God and do something.

MARY LYON

God helps them that helps themselves.

BENJAMIN FRANK.IN

Try first thyself, and after call in God, for to the worker God himself lends aid.

EURIPIDES

It behooves every man to remember that the work of the critic...is of altogether secondary importance, and that, in the end, progress is accomplished by the man who does...things.

THEODORE ROOSEVELT

Count that day lost whose slow descending sun views from thy hand no worthy action done.

JACOB BOBART

It is better to go down on the great seas which human hearts were made to sail than to rot at the wharves in ignoble anchorage.

HAMILTON WRIGHT MABIE

Activity back of a very small idea will produce more than inactivity and the planning of genius.

JAMES A. WARSHAM

It isn't what we say or think that defines us, but what we do.

JANE AUSTEN

Deeds, not words shall speak to me.
JOHN FLETCHER

God gives nothing to those who keep their arms crossed.
BAMARA PROVERB

Manliness consists not in bluff, bravado, or lordliness. It consists in daring to do the right and facing consequences, whether it is in matters social, political, or other. It consists in deeds, not in words.
MOHANDAS K. GANDHI

Words that do not match deeds are not important.
CHE GUEVARA

Action to be effective, must be directed to clearly conceived ends.
JAWAHARIAL NEHRU

'Tis what we do, not what we say, that makes us worthy of his grace.
GILDER

If you want a thing done, do it yourself.
JEAN-JACQUES ROUSSEAU

It is better to wear out than to rust out.
CUMBERLAND

All the beautiful sentiments in the world weigh less than a single lovely action.
JAMES RUSSELL LOWELL

We are always getting ready to live, but never living.
RALPH WALDO EMERSON

If he would move the world, he must first move himself.
SOCRATES

Action may not always bring happiness, but there is no happiness without action.
BENJAMIN DISRAELI

Either lead, follow, or get out of the way.
SAYING

All hard work brings profit, but mere talk leads only to poverty.
BIBLE

The world cares very little what you or I know, but it does care a great deal about what you or I do.
BOOKER T. WASHINGTON

What a man knows should find its expression in what he does.
CHRISTIAN NESTELL BOVEE

It is the greatest of all mistakes, to do nothing because you can only do little.
SYDNEY SMITH

The beginning is the most important of the work.
PLATO

Be content to act, and leave the talking to others.
BALTASAR GRACIAN

One of these days in none of these days.
ENGLISH PROVERB

Never put off till tomorrow what you can do today.
THOMAS JEFFERSON

God considered not action, but the spirit of the action. It is the intention, not the deed wherein the merit or praise of the doer consists.
PETER ABELAND

First, say to yourself what you would be; and then do what you have to do.
EPICTETUS

Inaction breeds doubt and fear. Action breeds confidence and courage. If you want to conquer fear, do not sit home and think about it. Go out and get busy.
DALE CARNEGIE

You see, in life, lots of people know what to do, but few people actually do what they know. Knowing is not enough! You must take action.
ANTHONY ROBBINS

What you do is what matters, not what you think or say or plan.
JASON FRIED

People may doubt what you say, but they will believe what you do.
LEWIS CASS

Trust only movement. Life happens at the level of events not of words. Trust movement.
ALFRED ADLER

You will never stub your toe standing still. The faster you go, the more chance there is of stubbing your toe, but the more chance you have of getting somewhere.
CHARLES F. KETTERING

Lose no time; be always employed in something useful.
BENJAMIN FRANKLIN

It is by acts and not by ideas that people live.
ANATOLE FRANCE

ADVERSITY

The beauty of the soul shines out when a man bears with composure one heavy mischance after another, not because he does not feel them, but because he is a man of high and heroic temper.

ARISTOTLE

Adversity is the first path to truth.

LORD BYRON

No man can smile in the face of adversity and mean it.

EDGAR WATSON HOWE

Adversity weakens the weak and strengthens the strong.

ANONYMOUS

He knows not his own strength that hath not met adversity.

BENJAMIN JONSON

People don't ever seem to realize that doing what's right's no guarantee against misfortune.

WILLIAM MCFEE

That which does not kill me makes me stronger.

FRIEDRICH NIETZSCHE

The drowning man is not troubled by rain.

PERSIAN PROVERB

Learn to see in another's calamity the ills which you should avoid.
PUBLILIUS SYRUS

Fire is the test of gold; adversity, of strong men.
LUCIUS ANNAEUS SENECA

Sweet are the uses of adversity, which, like the toad, ugly and venomous, wears yet a precious jewel in his head.
SHAKESPEARE

By trying, we can easily learn to endure adversity. Another man's, I mean.
MARK TWAIN

In prosperity, caution; in adversity, patience.
DUTCH PROVERB

It has done me good to be somewhat parched by the heat and drenched by the rain of life.
HENRY WADSWORTH LONGFELLOW

Adversity reveals and shapes character.
ANONYMOUS

He knows not the value of a day of pleasure who has not seen adversity.
SA'DI

If we had no winter, the spring would not be so pleasant; if we did not sometimes taste adversity, prosperity would not be so welcome.
ANNE BRADSTREET

God sometimes puts us on our backs so that we may look upward.
ANONYMOUS

The brightest crowns that are worn in heaven have been tried, and smelted, and polished, and glorified through the furnace of tribulation.
EDWIN HUBBEL CHAPIN

Stars may be seen from the bottom of a deep well, when they cannot be discerned from the top of a mountain. So are many things learned in adversity which the prosperous man dreams not of.
CHARLES SPURGEON

The good are better made by ill, as odours crushed are sweeter still.
SAMUAL ROGERS

Adversity makes men; prosperity, monsters.
FRENCH PROVERB

Advise and counsel him; if he does not listen, let adversity teach him.
JAPANESE PROVERB

Our strength often increases in proportion to the obstacles which are imposed upon it.
RENE RAPIN

Adversity is the diamond dust Heaven polishes its jewels with.
ROBERT LEIGHTON

Watch a man in times of ... adversity to discover what kind of man he is; for then at last words of truth are drawn from the depths of his heart, and the mask is torn off ...
LUCRETIUS

Adversity introduces a man to himself.
HORACE

Adversity does not break men; it makes them. Opposition and failure bring out what is in man.
COUNCILLOR

There is no education like adversity.
BENJAMIN DISRAELI

Let us be of good cheer, however, remembering that the misfortunes hardest to bear are those which never come.

JAMES RUSSELL LOWELL

Adversity makes fools lose religion; wise men use religion.

ROGER BABSON

The ultimate measure of a man is not where he stands in moments of comfort and convenience, but where he stands at times of challenges and controversy.

MARTIN LUTHER KING, JR.

Better be wise by the misfortunes of others than by your own.

AESOP

Adversity, if for no other reason, is of benefit, since it is to bring a season of sober reflection. Men see clearer at such times. Storms purify the atmosphere.

HENRY WARD BEECHER

"Times that try men's souls" are, by the same token, times that build the strength of men's soul.

ADOLPH PHILIP GOUTHEY

Adversity is sometimes hard upon a man; but for one man who can stand prosperity, there are a hundred that will stand adversity.

THOMAS CARLYLE

The diamond cannot be polished without friction, nor the man perfected without trials.

CHINESE PROVERB

Adversity leads the wise to prosperity.

GLENN FRANK

Do not be afraid of defeat. You are never so near to victory as when defeated in a good cause.

HENRY WARD BEECHER

I'll say this for adversity: people seem to be able to stand it, and that's more than I can say for prosperity.
KIN HUBBARD

Misfortune comes to all men.
CHINESE PROVERB

In the darkest hour the soul is replenished and given strength to continue and endure.
HEART WARRIOR CHOSA

He that can't endure the bad will not live to see the good.
YIDDISH PROVERB

One day in retrospect the years of struggle will strike you as the most beautiful.
SIGMUND FREUD

Come what come may, time and the hour runs through the roughest day.
WILLIAM SHAKESPEARE

Never let life's hardships disturb you...no one can avoid problems, not even saints or sages.
NICHIREN DAISHONEN

Let nothing disturb thee, let nothing affright thee, all things are passing, God changeth never.
HENRY WADSWORTH LONGFELLOW

The mass of men lead lives of quiet desperation.
HENRY DAVID THOREAU

Thy fate is the common fate of all, into each life some rain must fall, some days must be dark and dreary.
HENRY WADSWORTH LONGFELLOW

We do not live an equal life, but one of contrasts and patchwork; now a little joy, then a sorrow, now a sin, then a generous or brave action.

RALPH WALDO EMERSON

The difficulties and struggles of today are but the price we must pay for the accomplishments and victories of tomorrow.

WILLIAM J. H. BOETCKER

Difficulties should act as a tonic. They should spur us to greater exertion.

B. C. FORBES

Difficulties are meant to rouse, not discourage. The human spirit is to grow strong by conflict.

WILLIAM ELLERY CHANNING

The gem cannot be polished without friction, nor man perfected without trials.

CONFUCIUS

Many men owe the grandeur of their lives to their tremendous difficulties.

CHARLES SPURGEON

Times of general calamity and confusion have ever been productive of the greatest minds. The purist ore is produced from the hottest furnace, and the brightest thunderbolt is elicited from the darkest storms.

CHARLES CALEB COLTON

It is the surmounting of difficulties that makes heroes.

KOSSUTH

Unless a man has been kicked around a little, you can't really depend him to amount to anything.

WILLIAM FEATHER

Adversity is another way to measure the greatness of individuals. I never had a crisis that didn't make me stronger.

LOU HOLTZ

Of all the advantages which come to any young man...poverty is the greatest.
JOSIAH GILBERT HOLLAND

I would never have amounted to anything were it not for adversity. I was forced to come up the hard way.
JAMES CASH PENNEY

I thank God for my handicaps for, through them, I have found myself, my work, and my God.
HELEN KELLER

Who hath not know ill fortune, never knew himself, or his own virtue.
MALLETT

Adversity is the trial of principle. Without it a man hardly knows whether he is honest or not.
HENRY FIELDING

Difficulties are things that show what men are.
EPICTETUS

You can learn little from victory. You can learn everything from defeat.
CHRISTY MATHEWSON

A smooth sea never made a skillful mariner.
ENGLISH PROVERB

From their errors and mistakes, the wise and good learn wisdom for the future.
PLUTARCH

These things that hurt, instruct.
BENJAMIN FRANKLIN

Life can be real tough...you can either learn from your problems, or keep repeating them over and over.
MARIE OSMOND

Adversity reveals genius, prosperity conceals it.

HORACE

The greater the obstacle, the more glory in overcoming it.

MOLIERE

The harder the conflict, the more glorious the triumph. What we obtain too cheaply, we esteem too lightly; 'tis dearness only that give everything its value.

THOMAS PAINE

You are beaten to earth? Well, well what's that? Come up with a smiling face, it's nothing against you to fall down flat but to lie there – that's the disgrace.

EDMUND VANCE COOKE

Bad times have a scientific value. These are occasions a good learner would not miss.

RALPH WALDO EMERSON

It is certain that whatever seeming calamity happens to you, if you thank and praise God for it, you will turn it into a blessing.

WILLIAM LAW

I think as I look back over my life, that there was hardly a single...instance where things seemed to go against me, in which I cannot even now see that by God's profound mercy they really went for me all the while.

FRANCIS PAGET

People who escape trouble miss growth.

C. M. WARD

I don't say embrace trouble. That's as bad as treating it as an enemy. But I do say meet it as a friend, for you'll see a lot of it and had better be on speaking terms with it.

OLIVER WENDELL HOLMES, JR.

Adversity has the effect of eliciting talents which, in prosperous circumstances, would have lain dormant.

HORACE

No pain, no palm; no thorns, no throne; no gall, no glory; no cross, no crown.
WILLIAM PENN

Hardship and opposition are the native soil of manhood and self-reliance.
NEAL

Great occasions do not make heroes or cowards; they simply unveil them to the eyes of men. Silently and imperceptibly, as we wake or sleep, we grow strong or we grow weak, and at last some crisis shows us what we have become.
BISHOP WESTCOTT

Great trials seem to be a necessary preparation for great duties.
THOMSON

Nothing happens to anybody which he is not fitted by nature to bear.
MARCUS AURELIUS

You may not control all the events that happen to you but you can decide not to be reduced by them.
MAYA ANGELOU

Hardship often prepares an ordinary person for an extraordinary destiny.
C. S. LEWIS

Smooth seas do not make skillful sailors.
AFRICAN PROVERB

Afflictions are the steps to heaven.
ELIZABETH SETON

Rightly conceived, time is the friend of all who are in any way in adversity, for its mazy road winds in and out of the shadows sooner or later into sunshine, and when one is at its darkest point one can be certain that presently it will grow brighter.
ARTHUR BRYANT

The virtue of prosperity is temperance; the virtue of adversity is fortitude, which in morals is the more heroical virtue.

FRANCIS BACON

I was the son of an immigrant. I experienced bigotry, intolerance and prejudice, even as so many of you have. Instead of allowing these things to embitter me, I took them as spurs to more strenuous effort.

BERNARD BARUCH

Men are polished, through act and speech, each by each, as pebbles are smoothed on the rolling beach.

TROWBRIDGE

Little minds are too much hurt by little things; great minds are quite conscious of them, and despise them.

FRANCOIS DE LA ROCHEFOUCAULD

The most disastrous times have produced the greatest minds. The purest metal comes of the most ardent furnace, the most brilliant lighting comes of the darkest clouds.

CHATEAUBRIAND

Who has never tasted what is bitter does not know what is sweet.

GERMAN PROVERB

He that has never known adversity is but half acquainted with others, or with himself.

CHARLES CALEB COLTON

If you would not have affliction visit you twice, listen at once to what it teaches.

JAMES BURGH

Victories that are cheap, are cheap. Those only are worth having which come as the result of hard fighting.

HENRY WARD BEECHER

There has never yet been a man in our history who led a life of ease whose name is worth remembering.

THEODORE ROOSEVELT

Prosperity is not without many fears and distastes, and adversity is not without comforts and hopes.

FRANCIS BACON

The block of granite which was an obstacle on the pathway of the weak, becomes a steppingstone on the pathway of the strong.

GEORGE HENRY LEWES

Little minds are tamed and subdued by misfortune; but great minds rise above it.

WASHINGTON IRVING

In the day of prosperity be joyful, but in the day of adversity consider.

BIBLE

If adversity hath killed his thousand, prosperity hath killed his ten thousand: therefore adversity is to be preferred; the one deceives, the other instructs; the one is miserably happy, the other happily miserable; and therefore many philosophers have voluntarily sought adversity and commend it in their precepts.

ROBERT BURTON

At the timberline were the storms strike with the most fury, the sturdiest of trees are found.

ANONYMOUS

Adversity has ever been considered as the state in which a man most easily becomes acquainted with himself, being free from flatterers.

SAMUEL JOHNSON

Difficulties strengthen the mind, as well as labor does the body.

LUCIUS ANNAEUS SENECA

Prosperity doth best discover vice; but adversity doth best discover virtue.

FRANCIS BACON

That which we acquire with most difficulty we retain the longest, as those who have earned a fortune are commonly more careful of it than those who have inherited one.

CHARLES CALEB COLTON

Doing what's right is no guarantee against misfortune.
WILLIAM MCFEE

Greater dooms win greater destinies.
HERACLITUS

In misfortune, what friend remains a friend?
EURIPIDES

The misfortune of the wise is better than the prosperity of the fool.
EPICURUS

Challenges are what makes life interesting; overcoming them is what makes life meaningful.
JOSHUA J. MARINE

It is a good rule to face difficulties at the time they arise and not allow them to increase unacknowledged.
EDWARD W. ZIEGLER

Trouble is only opportunity in work clothes.
HENRY J. KAISER

The bravest sight in the world is to see a great man struggling against adversity.
LUCIUS ANNAEUS SENECA

Into each life some rain must fall.
HENRY WADSWORTH LONGFELLOW

As a rule, adversity reveals genius and prosperity conceals it.
HORACE

Strength comes from struggle; weakness from ease.
B. C. FORBES

Believe that pain is in the nature of life as is pleasure, and believe further that without struggle there can be no success either in achievement or character. Make trouble your friend. It will do something for your inner, emotional, psychic life that nothing else can possibly do.

JOHN MILLER

To know that struggle will come, to prepare for it, to know that this is what we were made for, is an indispensable basis for any victory in life.

L. R. DITZEN

ADVICE

There is nothing which we receive with so much reluctance as advice.
JOSEPH ADDISON

Fools need advice most, but wise men only are the better for it.
BENJAMIN FRANKLIN

The light that a man receiveth by counsel from another is drier and purer than that which cometh from his own understanding and judgement, which is ever infused and drenched in his affections and customs.
FRANCIS BACON

It can be no dishonor to learn from others when they speak good sense.
SOPHOCLES

Ask counsel of him who governs himself well.
LEONARDO DA VINCI

In those days Mr. Baldwin was wiser than he is now; he used frequently to take my advice.
WINSTON CHURCHILL

Advice...always gives a temporary appearance of superiority.
SAMUEL JOHNSON

The advice if the elders to young men is very apt to be as unreal as a list of the hundred best books.
OLIVER WENDELL HOLMES, JR.

In the multitude of counsellors there is safety.
BIBLE

Advice after injury is like medicine after death.
DANISH PROVERB

It is not often that any man can have so much knowledge of another, as is necessary to make instruction useful.
SAMUEL JOHNSON

We give nothing so freely as advice.
LA ROCHEFOUCAULD

A hundred sage counsels are lost upon one who cannot take advice; a hundred bits of wisdom are lost upon the unintelligent.
PANCHATANTRA

Though men give you their advice gratis, you will often be cheated if you take it.
GEORGE DENNISON PRENTICE

In giving advice seek to help, not to please, your friend.
SOLON

No enemy is worse than bad advice.
SOPHOCLES

Many receive advice, only the wise profit by it.
PUBLILIUS SYRUS

To accept good advice is but to increase one's own ability.
JOHANN WOLFGANG GOETHE

A lawyer's advice is expensive, but it will cost you more if you consult yourself.
HORACE

How can they advise, if they see but a Part?
BENJAMIN FRANKLIN

If the counsel be good, no matter who gave it.
THOMAS FULLER

When we are confronted with problems, the counsel of someone who has mastered similar problems can be of great help.
PANTANJALI

Give not advice without being ask'd, and when desired, do it briefly.
GEORGE WASHINGTON

Listen to everything a man has to say about what he knows, but don't let him advise you about what he doesn't know. And usually he doesn't know too much about what's best for you.
BARNEY BALABAN

Advice: It's more fun to give than to receive.
MALCOLM FORBES

Men give away nothing so liberally as advice.
FRANCOIS DE LA ROCHEFOUCAULD

How is it possible to expect that mankind will take advice when they will not so much as take warning?
JONATHAN SWIFT

Never trust the advice of a man in difficulties.
AESOP

Get the advice of everybody whose advice is worth having-they are very few-and then do what you think best yourself.
CHARLES STEWART PARNELL

The way of a fool seems right to him, but a wise man listens to advice.
BIBLE

He that will not be counseled cannot be helped.
THOMAS FULLER

Do not offer advice which has not been seasoned by your own performance.
HENRY S. HASKINS

Give neither advice nor salt, until you are asked for it.
ENGLISH PROVERB

The people sensible enough to give good advice are usually sensible enough to give none.
EDEN PHILLPOTTS

It takes a great man to give sound advice tactfully, but a greater to accept it graciously.
LOGAN PEARSALL SMITH

Beware of him who gives thee advice according to his own interests.
TALMUD

When we ask advice we are usually looking for an accomplice.
CHARLES DE LA GRANGE

AGE

Old age isn't so bad when you consider the alternative.
MAURICE CHEVALIER

I love everything that is old: old friends, old times, old manners, old books, old wine.
OLIVER GOLDSMITH

After the age of eighty, all contemporaries are friends.
MADAME DE DINO

When you win, you're an old pro. When you lose, you're and old man.
TY COBB

I am old enough to tell the truth. It is one of the privileges of age.
GEROGES CLEMENCEAU

To grow old is to move from passion to compassion.
ALBERT CAMUS

We must not take the faults of our youth into our old age, for old age brings with it its own defects.
JOHANN WOLFGANG VON GOETHE

An inordinate passion for pleasure is the secret of remaining young.
OSCAR WILDE

A man's as old as he's feeling, a woman as old as she looks.
MORTIMER COLLINS

Twenty years a child; twenty years running wild; twenty years a mature man – and after that, praying.
IRISH PROVERB

Probably the happiest period in life most frequently is in middle age, when the eager passions of youth are cooled and the infirmities of age not yet begun.
THOMAS ARNOLD

Old men for counsel, young men for action.
ADOLPH PHILIP GOUTHEY

Only years make men. Rarely do the great men of history distinguish themselves before they are fifty, and between fifty and eighty they do their best work – both as regards quality and quantity.
ADOLPH PHILIP GOUTHEY

After a certain number of years, our faces become our biographies.
CYNTHIA OZICK

As we grow old, the beauty steals inward.
E. BRONSON ALCOTT

The older I get, the greater power I seem to have to help the world; I am like a snowball – the further I am rolled, the more I gain.
SUSAN B. ANTHONY

To me, old age is always fifteen year older than I am.
BERNARD M. BARUGH

Old age takes away from us what we have inherited and gives us what we have earned.
GERALD BRENAN

Getting old ain't for sissies.
BETTE DAVIS

Wrinkles – the service stripes of life.
ANONYMOUS

One of the delights known to age, and beyond the grasp of youth, is that of 'not going'!
J. B. PRIESTLEY

Times go by: reputation increases, ability declines.
DAG HAMMARSKJOLD

Most men spend the first half of their lives making the second half miserable.
JEAN DE LA BRUYERE

A youth without fire is followed by an old age without experience.
CHARLES CALEB COLTON

Few people know how to be old.
FRANCOIS DE LA ROCHEFOUCAULD

In youth the days are short and the years are long; in old age the years are short and the days long.
NIKITA PANIN

Young men think old men are fools; but old men know young men are fools.
GEORGE CHAPMAN

All would live long, but none would be old.
BENJAMIN FRANKLIN

As for old age, embrace and love it. It abounds with pleasure if you know how to use it. The gradually declining years are among the sweetest in a man's life, and I maintain that, even when they have reached the extreme limit, they have pleasure still.
LUCIUS ANNAEUS SENECA

If you do not have to worry about money matters, then old age may bring the joy of old books and old friends. If you love birds and animals, trees, grass, and blue skies – if you like good humor and beautiful pictures – then the hours may be brimful of golden happiness.

GRENVILLE KLEISER

If wrinkles must be written upon our brows, let them not be written upon the heart. The spirit should not grow old.

JAMES A. GARFIELD

How beautiful can time with goodness make an old man look.

DOUGLASS WILLIAM JERROD

To keep the heart unwrinkled, to be hopeful, kindly, cheerful, reverent – that is to triumph over old age.

THOMAS BAILEY

Within, I do not find wrinkles and used heart, but unspent youth.

RALPH WALDO EMERSON

To know how to grow old is the master work of wisdom, and one of the most difficult chapters in the great art of living.

HENRI FREDERIC AMIEL

Nearly two-thirds of all the greatest deeds ever performed by human beings – the victories in battle, the greatest books, the greatest pictures and statues – have been accomplished after the age of sixty.

ALBERT E. WIGGAM

If the young only knew; if the old only could.

FRENCH SAYING

Oh to be seventy again.

OLIVER WENDELL HOLMES, JR.

An old man loved is winter with flowers.

GERMAN PROVERB

When a man's friends begin to compliment him about looking young, he may be sure that they think he is growing old.
WASHINGTON IRVING

My diseases are an asthma and a dropsy, and what is less curable, seventy-five.
SAMUEL JOHNSON

A person is not old until regrets take the place of hopes and plans.
SCOTT NEARING

Nothing is more beautiful than cheerfulness in an old face.
JEAN PAUL FRIEDRICH RICHTER

The whiter my hair becomes, the more ready people are to believe what say.
BERTRAND RUSSELL

Wrinkles should merely indicate where the smiles have been.
MARK TWAIN

All of a sudden, I'm older than my parents were when I thought they were old.
LOIS WYSE

There is no fool like an old fool.
ENGLISH SAYING

Old Boys have their Playthings as well as young Ones; the Difference is only in the price.
BENJAMIN FRANKLIN

They who would be young when they are old must be old when they are young.
JOHN RAY

From birth to age 18, a girl needs good parents, from 18 to 35 she needs good looks, from 35 to 55 she needs a good personality, and from 55 on she needs cash.
SOPHIE TUCKER

I am not young enough to know everything.

OSCAR WILDE

A comfortable old age is the reward of a well spent youth. Instead of its bringing sad and melancholy prospects of decay, it would give us hopes of eternal youth in a better world.

MAURICE CHEVALIER

A man growing old becomes a child again.

SOPHOCLES

After you're older, two things are possibly more important than any others: health and money.

HELEN GURLEY BROWN

Age is a very high price to pay for maturity.

TOM STOPPARD

Anyone who stops learning is old, whether at twenty or eighty. Anyone who keeps learning stays young. The greatest thing in life is to keep your mind young.

HENRY FORD

As men get older, the toys get more expensive.

MARVIN DAVIS

Old age is like a plane flying through a storm. Once you're aboard, there's nothing you can do.

GOLDA MEIR

Old age, believe me, is a good and pleasant thing. It is true you are gently shouldered off the stage, but then you are given such a comfortable front stall as spectator.

CONFUCIUS

We pay when old for the excesses of youth.

J. B. PRIESTLEY

Youth is the best time to be rich, and the best time to be poor.
EURIPIDES

A man is not old until regrets take the place of dreams.
JOHN BARRYMORE

At twenty a man is full of fight and hope. He wants to reform the world. When he's seventy he still wants to reform the world, but he knows he can't.
CLARENCE DARROW

I used to think that the main-spring was broken by 80, although my father kept on writing. I hope I was wrong for I am keeping on in the same way. I like it and want to produce as long as I can.
OLIVER WENDELL HOLMES, JR.

Of all the faculties of the human mind that of memory is the first which suffers decay from age.
THOMAS JEFFERSON

To be seventy years old is like climbing the Alps. You reach a snow-crowned summit, and see behind you the deep valley stretching miles and miles away, and before you other summits higher and whiter, which you may have strength to climb, or may not. Then you sit down and meditate and wonder which it will be.
HENRY WADSWORTH LONGFELLOW

I promise to keep on living as though I expected to live forever. Nobody grows old by merely living a number of years. People grow old only by deserting their ideals. Years may wrinkle the skin, but to give up interest wrinkles the soul.
DOUGLAS MACARTHUR

No one grows old by living – only by losing interest in living.
MARIE RAY

Every man desires to live long; but no man would be old.
JONATHAN SWIFT

At 20 years of age, the will reigns; at 30, the wit; and at 40, the judgement.
BENJAMIN FRANKLIN

Each part of life has its own pleasures. Each has its own abundant harvest, to be garnered in season. We may grow old in body, but we need never grow old in mind and spirit. We must make a stand against old age. We must atone for its faults by activity. We must exercise the mind as we exercise the body, to keep it supple and buoyant. Life may be short, but it is long enough to live honorably and well. Old age is the consummation of life, rich in blessings.
MARCUS TULLIUS CICERO

I shall grow old, but never lose life's zest, because the road's last turn will be the best.
HENRY VAN DYKE

That man never grows old who keeps a child in his heart. A healthy old fellow, who is not a fool, is the happiest creature living.
SIR RICHARD STEELE

Age appears to be best in four things, - old wood best to burn, old wine to drink, old friends to trust, and old authors to read.
FRANCIS BACON

Youth will never live to age unless they keep themselves in health with exercise, and in heart with joyfulness.
PHILIP SIDNEY

Age considers; youth ventures.
HERMANN RAUPACH

When young, one is confident to be able to build palaces for mankind, but when the time comes one has one's hands full just to be able to remove their trash.
JOHANN WOLFGANG VON GOETHE

The woman who tells her age is either too young to have anything to lose or too old to have anything to gain.
CHINESE PROVERB

Nobody loves life like him who is growing old.
SOPHOCLES

It is time to be old. To take in sail.
RALPH WALDO EMERSON

No wise man ever wished to be younger.
JONATHON SWIFT

AMBITION

A man's worth is no greater than the worth of his ambitions.
MARCUS AURELIUS

Keep away from those who try to belittle your ambitions. Small people always do that, but the really great make you believe that you, too, can become great.
MARK TWAIN

The people who are crazy enough to think they can change the world are the ones who do.
STEVE JOBS

There is one weakness in people for which there is no remedy. It is the universal weakness of lack of ambition.
NAPOLEON HILL

What shall it profit a man, if he shall gain the whole world, and lose his own soul?
BIBLE

No bird soars too high, if he soars with his own wings.
WILLIAM BLAKE

All ambitions are lawful except those which climb upward on the miseries or credulities of mankind.
JOSEPH CONRAD

A feeble man can see the farms that are fenced and tilled, the houses that are built. The strong man sees the possible houses and farms. His eye makes estates as fast as the sun breeds clouds.
RALPH WALDO EMERSON

The greatest evil which fortune can inflict on men is to endow them with small talents and great ambition.

VAUVENARGUES

Whether life is smooth or rough, ambition we must have, or die at the hands of our own laziness.

ADOLPH PHILIP GOUTHEY

A man will remain a rag-picker as long as he has only the vision of a rag-picker.

ORISON SWETT MARDEN

If you would hit the mark, you must aim a little above it.

HENRY WADSWORTH LONGFELLOW

The successful man has ambition: before an engine has any power, it must have a fire under the boilers. Ambition was the fire that stirred Edison, Lindbergh, and other successful men who have been more interested in achievement than in public applause.

A. B. ZU TAVERN

Every man is capable of being something better than he is.

ROY L. SMITH

If I had not had so much ambition and had not tried to do so many things, I probably would have been happier, but less useful.

THOMAS ALVA EDISON

Ambition is the fuel of achievement.

JOSEPH EPSTEIN

Nothing humbler than ambition, when it is about to climb.

BENJAMIN FRANKLIN

You are ambitious, which, within reasonable bounds, does good rather than harm.

ABRAHAM LINCOLN

Nothing great will ever be achieved without great men, and men are great only if they are determined to be so.
CHARLES DE GAULLE

Ambition is the grand enemy of all peace.
JOHN COWPER POWYS

Ambition! Powerful source of good and ill!
EDWARD YOUNG

Hitch your wagon to a star.
RALPH WALDO EMERSON

Without ambition, one starts nothing. Without work, one finishes nothing. The prize will not be sent to you. You have to win it.
RALPH WALDO EMERSON

Intelligence without ambition is a bird without wings.
WALTER H. COTTINGHAM

A young man without ambition is an old man waiting to be.
STEVEN BRUST

Ambition beats genius 99 percent of the time.
JAY LENO

A man without ambition is dead. A man with ambition but no love is dead. A man with ambition and love for his blessings here on earth is ever so alive.
PEARL BAILEY

It is a good thing to rise in the world. The ambition to do so is the very salt of the earth. It is the parent of all enterprise, and the cause of all improvement.
ANTHONY TROLLOPE

A dream without ambition is like a car without gas...you're not going anywhere.
SEAN HAMPTON

Big results require big ambitions.
HERACLITUS

A slave has but one master; an ambitious man has as many masters as there are people who may be useful in bettering his position.
JEAN DE LA BRUYERE

Every human mind is a great slumbering power until awakened by keen desire and by definite resolution to do.
EDGAR F. ROBERTS

Ambition is the germ from which all growth of nobleness proceeds.
T. D. ENGLISH

You will become as small as your controlling desire; as great as your dominant aspiration.
JAMES ALLEN

Nothing arouses ambition so much in the heart as the trumpet-clang of another's fame.
BALTASAR GRACIAN

You can't hold a man down without staying down with him.
BOOKER T. WASHINGTON

Most people would succeed in small things if they were not troubled with great ambition.
HENRY WADSWORTH LONGFELLOW

Ambition is so powerful a passion in the human breast that however high we reach we are never satisfied.
NICCOLO MACHIAVELLI

Ambition's a good thing if you've got it headed in the right direction.
JOSH WISE

ANGER

The greatest remedy for anger is delay.
LUCIUS ANNAEUS SENECA

If you are patient in one moment of anger, you will escape a hundred days of sorrow.
CHINESE PROVERB

No man can think clearly when his fists are clenched.
GEORGE JEAN NATHAN

A soft answer turneth away wrath; but grievous words stir up anger.
BIBLE

How many a day has been saddened and darkened by an angry word.
JOHN LUBBOCK

Anger manages everything badly.
P. STATIUS

Never answer a letter while you are angry.
CHINESE PROVERB

Anger resteth in the bosom of fools.
BIBLE

Anger is a bad counsellor.
FRENCH PROVERB

Anger is never without a reason, but seldom with a good one.
BENJAMIN FRANKLIN

When angry, count to four before you speak; if very angry, an hundred.
THOMAS JEFFERSON

Always shun whatever may make you angry.
PUBLILIUS SYRUS

Anger itself is much more hurtful for us than the injury that provokes it.
LUCIUS ANNAEUS SENECA

Anger is a wind which blows out the lamp of the mind.
ROBERT GREEN INGERSOLL

He that is soon angry dealeth foolishly.
BIBLE

He that is slow to wrath is of great understanding: but he that is hasty of spirit exalteth folly.
BIBLE

How much more grievous are the consequences of anger than the causes of it.
MARCUS AURELIUS

Surround yourself with those who are slow to anger, not those who are free from anger.
J. S. FELTS

People who fly into a rage always make a bad landing.
WILL ROGERS

Anyone who angers you conquers you.
SISTER KENNY

No matter how much someone deserves your anger, the anger itself does not hurt that person as much as it hurts you.
NINA WALTER

Anger is a thief that seizes control of man's faculties and uses them blindly and destructively. Usually a man who loses his temper also temporarily loses his ability to think logically.
LOWELL FILLMORE

Anger is momentary passion, so control your passion or it will control you.
HORACE

Holding on to anger is like grasping a hot coal with the intent of throwing it at someone else; you are the one who gets burned.
BUDDHA

Whatever is begun in anger ends in shame.
BENJAMIN FRANKLIN

For every minute you remain angry, you give up sixty seconds of peace of mind.
RALPH WALDO EMERSON

The angry people are those people who are most afraid.
DR. ROBERT ANTHONY

Anger dwells only in the bosom of fools.
ALBERT EINSTEIN

Anger is an acid that can do more harm to the vessel in which it is stored than to anything on which it is poured.
MARK TWAIN

Every time you get angry, you poison your own system.
ALFRED ARMAND MONTAPERT

When anger rises, think of the consequences.
CONFUCIUS

Anybody can become angry – that is easy. But to be angry with the right person, and to the right degree, and at the right time, and for the right purpose, and in the right way – that is not within everybody's power and is not easy.
ARISTOTLE

What was anger when it was new became hatred when it was turned into long continuance. Anger is a weed, hatred, a tree.
SAINT AUGUSTINE

Anger blows out the lamp of the mind. In the examination of a great and important question, everyone should be serene, slow-pulsed, and calm.
ROBERT GREEN INGERSOLL

The best fighter is never angry.
LAO TZU

Hesitation is the best cure for anger.
LUCIUS ANNAEUS SENECA

It is easy to fly into a passion - anybody can do that – but to be angry with the right person and to the right extent and at the right time and with the right object and in the right way – that is not easy, and it is not everyone who can do it.
ARISTOTLE

No person is important enough to make me angry.
CARLOS CASTANEDA

There is no sight so ugly as the human face in anger.
LOUISE FITZHUGH

A man is about as big as the things that make him angry.
WINSTON CHURCHILL

Never answer an angry word with an angry word. It's the second one that makes the quarrel.

W. A. NANCE

People in a temper often say a lot of silly, terrible things they mean.

PENELOPE GILLIAT

To rule one's anger is well; to prevent it is still better.

TYRON EDWARDS

ANXIETY

Do not look forward to what might happen tomorrow; the same Everlasting Father who cares for you today will take care of you tomorrow and every day. Either He will shield you from suffering, or He will give you unfailing strength to bear it. Be at peace then and put aside all anxious thoughts and imaginations.

FRANCIS DE SALES

Anxiety is the poison of human life.

HUGH BLAIR

Nothing in the affairs of men is worthy of great anxiety.

PLATO

Anxiety is the rust of life, destroying its brightness and weakening its power. A childlike and abiding trust in Providence is its best preventative and remedy.

TRYON EDWARDS

Anxiety is the interest paid on trouble before it is due.

DEAN WILLIAM R. INGE

If you want to conquer the anxiety of life, live in the moment, live in the breath.

AMIT RAY

The more you pray, the less you'll panic. The more you worship, the less you worry. You'll feel more patient and less pressured.

RICK WARREN

Worry often gives a small thing a big shadow.

SWEDISH PROVERB

What else does anxiety about the future bring you but sorrow upon sorrow?
THOMAS A' KEMPIS

Do not anticipate trouble or worry about what may never happen. Keep in the sunlight.
BENJAMIN FRANKLIN

Nothing diminishes anxiety faster than action.
WALTER ANDERSON

Surrender to what is, let go what was, and have faith in what will be.
SONIA RICOTTI

How much pain have cost us the evils which have never happened.
THOMAS JEFFERSON

Everyone remembers the remark of the old man at the point of death, that his life had been full of troubles - most of which had never happened.
WINSTON CHURCHILL

For us, there is only the trying. The rest is not our business.
T. S. ELIOT

There must be quite a few things that a hot bath won't cure, but I don't know many of them.
SYLVIA PLATH

There is only one way to happiness and that is to cease worrying about things which are beyond the power of our will.
EPICTETUS

Do what you can, with what you've got, where you are.
THEODORE ROOSEVELT

Most men, however brave, have some anxiety or fear in them.

BABUR

Why worry one's head over a thing that is inevitable? Why die before one's death?

MOHANDAS K. GANDHI

Anonymous: Who suffers most from anxiety?

Bion: He who is ambitious of the greatest property.

BION

Do not be anxious about tomorrow, for tomorrow will be anxious for itself. Let the day's own trouble be sufficient for the day.

BIBLE

Nothing in life is more remarkable than the unnecessary anxiety which we endure, and generally create ourselves.

BENJAMIN DISRAELI

Every tomorrow has two handles. We can take hold of it with the handle of anxiety or the handle of faith.

HENRY WARD BEECHER

It is not the cares of today, but the cares tomorrow, that weigh a man down. For the needs of today we have corresponding strength given. For the morrow we are told to trust. It is not ours yet.

GEORGE MACDONALD

Take therefore no thought of the morrow; for the morrow shall take thought for the things of itself.

BIBLE

There is little peace or comfort in life if we are always anxious as to future events. He that worries himself with the dread of possible contingencies will never be at rest.

SAMUEL JOHNSON

Why are ye fearful, O ye of little faith.

BIBLE

He is well along the road to perfect manhood who does not allow the thousand little worries of life to embitter his temper, or disturb his equanimity. An undivided heart which worships God alone, and trusts him as it should, is raised above anxiety for earthly wants.

JOHN CUNNINGHAM GEIKIE

The beginning of anxiety is the end of faith, and the beginning of true faith is the end of anxiety.

GEORGE MULLER

Learn to do thy part, and leave the rest to God.

JOHN HENRY NEWMAN

It has been well said that are anxiety does not empty tomorrow of its sorrows, but only empties today of its strength.

CHARLES SPURGEON

APPEARANCE

Beware as long as you live, of judging men by their outward appearance.
JEAN DE LA FONTAINE

Man looketh on the outward appearance, but the Lord looketh on the heart.
BIBLE

Appearances are very deceitful.
FRENCH PROVERB

Appearances do not make the man, but it will pay any man to make the best appearance possible.
ROY L. SMITH

It's not the garb he wears that makes the monk.
BLAISE PASCAL

Outside show is a poor substitute for inner worth.
AESOP

All is not gold that glitters.
JOHN HEYWOOD

If it walks like a duck, and quacks like a duck, then it probably is a duck.
ANONYMOUS

The Lord seeth not as man seeth; for man looketh on the outward appearance, but the Lord looketh on the heart.

BIBLE

They are not all saints who use holy water.

ENGLISH PROVERB

A good presence is letters of recommendation.

THOMAS FULLER

A man, in order to establish himself in the world, does everything he can to appear established there.

FRANCOIS DE LA ROCHEFOUCAULD

Be content to seem what you really are.

MARTIAL

Long whiskers cannot take the place of brains.

RUSSIAN PROVERB

Half of the work that is done in the world is to make things appear what they are not.

E. R. BEADLE

Keeping your clothes well pressed will keep you from looking hard pressed.

COLEMAN COX

Looking the part helps get the chance to fill it. But if you fill the part, it matters not if you look it.

MALCOLM FORBES

The time men spend in trying to impress others they could spend in doing the things by which others would be impressed.

FRANK ROMER

We do not see things as they are, we see things as we are.

TALMUDIC SAYING

Eat to please yourself, dress to please other.
BENJAMIN FRANKLIN

Always dress neatly, taking care to have good materials. It is astonishing how much people judge by dress.
JOHN LUBBOCK

The bosom can ache beneath diamond brooches; and many a blithe heart dances under coarse wool.
EDWIN HUBBEL CHAPIN

Things do not pass for what they are, but for what they seem. Most things are judged by their jackets.
BALTASAR GRACIAN

What I have to say is far more important than how long my eyelashes are.
ALANIS MORISSETTE

Every person is responsible for his own looks after 40.
ABRAHAM LINCOLN

There's one thing about baldness, it's neat.
DON HEROLD

People that seem so glorious are all show; underneath they are like everyone else.
EURIPIDES

How things look on the outside of us depends on how things are on the inside of us.
HENRY WARD BEECHER

Handsome is that handsome does.
HENRY FIELDING

Don't judge men's wealth or godliness by their Sunday appearance.
BENJAMIN FRANKLIN

We don't see things as they are, we see things as we are.
ANAIS NIN

After all, you can't expect men not to judge by appearances.
ELLEN GLASGOW

Of all the things you wear, your expression is the most important.
JANET LANE

Those who make their dress a principal part of themselves, will, in general, become of no more value than their dress.
WILLIAM HAZLITT

Charms strike the sight, but merit wins the soul.
ALEXANDER POPE

Take nothing on its looks; take everything on evidence. There's no better rule.
CHARLES DICKENS

It is an interesting question how far men would retain their relative rank if they were divested of their clothes.
HENRY DAVID THOREAU

APPRECIATION

Wise men appreciate all men, for they see the good in each and know how hard it is to make anything good.

BALTASAR GRACIAN

I would rather be able to appreciate things I cannot have than to have things I am not able to appreciate.

ELBERT HUBBARD

Ignorant men don't know what good they hold in their hands until they've flung it away.

SOPHOCLES

The best things in life are appreciated most after they have been lost.

ROY L. SMITH

Don't be stingy with words of appreciation when they are justly due. Everyone likes to be told that he is admired, respected, and appreciated, and liked.

NICOLAS CAUSSIN

As we express our gratitude, we must never forget that the highest appreciation is not to utter words, but to live by them.

JOHN F. KENNEDY

Make it a habit to tell people thank you. To express your appreciation, sincerely and without the expectation of anything in return. Truly appreciate those around you, and you'll soon find many others around you. Truly appreciate life, and you'll find that you have more of it.

RALPH MARSTON

Recognition is a reward in itself. Any form of appreciation, even a small word, is important.
VIKRANT MASSEY

Dwell on the beauty of life. Watch the stars, and see yourself running with them.
MARCUS AURELIUS

Next to excellence is the appreciation of it.
WILLIAM MAKESPEACE THACKERAY

The deepest principle in human nature is the craving to be appreciated.
WILLIAM JAMES

Prioritize yourself. Make yourself happy and, most of all. Live, love, and appreciate what life has offered you.
WAZIM SHAW

Someone who feels appreciated will do more than someone who is simply being paid.
J. S. FELTS

Abundance and prosperity begin with gratitude and appreciation.
ANTHON ST. MAARTEN

Appreciation is true wealth.
JAJA REQUA

The most impoverished people of all are those who have everything but appreciate nothing.
CRAIG D. LOUNSBROUGH

Those things you have but stupidly don't appreciate are on someone else's wish list... be grateful.
SAMIHA TOTANJI

It is easy to not appreciate something until you almost lose it.
MATT FOX

Each morning before you rise, before you even open your eyes, acknowledge the truth of this wisdom seed…that you possess it all and you have all you need.

JASON VERSEY

Appreciate your own courage and strength, especially during difficult times.

AKIROQ BROST

Sleep, riches and health to be truly enjoyed must be interrupted.

JEAN PAUL RICHTER

ATTITUDE

Attitude is a little thing that makes a big difference.
WINSTON CHURCHILL

There is little difference in people, but that little difference makes a big difference.
The little difference is attitude. The big difference is whether it is positive or negative.
W. CLEMENT STONE

The people who get on in this world are the people who get up and look for the
circumstances they want and, if they can't find them, make them.
GEORGE BERNARD SHAW

The greatest discovery of my generation is that human beings can alter their lives by
altering their attitudes of mind.
WILLIAM JAMES

A great attitude to have in life is to learn how to be prepared for the worse – but also
know how to expect the best in life.
DYLAN J. CAMERON

Your attitude will determine your success in life. You are the one who decides what
type of attitude you have, it is your choice.
CATHERINE PULSIFER

Your attitude towards life influences your happiness, not what happens to you.
THIBAUT MEURISSE

Our attitude toward life counts more than our ancestry.
ROY L. SMITH

Our attitudes determine whether we experience peace or fear, freedom or limitation, and to a large extent, whether we are well or sick.

GERALD JAMPOLSKY

Whether you think you can or whether you think you can't, you're right.

HENRY FORD

Everything is in your mind. Your ability to succeed, to fail to win, to lose is just a matter of attitude.

SCOTT OTERI

The best people in sales are those who are always in control of their own attitude. They remain calm, positive, cheerful, and engaging whatever the situation may be.

DAN GOLDBERG

Skills can be taught and developed but attitudes are difficult to change and ultimately are the responsibility of each person.

GARY SCHULZ

If you don't like something, change it. If you can't change it, change your attitude.

MAYA ANGELOU

No matter what happens in your life, find the good. Your attitude can be either positive or negative. The choice is up to you.

CATHERINE PULSIFER

The one that changes thoughts changes attitude.

ALBERLIN TORRES

People may hear your words, but they feel your attitude.

JOHN MAXWELL

Our attitudes control our lives, attitudes are a secret power working twenty-four hours a day, for good or bad. It is of paramount importance that we know how to harness and control this great force.

CHARLES SIMMONS

Your day is going to be good or bad it depends on your attitude.
PRIYANSHU SINGH

To one man, the world is barren, dull and superficial, to another rich, interesting and full of meaning.
ARTHUR SCHOPENHAUER

Every man has his choice of becoming a fountain of joy, or a fountain of sorrow. Our attitudes determine our altitudes.
ROY L. SMITH

Attitudes are more important than aptitudes. Attitudes affect your body, we create the climate in and around us by our attitudes; have a beautiful, warm and friendly attitude. Everything in your life will depend on your attitude.
ALFRED ARMAND MONTAPERT

A positive attitude is definitely one of the keys to success. My definition of a positive attitude is a simple one: Looking for the good in all circumstances.
CATHERINE PULSIFER

It's not what happens to you, but how you react to it that matters.
EPICTETUS

No one will hit you harder than life itself. It doesn't matter how hard you get hit. It's about how much you can take, and keep fighting, how much you can suffer and keep moving forward. That's how you win.
SYLVESTER STALLONE

Man's rise or fall, success or failure, happiness or unhappiness depends on his attitude...a man's attitude will create the situation he imagines.
JAMES ALLEN

Could we change our attitude, we should not only see life differently, but life itself would come to be different. Life would undergo a change of appearance because we ourselves had undergone a change in attitude.
KATHERINE MANSFIELD

Nothing can stop the man with the right mental attitude from achieving his goal; nothing on earth can help the man with the wrong attitude.

W. W. ZIEGE

The last, if not the greatest, of the human freedoms: to choose their own attitude in any given circumstances.

BRUNO BETTELHEIM

We are not troubled by things, but by the opinion which we have of things.

EPICTETUS

Things are in their essence what we choose to make them. A thing is, according to the mode in which one looks at it.

OSCAR WILDE

Man is only miserable so far as he thinks himself so.

SANNAZARE

So long as one does not despair, so long one doesn't look upon life bitterly, things work out fairly well in the end.

GEORGE MOORE

The meaning of things lies not in the things themselves, but in our attitude towards them.

ANTOINE DE SAINT-EXUPERY

Little things affect little minds.

BENJAMIN DISRAELI

There is nothing either good or bad, but thinking makes it so.

WILLIAM SHAKESPEARE

Nothing is miserable unless you think it so.

BOETHIUS

Your living is determined not so much by what life brings to you as by the attitude you bring to life; not so much by what happens to you as by the way your mind looks at what happens.

JOHN MILLER

Nothing is so commonplace as to wish to be remarkable.

OLIVER WENDELL HOLMES

Men are not prisoners of fate, but only prisoners of their own minds.

FRANKLIN D. ROOSEVELT

No life is so hard that you can't make it easier by the way you take it.

ELLEN GLASGOW

When you change the way you look at things, the things you look at change.

WAYNE W. DYER

In one minute you can change your attitude and in that minute you can change your entire day.

SPENCER JOHNSON

Instead of giving myself reasons why I can't, I give myself reasons why I can.

ANONYMOUS

Attitude is that 'single string' that keeps me going or cripples my progress It alone fuels my fire or assaults my hope. When my attitudes are right, there's no barrier too high, no valley too deep, no dream too extreme, no challenge too great for me.

CHARLES R. SWINDOLL

Our success or our failure is the result of our mental condition – our thoughts about people and about ourselves – our attitudes toward people and toward ourselves.

DAN CUSTER

BEAUTY

Another kind of beauty is possibly the highest type of all. Beauty of spirit, as revealed by the expression on the face of a human being. By the merry twinkle in the eye, by the smile on the lips – all indicating happiness and contentment within. This is probably the greatest beauty we will ever see.

WILLIAM ROSS

Beauty without virtue is a flower without perfume.

FRENCH PROVERB

Beauty is a short-lived reign.

SOCRATES

Rare is the union of beauty and modesty.

JUVENAL

Beauty is one of the rare things that do not lead to doubt of God.

JEAN ANOUILH

A poor beauty finds more lovers than husbands.

ENGLISH PROVERB

Though we travel the world over to find the beautiful, we must carry it within us, or we find it not.

RALPH WALDO EMERSON

There is no cosmetic for beauty like happiness.

MARIA MITCHELL

Rarely do great beauty and great virtue dwell together.
PETRARCH

Take care of your inner, spiritual beauty. That will reflect in your face.
DOLORES DEL RIO

Beauty is when you can appreciate yourself. When you love yourself, that's when you're most beautiful.
ZOE KRAVITZ

Everything has beauty, but not everyone sees it.
CONFUCIUS

Outer beauty turns the head, inner beauty turns the heart.
HELEN J. RUSSELL

Beauty and wisdom are seldom found together.
PETRONIUS

A pretty face may be enough to catch a man, but it takes character and good nature to hold him.
THOMAS MORE

Beauty is how you feel inside, and it reflects in your eyes. It is not something physical.
SOPHIA LOREN

In youth and beauty, wisdom is but rare!
HOMER

There is no personal achievement in being born beautiful.
LORETTA YOUNG

Love built on beauty, soon as beauty, dies.
JOHN DONNE

The problem with beauty is that it's like being born rich and getting poorer.
JOAN COLLINS

How goodness heightens beauty!
MILAN KUNDERA

Think of all the beauty still left around you and be happy.
ANNE FRANK

It is amazing how complete is the delusion that beauty is goodness.
LEO TOLSTOY

Cheerfulness and contentment are great beautifiers, and are famous preservers of good looks.
CHARLES DICKENS

Beauty is a short success, but while it lasts it is quite pretty.
JOSH BILLINGS

More women are wooed for their complexions than for their characters.
ARNOLD HAULTAIN

Frankly, I like the fact that I no longer fit the young beauty type - people take me seriously now.
CYBIL SHEPHERD

Beauty is in the heart of the beholder.
H. G. WELLS

Beauty is a greater recommendation than any letter of introduction.
ARISTOTLE

Beauty is only temporary, but your mind lasts a lifetime.
ALICIA MACHADO

Beauty is in the eye of the beholder.

OLD PROVERB

In all ranks of life the human heart yearns for the beautiful; and the beautiful things that God makes are his gifts to all alike.

HARRIET BEECHER STOWE

The thought that is beautiful is the thought to cherish. The word that is beautiful is worthy to endure. The act that is beautiful is eternally and always true and right. Only beware that your appreciation of beauty is just and true; and to that end. I urge you to live intimately with beauty of the highest type, until it has become a part of you, until you have within you that fineness, that order that calm, which puts you in tune with the finest things of the universe, and which links you with that spirit that is the enduring life of the world.

BERTHA BAILEY

Beauty is power; a smile is its sword.

CHARLES READE

The longer I live the more beautiful life becomes. The earth's beauty grows on men. If you foolishly ignore beauty, you'll soon find yourself without it. Your life will be impoverished. But if you wisely invest in beauty, if will remain with you all the days of your life.

FRANK LLOYD WRIGHT

We do not sufficiently cultivate in children, or, for that matter, in ourselves either, the sense of beauty. Yet what pleasure is so pure, so costless, so accessible, indeed so ever present with us.

JOHN LUBBOCK

BLESSINGS

We do not learn to value our blessings till we have lost them.
JOHANN GOTTFRIED VON HERDER

God bless you.
SAYING

Take, I pray thee, my blessing that is brought to thee; because God hath dealt graciously with me, and because I have enough.
BIBLE

Reflect that life, like every other blessing, derives its value from its use alone.
SAMUEL JOHNSON

Blessings we enjoy daily; and for the most of them, because they be so common, most men forget to pay their praise.
IZAAK WALTON

The unthankful heart...discovers no mercies; but let the thankful heart sweep through the day and, as the magnet finds the iron, so it will find, in every hour, some heavenly blessings!
HENRY WARD BEECHER

When I first open my eyes upon the morning meadows and look out upon the beautiful world, I thank God I am alive.
RALPH WALDO EMERSON

Each day comes bearing its own gifts. Untie the ribbons.
RUTH ANN SCHABACKER

The best things are nearest: breath in your nostrils, light in your eyes, flowers at your feet, duties at your hand, the path of God just before you. Then do not grasp at the stars, but do life's plain, common work as it comes, certain that daily duties and daily bread are the sweetest things in life.

ROBERT LOUIS STEVENSON

Why do some people always see beautiful skies and grass and lovely flowers and incredible human beings, while others are hard-pressed to find anything or any place that is beautiful?

LEO BUSCAGLIA

Most human beings have an almost infinite capacity for taken things for granted.

ALDOUS HUXLEY

Not being beautiful was the true blessing. ...Not being beautiful forced me to develop my inner resources. The pretty girl has a handicap to overcome.

GOLDA MEIR

To be alive, to be able to see, to walk...it's all a miracle. I have adapted the technique of living life from miracle to miracle.

ARTHUR RUBINSTEIN

To have a full stomach and fixed income are no small things.

ELBERT HUBBARD

Great blessings come from Heaven; small blessings come from man.

CHINESE PROVERB

There are two blessings which most people misuse – health and leisure.

MUHAMMAD

Sometimes we must look outside our own backyards to realize how big the world is and how blessed we are.

EUGENE BUTLER

Concentrate on counting your blessings and you'll have little time to count anything else.

WOODROW KROLL

Blessed are they who see beautiful things in humble places where other people see nothing.

CAMILLE PISSARRO

If we counted our blessings instead of our money, we would all be rich.

LINDA POINDEXTER

When you arise in the morning, think of what a precious privilege it is to be alive - to breathe, to think, to enjoy, to love.

MARCUS AURELIUS

Enjoy the little things, for one day you may look back and realize they were the big things.

ROBERT BRAULT

Take full account of the excellencies which you possess, and in gratitude remember how you would hanker after them, if you had them not.

MARCUS AURELIUS

If you would but exchange places with the other fellow, how much more you could appreciate your own position.

VICTOR E. GARDNER

God's gifts put man's best dreams to shame.

ELIZABETH BARRETT BROWNING

The best of blessings - a contented mind.

LATIN PROVERB

BOOKS

In that Mankind has done, thought, gained or been, it is lying as in magic perseveration in the pages of Books. They are chose possession of men.
THOMAS CARLYLE

Books are the legacies that a great genius leaves to man-kind.
JOSEPH ADDISON

It is chiefly through books that we enjoy intercourse with superior minds. In the best books, great men talk to us, give us their most precious thoughts.
WILLIAM ELLERY CHANNING

All that mankind has done, thought, gained, or been – it is lying as in magic preservation in the pages of books.
THOMAS CARLYLE

Books are the true levellers. They give to all, who will faithfully use them, the society, the spiritual presence, of the best and greatest of our race.
WILLIAM ELLERY CHANNING

The choice of books, like that of friends, is a serious duty. We are as responsible for what we read as what we do.
JOHN LUBBOCK

A reader lives a thousand lives before he dies, said Jojen. The man who never reads lives only one.
GEORGE R. R. MARTIN

My books are friends that never fail me.
THOMAS CARLYLE

It is a man's duty to have books. A library is not a luxury, but one of the necessaries of life.
HENRY WARD BEECHER

Books are the treasured wealth of the world and the fit inheritance of generations and nations.
HENRY DAVID THOREAU

No furniture is so charming as books.
SYDNEY SMITH

Book lovers never go to bed alone.
ANONYMOUS

You are the same today as you will be five years from now except for two things … the people you meet and the books you read.
CHARLES E. JONES

Some good book is usually responsible for the success of every really great man.
ROY L. SMITH

Books are the quietest and most constant of friends; they are the most accessible and wisest of counsellors, and the most patient of teachers.
CHARLES ELIOT

A drop of ink may make a million think.
LORD BYRON

When I am reading a book, whether wise or silly, it seems to me to be alive and talking to me.
JONATHAN SWIFT

Next to acquiring good friends, the best acquisition is that of good books.
CHARLES CALEB COLTON

That is a good book which is opened with expectation, and closed with profit.
E. BONSON ALCOTT

The first time I read an excellent book, it is to me just as if I had gained a new friend. When I read over a book I have perused before, it resembles the meeting with an old one.
OLIVER GOLDSMITH

To add a library to a house is to give that house a soul.
MARCUS TULLIUS CICERO

In books we have the choicest thoughts of the ablest men in their best dress.
JOHN AIKIN

Books are nourishment to the mind.
ITALIAN PROVERB

A room without books is like a body without soul.
MARCUS TULLIUS CICERO

A book by its counsel teaches a wise man how to live.
PHAEDRUS

Books, like friends should be few and well chosen.
KEVIN PATTERSON

It is from books that wise men derive consolation in the troubles of life.
VICTOR HUGO

No matter what his rank or position may be, the lover of books is the richest and happiest of the children of men.
J. A. LANGFORD

A good book contains more real wealth than a good bank.

ROY L. SMITH

Some books are to be tasted; others swallowed; and some to be chewed and digested.

FRANCIS BACON

Everyone who knows how to read has it in their power to magnify themselves, to multiply the ways in which they exist, to make their life full, significant, and interesting.

ALDOUS HUXLEY

In the highest civilization the book is still the highest delight.

RALPH WALDO EMERSON

The habit of reading is the only enjoyment in which there is no alloy; it lasts when all other pleasures fade.

ANTHONY TROLLOPE

He that loveth a book, will never want a faithful friend, a wholesome counsellor, a cheerful companion, an effectual comforter.

BARROW

Just the knowledge that a good book is awaiting one at the end of the day makes that day happier.

KATHLEEN NORRIS

When I consider what some books have done for the world, and what they are doing, how they keep up our hope, awaken new courage and faith, soothe pain, give an ideal; life to those hours are cold and hard, bind together distant ages and foreign lands, create new worlds of beauty, bring down truth from heaven; I give eternal blessings for this gift, and thank God for books.

JAMES FREEMAN

Some books leave us free and some books make us free.

RALPH WALDO EMERSON

Books are the food of youth, the delight of old age; the ornament of prosperity, the refuge and comfort of adversity; a delight at home, and no hindrance abroad; companions by night, in travelling, in the country.

CICERO

When we are collecting books, we are collecting happiness.

VINCENT STARRETT

Nothing can supply the place of books. They are cheering or soothing companions in solitude, illness, affliction. The wealth of both continents would not compensate for the good they impart.

WILLIAM ELLERY CHANNING

One must always be careful of books, "said Tessa,"and what is inside them, for words have the power to change us.

CASSANDRA CLARE

It is what you read when you don't have to that determines what you will be when you can't help it.

OSCAR WILDE

When a book raises your spirit and inspires you with noble and manly thoughts, seek for no other test of its excellence. It is good and made by a good workman.

JEAN DE LA BRUYERE

'Tis the good reader that makes the good book.

RALPH WALDO EMERSON

Books are the most mannerly of companions, accessible at all times, in all moods, frankly declaring the author's mind, without offence.

A. BRONSON ALCOTT

A man is known by the books he reads.

RALPH WALDO EMERSON

When you reread a classic you do not see more in the book than you did before; you see more in you than there was before.

CLIFTON FADIMAN

Books cannot change. A thousand years hence they are what you find them today, speaking the same words, holding forth the same comfort.

EUGENE FIELD

Read much, but not many books.

BENJAMIN FRANKLIN

I cannot live without books.

THOMAS JEFFERSON

The pleasant books, that silently among our household treasures take familiar places, and are to us as if a living tongue spake from the printed leaves or pictured faces!

HENRY WADSWORTH LONGFELLOW

Wear the old coat and buy the new book.

AUSTIN PHELPS

Books must be read as deliberately and reservedly as they are written.

HENRY DAVID THOREAU

No man can be called friendless when he has God and the companionship of good books.

SAMUEL ZWEMER

It is with books as with men: a very small number play a great part.

VOLTAIRE

Books worth reading once are worth reading twice; and what is most important of all, the masterpieces of literature are worth reading a thousand times.

JOHN MORLEY

A good book is the precious lifeblood of a master spirit, embalmed and treasured up on purpose to life beyond life.

JOHN MILTON

Handle a book as a bee does a flower, extract its sweetness but do not damage it.

JOHN MUIR

Reading maketh a full man, conference a ready man, and writing an exact man.

FRANCIS BACON

They are for company the best friends, in doubts counsellors, in damps comforters, time's perspective, the home-traveler's ship or horse, the busy man's best recreation, the opiate of idle weariness, the mind's best ordinary, nature's garden, and the seed-plot of immortality.

BULSTRODE WHITELOCKE

Consider what you have in the smallest chosen library. A company of the wisest and wittiest men that cold be picked out of all civil countries, in a thousand years, have set in best order the results of their learning and wisdom. The men themselves were hid and inaccessible, solitary, impatient of interruption, fenced by etiquette; but the thought which they did not uncover to their bosom friend is here written out in transparent words to us, the strangers of another age.

RALPH WALDO EMERSON

Books make up no small part of human happiness.

FREDERICK THE GREAT

The true university of these days is a collection of books.

THOMAS CARLYLE

To produce a mighty book, you must choose a mighty theme.

HERMAN MELVILLE

Books never pall on me. They discourse with us, they take counsel with us, and are united to us by a certain living chatty familiarity. And not only does each book inspire the sense that it belongs to its readers, but it also suggests the name of others, and one begets the desire of the other.

PETRARCH

A house without books is like a room without windows.

HORACE MANN

A book is a garden, an orchard, a storehouse, a party, a company by the way, a counsellor, a multitude of counsellors.

HENRY WARD BEECHER

Of all the things which man can do or make here below, by the far the most momentous, wonderful, and worthy are the things we call books.

THOMAS CARLYLE

When I am attacked by gloomy thoughts, nothing helps me so much as running to my books. They quickly absorb me and banish the clouds from my mind.

MICHEL DE MONTAIGNE

Books are yours, within whose silent chambers treasure lies preserved from age to age; more precious far than that accumulated store of gold and orient gems which, for a day of need, the sultan hides deep in ancestral tombs. These hoards of truth you can unlock at will.

WILLIAM WORDSWORTH

Book love, my friends, is your pass to the greatest, the purest, and the most perfect pleasure that God has prepared for his creatures. It lasts when all other pleasures fade. It will support you when all other recreations are gone. It will last you until your death. It will make your hours pleasant to you as long as you live.

ANTHONY TROLLOPE

Books, like proverbs, receive their chief value from the stamp and esteem of ages through which they passed.

SIR WILLIAM TEMPLE

The love of books, the golden key that opens the enchanted door.

ANDREW LANG

The man who does not read good books has no advantage over the man who can't read.

SAYING

Reading is to the mind what exercise is to the body.
JOSEPH ADDISON

Books are standing counselors and preachers, always at hand, and always disinterested; having this advantage over oral instructors, that they are ready to repeat the lessons as often as we please.
ROBERT CHAMBERS

The reading of all good books is like conversation with the finest men of past centuries.
RENE DESCARTES

The books which help you most are those which make you think the most.
THEODORE PARKER

I am a part of all I have read.
JOHN KIERAN

Reading is like permitting a man to talk a long time, and refusing you the right to answer.
EDGAR WATSON HOWE

We should be as careful of the books we read, as of the company we keep. The dead very often have more power than the living.
TRYON EDWARDS

It is not the number of books you read, nor the variety of sermons you hear, nor the amount of religious conversations in which you mix, but it is the frequency and earnestness with which you meditate on these till the truth in them becomes your own and part of your being, that ensures your growth.
FREDERICK W. ROBERTSON

Books are the open avenues down which, like kings coming to be crowned, great ideas and inspirations move to the abbey of man's soul. There are some people still left who understand perfectly what Fenelon meant when he said, "if the crowns of all the kingdoms of the empire were laid down at my feet in exchange for my books and my love of reading, I would spurn them all."
ERNEST DRESSEL NORTH

While you converse with lords and dukes, I have their betters here – my books.
THOMAS SHERIDAN

A book is like a garden carried in the pocket.
CHINESE PROVERB

When we read we may not only be kings and live in palaces, but, what is far better, we may transport ourselves to the mountains or the seashore, and visit the most beautiful parts of the earth, without fatigue, inconvenience, or expense.
JOHN LUBBOCK

Many times the reading of a book has made the future of a man.
RALPH WALDO EMERSON

True books have been written in all ages by their greatest men; by great leaders, great statesmen, and great thinkers. These are all of your choice, and life is short. Will you jostle with the common crowd, for entree here and audience there, when all the while this eternal court is open to you, with its society as the world, multitudinous as its day, the chosen and the mighty of every time and place?
JOHN RUSKIN

I would rather be a poor man in a garret with plenty of books than a king who did not love reading.
MACAULAY

I would prefer to have one comfortable room well stocked with books to all you could give me in the way of decoration which the highest art can supply.
JOHN BRIGHT

Except a living man there is nothing more wonderful than a book! – a message to us from the dead – from human souls we never saw, and who lived perhaps thousands of miles away; and yet these words on those little sheets of paper speak to us, amuse us, and comfort us.
CHARLES KINGSLEY

The best effect of any book is that it excites the reader to self activity.
THOMAS CARLYLE

Reading furnishes the mind only with materials of knowledge; it is thinking makes what we read ours. So far as we apprehend and see the connection of ideas, so far it is ours; without that it is so much loose matter floating in our brains.

JOHN LOCKE

When you read the best books, you will have as the guests of your mind the best thoughts of the best men.

GRENVILLE KLEISER

BUSINESS

Business is managing risk.
LARRY JOHN PHILLIPS

It's not the strongest species that survives, nor the most intelligent, but the most responsive to change.
CHARLES DARWIN

It either is or ought to be evident to everyone that business has to prosper before anybody can get any benefit from it.
THEODORE ROOSEVELT

A man without a smiling face must not open a shop.
CHINESE PROVERB

Seest thou a man diligent in his business? He shall stand before kings.
BIBLE

Everyone wants to live on top of the mountain, but all the happiness and growth occurs while you're climbing it.
ANDY ROONEY

In the end, all business operations can be reduced to three things: people, product, and profits. People come first.
LEE IACOCCA

One man's wage rise is another man's price increase.
HAROLD WILSON

It's very easy to be different, but very difficult to be better.
JONATHAN IVE

Whenever you see a successful business, someone once made a courageous decision.
PETER DRUCKER

Many companies get trapped by the paradox of hitting numbers "now" versus improving sales for the future quarters or years ahead.
TIFFANI BOVA

If you don't build your dream, someone else will hire you to help build theirs.
DHIRUBHAI AMBANI

Do what thou lovest; paint or sing or carve. Do what thou lovest, though the body starve! Who works for glory oft may miss the goal. Who works for money merely starves the soul.
ANONYMOUS

Happy employees lead to happy customers, which leads to more profits.
VAUGHN AUST

Companies that grow for the sake of growth or that expand into areas outside of their core business strategy often stumble. On the other hand, companies that build scale for the benefit of their customers and shareholders more often succeed over time.
JAMIE DIMON

Logic will get you from A to B. Imagination will take you everywhere.
ALBERT EINSTEIN

Never lower your price. Add value.
GRANT CARDONE

Your most unhappy customers are your greatest sources of learning.
BILL GATES

To be successful, you have to have your heart in your business, and your business in your heart.
THOMAS WATSON, SR.

If you cannot do great things do small things in a great way.
NAPOLEON HILL

Choose a job that you like, and you will never have to work a day in your life.
CONFUCIUS

If you really look closely, most overnight successes took a long time.
STEVE JOBS

I feel that luck is preparation meeting opportunity.
OPRAH WINFREY

I don't look to jump over 7-foot bars – I look for 1-foot bars that I can step over.
WARREN BUFFETT

It is always the start that requires the greatest effort.
JAMES CASH PENNEY

What do you need to start a business? Three simple things: know your product better than anyone, know your customer, and have a burning desire to succeed.
DAVE THOMAS

Entrepreneurship is not for the faint of heart.
ANONYMOUS

Failure is simply the opportunity to begin again, this time more intelligently.
HENRY FORD

Executive ability is deciding quickly and getting somebody else to do the work.
EARL NIGHTINGALE

Always deliver more than expected.
LARRY PAGE

To open a shop is easy; the difficult thing is keeping it open.
CHINESE PROVERB

Don't be afraid to give up the good to go for the great.
JOHN D. ROCKEFELLER

The company is only as good as the people it keeps.
MARY KAY ASH

Profit in business comes from repeat customers, customer's that boast about your project or service, and that brings friends with them.
W. EDWARDS DEMING

Fortunes are built during the down market and collected in the upmarket.
JASON CALACANIS

Anything that is measured and watched, improves.
BOB PARSONS

A task without a vision is drudgery; a vision without a task is a dream; a task with a vision is victory.
ANONYMOUS

Eat and drink with your relatives, do business with strangers.
GREEK PROVERB

A business that makes nothing but money is a poor business.
HENRY FORD

The employer generally gets the employees he deserves.
SIR WALTER BILBEY

Business without profit is not business any more than a pickle is candy.
CHARLES F. ABBOTT

Business is always a struggle. There are always obstacles and competitors. There is never an open road, except the wide road that leads to failure. Every great success has always been achieved by fight. Every winner has scars. The men who succeed are the efficient few. They are the few who have the ambition and the will-power to develop themselves.
HERBERT N. CASSON

Men who develop businesses of their own turn out to be the nation's most successful men.
WILLIAM BENTON

The biggest word in the language of business is not gross, but net.
HERBERT N. CASSON

The more people who own little businesses of their own, the safer our country will be, and the better off its cities and towns; for the people who have a stake in their country and their community are its best citizens.
JOHN HANCOCK

Whatever your duties or business in life may be, try to do it as well as it can be done.
JOHN LUBBOCK

CALMNESS

Man becomes calm in the measure that he understands himself as a thought-evolved being.

JAMES ALLEN

Calmness is the rarest quality in human life. It is the poise of a great nature, in harmony with itself and its ideals.

WILLIAM G. JORDAN

Calmness of mind is one of the beautiful jewels of wisdom. It is the result of long and patient effort in self-control. Its presence is an indication of ripened experience, and of a more than ordinary knowledge of the laws of thought.

JAMES ALLEN

Anyone can hold the helm when the sea is calm.

PUBLILIUS SYRUS

Nothing gives a person so much advantage over another as to remain always cool and unruffled under all circumstances.

THOMAS JEFFERSON

The mind is like water. When it's turbulent, it's difficult to see. When it's calm, everything becomes clear.

PRASAD MAHES

Remember to preserve a calm soul amid difficulties.

HORACE

Calm mind brings inner strength and self-confidence, so that's very important for good health.
DALAI LAMA

The true strength of a man is in calmness.
LEO TOLSTOY

Calmness is always Godlike.
RALPH WALDO EMERSON

The superior person is calm and composed; the lesser person is continuously worried and distressed.
CONFUCIUS

The greater the level of calmness of our mind, the greater our peace of mind, the greater our ability to enjoy a happy and joyful life.
DALAI LAMA

Man's greatest strength is shown in standing still.
EDWARD YOUNG

Quiet minds cannot be perplexed or frightened, but go on in fortune or misfortune at their own private pace, like a clock during a thunderstorm.
ROBERT LOUIS STEVENSON

Self-control is strength; right thought is mastery; calmness is power. Say unto your heart, "Peace, be still!"
JAMES ALLEN

The more tranquil a man becomes, the greater is his success, his influence, his power for good. Calmness of mind is one of the beautiful jewels of wisdom.
JAMES ALLEN

There is no joy but calm.
ALFRED TENNYSON

Calmness is the cradle of power.
JOSIAH GILBERT HOLLAND

Keep cool and you will command everyone.
JUSTINIAN

Happiness is a state of mind; happiness means calmness of mind...
ANONYMOUS

Never be in a hurry; do everything quietly and in a calm spirit. Do not lose your inner peace for anything whatsoever, even if your whole world seems upset.
FRANCIS DE SALES

In calmness lies true pleasure.
VICTOR HUGO

It's about finding the calmness in the chaos.
DONNA KAREN

Calmness is a huge gift. And once you master it, you will be able to respond in a useful way to every difficult situation that decides to walk into your heart.
GERI LARKIN

You can't force raging water to be calm. You have to leave it alone and let it return to its natural flow. Emotions are the same way.
THIBAUT

Calm your mind life becomes more crystal clear.
ANONYMOUS

The important thing is to know how to take all things quietly.
MICHAEL FARADAY

Nearer a man comes to a calm mind the closer he is to strength.
MARCUS AURELIUS

Those who act with few desires are calm, without worry or fear.
BUDDHA

Learn to calm down the winds of your mind, and you will enjoy great inner peace.
REMEZ SASSON

A man of calm is like a shady tree. People who need shelter come to it.
TOBA BETA

When you have inner calmness then you automatically succeed in what you do. The more silent you are from inside, your thoughts and actions become more powerful.
SRI SRI RAVI SHANKAR

To bear trials with a calm mind robs misfortune of its strength and burden.
LUCIUS ANNAEUS SENECA

Keep calm and carry on.
WINSTON CHURCHILL

Calmness is a human superpower. The ability to not overreact or take things personally keeps your mind clear and heart at peace.
MARCANDANGEL

One of the best lessons you can learn is to master how to remain calm.
CATHERINE PULSIFER

The ability to stay calm and focused in the midst of change is what distinguishes great leaders from those just collecting a paycheck.
TODD STOCKER

Don't chase the fast pace. Be calm and stay at peace, for it has 10x more power to take you places.
HIRAL NAGDA

Mistakes and pressure are inevitable; the secret to getting past them is to stay calm.
TRAVIS BRADBERRY

Remain calm, serene, always in command of yourself. You will then find out how easy it is to get along.
PARAMAHANSA YOGANANDA

The pursuit, even of the best things, ought to be calm and tranquil.
MARCUS TULLIUS CICERO

He who is of calm and happy nature will hardly feel the pressure of age, but to him who is of an opposite disposition youth and age are equally a burden.
PLATO

Your calm mind is the ultimate weapon against your challenges. So relax.
BRYANT MCGILL

To be calm is the highest achievement of the self.
ZEN PROVERB

No state is so bitter than a calm mind cannot find in it some consolation.
LUCIUS ANNAEUS SENECA

A calm and modest life brings more happiness than the pursuit of success combined with constant restlessness.
ALBERT EINSTEIN

Freedom is a calm mind.
SHANE PARRISH

It takes a calm mind to be able to consider things from different angles and points of view.
DALAI LAMA

To a mind that is still, the entire universe surrenders.
ZHUANGZI

Calm seas never made a good sailor.
FRANKLIN D. ROOSEVELT

Calm is a superpower.
BRENE BROWN

When the mind is calm, how quickly, how smoothly, how beautifully you will perceive everything.
PARAMAHANSA YOGANANDA

The measure of wisdom is how calm you are when facing any given situation.
NAVAL RAVIKANT

Nothing can disturb the calm peace of my soul.
JIDDU KRISHNAMURTI

Respect your calmness because it is the loudest voice of your strength.
ENERGY YODA

Cultivate a calm nature expectant of good.
CHARLES ELIOT

CARE

Caring – about people, about things, about life – is an act of maturity.
TRACY MCMILLAN

Caring about others, running the risk of feeling, and leaving an impact on people brings happiness.
HAROLD KUSHNER

Never be So busy as not to think of others.
MOTHER TERESA

Nobody cares how much you know, until they know how much you care.
THEODORE ROOSEVELT

Remember that children, marriages, and flower gardens reflect the kind of care they get.
H. JACKSON BROWN, JR.

Some people care too much. I think it's called love.
WINNIE THE POOH

Surround yourself with people who make you happy. People who make you laugh, who help you when you're in need. They are the ones worth keeping in your life. Everyone else is just passing through.
KARL MARX

The happiest people are those who do the most for others. The most miserable are those who do the least.

BOOKER T. WASHINGTON

Caring for others creates the spirit of a nation.

PAT NIXON

You can't live a perfect day without doing something for someone who will never be able to repay you.

JOHN WOODEN

Caring for others is the basis of worldly success.

SAKYONG MIPHAM

Only a life lived for others is a life worthwhile.

ALBERT EINSTEIN

Adult friendships are hard. Everyone is busy, and life happens. I've learned you gotta text people when you're thinking of them. A simple, "Thinking of you, hope all is well', really goes a long way."

ROB LOWE

The simple act of caring is heroic.

EDWARD ALBERT

Never believe that a few caring people can't change the world. For, indeed, that's all who ever have.

MARGARET MEAD

Taking care is one way to show your love. Another way is letting people take good care of you when you need it.

FRED ROGERS

To care for those who once cared for us is one of the highest honors.

TIA WALKER

My friend...care for your psyche...know thyself, for once we know ourselves, we may learn how to care for ourselves.

SOCRATES

Act like you care. Pray like you care. Speak, smile, reach out, and live like you care. The point is to make sure those in your life know beyond doubt that you do care.

RICHELLE E. GOODRICH

One's true religion is what one cares about most.

WALTER STARCKE

To be successful is to be helpful, caring, and constructive; to make everything and everyone you touch a little bit better.

NORMAN VINCENT PEALE

You really can change the world if you care enough.

MARIAN WRIIGHT EDELMAN

One person caring about another represents life's greatest value.

JIM ROHN

CHANGE

The absurd man is he who never changes.
AUGUSTE BARTHELEMY

A wise man changes his mind, a fool never.
SPANISH PROVERB

The world hates change, yet it is the only thing that has bought progress.
CHARLES F. KETTERIN

Blessed is the man who has discovered that there is nothing permanent in life but change.
ADOLPH PHILIP GOUTHEY

Be the change that you wish to see in the world.
MAHATMA GANDHI

Progress is impossible without change; and those who cannot change their minds cannot change anything.
GEORGE BERNARD SHAW

There is no way to make people like change. You can only make them feel less threatened by it.
FREDERICK HAYES

All appears to change when we change.
HENRI FREDERICK AMIEL

There can be change without progress, but not progress without change.
ANONYMOUS

The stationary condition is the beginning of the end.
HENRI FREDERICK AMIEL

There is danger in reckless change, but greater danger in blind conservatism.
HENRY GEORGE

All change is not growth; as all movement is not forward.
ELLEN GLASGOW

Give us the fortitude to endure the things which cannot be changed, and the courage to change the things which should be changed, and the wisdom to know one from the other.
BISHOP OLIVER J. HART

The only thing constant in life is change.
FRANCOIS DE LA ROCHEFOUCAULD

Everything passes; everything wears out; everything breaks.
FRENCH PROVERB

We change, whether we like it or not.
RALPH WALDO EMERSON

Nothing in this world is permanent.
GERMAN PROVERB

If you do what you've always done, you'll get what you've always gotten.
ANONYMOUS

Only in growth, reform, and change, paradoxically enough is true security to be found.
ANNE MORROW LINDBERGH

For many men, the acquisition of wealth does not end their troubles, it only changes them.

LUCIUS ANNAEUS SENECA

Change the fabric of your own soul and your own visions, and you change all.

VACHEL LINDSAY

Any change, even a change for the better, is always accompanied by drawbacks and discomforts.

ARNOLD BENNETT

The hearts of great men can be changed.

HOMER

A man's fortune must first be changed from within.

CHINESE PROVERB

If you do not change direction, you might end up where you are heading.

LAO TZU

Only I can change my life. No one can do it for me.

CAROL BURNETT

It is not the strongest of the species that survive, nor the most intelligent, but the one most responsive to change.

CHARLES DARWIN

Growth is painful. Change is painful. But nothing is as painful as staying stuck somewhere you don't belong.

N. R. NARAYANA MURTHY

Change before you have to.

JACK WELCH

Today is not yesterday; how can our works and thoughts, if they are always to be the fittest, continue always the same? Change, indeed, is painful, yet ever needful.

THOMAS CARLYLE

It's an ill plan that cannot be changed.

LATIN PROVERB

The most significant change in a person's life is a change of attitude. Right attitudes produce right actions.

WILLIAM J. JOHNSTON

I shall try to correct errors when shown to be errors, and I shall adopt new views so fast as they shall appear to be new views.

ABRAHAM LINCOLN

He that never changes his opinions, and never corrects his mistakes, will never be wiser on the morrow than he is today.

TRYON EDWARDS

The only man who can't change his mind is a man who hasn't got one.

EDWARD NOYES WESTCOTT

The foolish and the dead alone never change their opinion.

JAMES RUSSELL LOWELL

Change is not made without inconvenience, even from worse to better.

RICHARD HOOKER

Change is what people fear most.

FYODOR DOSTOYEVSKY

When you're through changing, you're through.

BRUCE BARTON

Be not the first by whom the new is tried, nor yet the last to lay the old aside.

ALEXANDER POPE

In a moving world readaptation is the price of longevity.
GEORGE SANTAYANA

No matter how far you have gone on a wrong road, turn back.
TURKISH PROVERB

Everyone thinks of changing the world, but no one thinks of changing himself.
LEO TOLSTOY

Who would be constant in happiness must often change.
CHINESE PROVERB

CHARACTER

For when the One Great Scorer comes to write against your name, he writes - not that you won or lost - but how you played the game.

CHRISTINE RICE

One of the most important lessons that experience teaches is that, on the whole, success depends more upon character than upon either intellect or fortune.

WILLIAM LECKY

Your character will be what you yourself choose to make it.

JOHN LUBBOCK

For everyone who exalts himself will be humbled, and he who humbles himself will be exalted.

BIBLE

A good name is more desirable than great riches; to be esteemed is better than silver or gold.

BIBLE

I have a dream that my four little children will one day live in a nation where they will not be judged by the color of their skin, but by the content of their character.

MARTIN LUTHER KING, JR.

When wealth is lost, nothing is lost; when health is lost, something is lost; when character is lost, all is lost.

BILLY GRAHAM

If you want to know what a man's like, take a good look at how he treats his inferiors, not his equals.

J. K. ROWLING

I believe in doing the right things; that is my character and personality.

GIANLUIGI BUFFON

Be more concerned with your character than your reputation, because character is what you really are, while reputation is merely what others think you are.

JOHN WOODEN

It is our duty to compose our character, not to compose books, and to win, not battles and provinces, but order and tranquility for our conquest of life.

MICHEL DE MONTAIGNE

Sports do not build character. They reveal it.

HEYWOOD BROWN

Each individual must develop his own character.

E. B. ZU TAVERN

The greatest legacy one can pass to one's children and grandchildren is not money or other material things accumulated in one's life, but rather a legacy of character and faith.

BILLY GRAHAM

The right way is not always the popular and easy way. Standing for right when it is unpopular is a true test of moral character.

MARGARET CHASE SMITH

If I keep my good character, I shall be rich enough.

PLATONIUS

Nearly all men can stand adversity, but if you want to test a man's character, give him power.

ABRAHAM LINCOLN

When you find a man you wish to marry Tessa, remember this: you will know what kind of man he is not by the things he says but by the things he does.

CASSANDRA CLARE

Talents are best nurtured in solitude. Character is best formed in the stormy billows of the world.

JOHANN WOLFGANG VON GOETHE

Character is what you are in the dark.

DWIGHT L. MOODY

Character is much easier kept than recovered.

THOMAS PAINE

Nothing endures but personal qualities.

WALT WHITMAN

Life is a grindstone, and whether it grinds man down or polishes him up depends on the stuff he's made of.

JOSH BILLINGS

You are what you are - and not what people think you are.

O. W. POLEN

Man is very much like a barrel of apples. The apples that are seen on the top are his reputation, but the apples that are down below represent his character.

FULTON J. SHEEN

If adversity develops character, prosperity demand it.

J. D. EPPINGA

Character is built into the spiritual fabric of personality hour by hour, day by day, year by year in much the same deliberate way that physical health is built into the body.

E. LAMAR KINCAID

Character is power; it makes friends, draws patronage and support, and opens a sure way to wealth, honor and happiness.

J. HOWE

The measure of a man's real character is what he would do if he knew he would never be found out.

MACAULAY

Any man worth his salt will stick up for what he believes right, but it takes a slightly bigger man to acknowledge instantly and without reservation that he is in error.

PEYTON C. MARCH

A man's character is the reality of himself. His reputation is the opinion others have formed of him. Character is in him; reputation is from other people.

HENRY WARD BEECHER

Character is not made in a crisis – it is only exhibited.

DR. ROBERT FREEMAN

A man's character is his fate.

HERACLITUS

In the end, we are all the sum total of our actions. Character cannot be counterfeited, nor can it be put on and cast off as if it were a garment to meet the whim of the moment. Like the markings on wood which are ingrained in the very heart of the tree, character requires time and nurture for growth and development.

MADAME CHIANG KAI-SHEK

A man is what he is, not what men say he is. His character no man can touch. His character is what he is before God. His reputation is what men say he is. That can be damaged. For reputation is for time. Character is for eternity.

JOHN B. GOUGH

Fame is a vapor, popularity an accident, riches take wings. Only one thing endures, and that is character.

HORACE GREELEY

I pray thee O God, that I may be beautiful within.
SOCRATES

The noblest contribution which any man can make for the benefit of posterity, is that of a good character. The richest bequest which any man can leave to the youth of his native land, is that of a shining, spotless example.
ROBERT C. WINTHROP

Character is nurtured midst the tempests of the world.
JOHANN WOLFGANG VON GOETHE

Put trust in character.
GREEK PROVERB

A man's fortunes are the fruit of his character.
RALPH WALDO EMERSON

A good character is the best tombstone. Those who loved you, and were helped by you, will remember you when forget-me-nots are withered. Carve your name on hearts, and not on marble.
CHARLES SPURGEON

Bad company corrupts good character.
BIBLE

Our deeds determine us, as much as we determine our deeds.
GEORGE ELIOT

Nor is it always in the most distinguished achievements that men's virtues or vices may be best discovered; but often an action of small note, a short saying, or a jest, may distinguished a person's real character more than the greatest sieges or the most important battles.
PLUTARCH

To enjoy the things we ought and to hate the things we ought has the greatest bearing on virtue of character.
ARISTOTLE

What thou art, that thou art; neither by words canst thou be made greater than what thou art in the sight of God.
THOMAS A' KEMPIS

There is no pillow as soft as a clear conscience.
FENCH PROVERB

You can construct the character of a man not only from what he does and says, but from what he fails to say and do.
NORMAN DOUGLAS

It is not what he has, nor even what he does, which directly expresses the worth of a man, but what he is.
HENRI FREDERIC AMIEL

Not education but character is man's greatest need and man's greatest safeguard.
HERBERT SPENCER

You can easily judge the character of a man by the way he treats those who can do nothing for him.
SAYING

Oh, young man, character is worth more than money, character is worth more than anything else in this wide world.
DWIGHT L. MOODY

Be your character what it will, it will be known; and nobody will take it upon your word.
EARL OF CHESTERFIELD

When the character of a man is not clear to you, look at his friends.
JAPANESE PROVERB

Be not anxious about what you have, but about what you are.
SAINT GEGORY I

You cannot dream yourself into a character; you must hammer and forge yourself one.
JAMES ANTHONY FROUDE

Old age and sickness bring out the essential characteristics of a man.
FELIX FRANKFURTER

Men are what their mothers made them.
RALPH WALDO EMERSON

When the character's right, looks are a greater delight.
OVID

What you have outside you counts less than what you have inside you.
B. C. FORBES

In matters of style, swim with the current; in matters of principle, stand like a rock.
THOMAS JEFFERSON

One can acquire everything in solitude except character.
STENDHAL

Character is what God and the angels know of us; reputation is what men and women think of us.
HORACE MANN

Character is long-standing habit.
PLUTARCH

Character building begins in our infancy, and continues until death.
ELEANOR ROOSEVELT

Good character is more to be praised than outstanding talent. Most talents are, to some extent, a gift. Good character, by contrast, is not given to us. We have to build it piece by piece – by thought, choice, courage and determination.
JOHN LUTHER

Character is habit long continued.
GREEK PROVERB

Character equals the sum of traits and habits that make up a person's mental and moral being.
HERBERT SPENCER

Character is the keystone of life. Character means the quality of the stuff of which anything is made. We can learn from others what is needed for character, but the actual carving we must do ourselves.
JOHN LUBBOCK

One of the most important lessons that experience teaches is that, on the whole, success depends more upon character than upon either intellect or fortune.
WILLIAM LECKY

You don't make your character in a crisis, you exhibit it.
OREN ARNOLD

CHEERFULNESS

Laughing cheerfulness throws the light of day on all the paths of life.
JEAN PAUL

The unselfish effort to bring cheer to others will be the beginning of a happier life for ourselves.
HELEN KELLER

Cheerfulness is the best promoter of health, and is as friendly to the mind as to the body.
JOSEPH ADDISON

The best way to cheer yourself up is to try to cheer someone else up.
MARK TWAIN

The most certain sign of wisdom is cheerfulness.
MICHEL DE MONTAIGNE

You find yourself refreshed in the presence of cheerful people. Why not make an honest effort to confer that pleasure on others?
LYDIA M. CHILD

Wondrous is the strength of cheerfulness, and its power of endurance - the cheerful man will do more in the same time, will do it; better, will preserve it longer, than the sad or sullen.
THOMAS CARLYLE

There is no personal charm so great as the charm of a cheerful temperament.
HENRY VAN DYKE

A merry heart maketh a cheerful countenance.
KING SOLOMON

To be seventy years young is sometimes far more cheerful and hopeful than to be forty years old.
OLIVER WENDELL HOLMES

Childhood itself is scarcely more lovely than a cheerful, kindly, sunshiny old age.
LYDIA M. CHILD

A cheerful frame of mind, reinforced by relaxation...is the medicine that puts all ghosts of fear on the run.
GEORGE MATTHEW ADAMS

When the mind has once formed the habit of holding cheerful happy, prosperous pictures, it will not be easy to form the opposite habit.
ORISON SWETT MARDEN

Learn the sweet magic of a cheerful face.
OLIVER WENDELL HOLMES

A cheerful heart and a cheerful mind are powerful tools.
ANONYMOUS

Some men are born old, and some men never seem so. If we keep well and cheerful, we are always young and at last die in youth even when in years would count as old.
TYRON EDWARDS

A cheerful look makes a dish a feast.
GEORGE HERBERT

A merry heart doeth good like a medicine.
BIBLE

Cheerfulness is the great lubricant of the wheels of life. It lightens labor, diminishes difficulties, and mitigates misfortunes. Cheerfulness gives a creative power which the pessimist never possesses. A sunny, hopeful, optimistic disposition sweetens life, lightens its inevitable drudgery, and eases the jolts along the road.

COUNCILLOR

A cheerful disposition sweetens the day, and smooths the road of life.

HENRY MILLER

A face without a smile is like a lantern without a light.

ERNEST REEVES

Joyous people are not only the happiest, but the longest lived, the most useful and most successful.

ORISON SWETT MARDEN

Great joy is only earned by great exertion.

JOHANN WOLFGANG VON GOETHE

CHOICE

Nothing ranks a man so quickly as his skill in selecting things that are really worthwhile. Every day brings the necessity of keen discrimination. Not always is it a choice between good and bad, but between good and best.

ADOLPH PHILIP GOUTHEY

An individual chooses and makes himself.

JEAN-PAUL SARTRE

Most of us can, as we choose, make of this world either a palace or a prison.

JOHN LUBBOCK

Choice, not chance, determines human destiny.

BALTASAR GRACIAN

When you have to make a choice and don't make it, that is in itself a choice.

WILLIAM JAMES

This power to choose is what makes each one of us an individual, a god in his own right and our choices determine what happens to us – what our future will be – happy or unhappy, success or failure.

DAN CUSTER

As a man thinketh so is he, and as a man chooseth so is he.

RALPH WALDO EMERSON

The difficulty in life is the choice.

GEORGE MOORE

There is no better measure of a person than what he does when he is absolutely free to choose.

WILMA ASKINAS

My own view of history is that human beings do have genuine freedom to make choices. Our destiny is not predetermined for us; we determine it for ourselves.

ARNOLD J. TOYNBEE

The more decisions that you are forced to make alone, the more you are aware of your freedom to choose.

THORTON WILDER

You don't get to choose how you're going to die. Or when. You can only decide how you're going to live. Now.

JOAN BAEZ

Life is a matter of choices, and every choice you make makes you.

JOHN MAXWELL

When something bad happens you have three choices. You can either let it define you, let it destroy you, or you can let it strengthen you.

DR. SEUSS

Everything you are comes from your choices.

JEFF BEZOS

You and only you are responsible for your life choices and decisions.

ROBERT T. KIYOSAKI

Our lives are fashioned by our choices. First we make our choices. Then our choices make us.

ANNE FRANK

Make a choice of what you want, who you want to be and how you're going to do it. The universe will get out of the way.

WILL SMITH

You are free to choose, but the choices you make today will determine what you have, be, and do in the tomorrow of your life.

ZIG ZIGLAR

We always have a choice.

ANTHONY ROBBINS

In the long run, we shape our lives, and we shape ourselves. The process never ends until we die. And the choices we make are ultimately our own responsibility.

ELEANOR ROOSEVELT

I've realized that being happy is a choice.

ANGELINA JOLIE

We are our choices.

JEAN-PAUL SARTRE

Success is not an accident, success is a choice.

STEPHEN CURRY

The choices we make are ultimately our responsibility.

ELEANOR ROOSEVELT

You can't make someone else's choices. You shouldn't let someone else make yours.

COLIN POWELL

Joy does not simply happen to us. We have to choose joy and keep choosing it every day.

HENRI J. M. NOUWEN

Destiny is not a matter of chance, it is a matter of choice; it is not a thing to be waited for, it is thing to be achieved.

WILLIAM JENNINGS BRYAN

Every choice you make is creating your future. Choose wisely.

JOE TICHIO

You always do what you want to do. This is true with every act. You may say that you had to do something, or that you were forced to, but actually, whatever you do, you do by choice. Only you have the power to choose for yourself.

W. CLEMENT STONE

Your current life id the result of your previous choices, if you want something different, begin to choose differently.

JOE TICHIO

It is our choices that show what we are truly are, far more than our abilities.

J. K. ROWLING

We cannot have everything we want. The businessman in pursuit of financial success often has to neglect his athletic and cultural interests. Men who elect to serve the spiritual, the cultural, or the political interests of society – ministers, writers, artists, soldiers, teachers, statesmen, and public servants in general – usually have to relegate monetary well-being to secondary importance.

COUNCILLOR

We live by making choices.

DAVID FINE

So it is, life is actually made up of our choices. We are the sum total of them, and if we hold to an attitude of love and thanksgiving for all the good things within our grasp we may have what all ambitious people long for – success.

DELMA NEELEY

CIRCUMSTANCE

Circumstances do not make a man; they only reveal him to himself.
JAMES ALLEN

Circumstances may prevent you from building a fortune, but they have no power to prevent you from building character.
ARISTOTLE

What you did yesterday creates today's circumstances.
THOMAS BLANDI

Men are anxious to improve their circumstances, but are unwilling to improve themselves; they therefore remain bound.
JAMES ALLEN

You think me the child of circumstances; I make my circumstances.
RALPH WALDO EMERSON

Things do not happen in this world – they are brought about.
HAYS

The ideal man bears the accidents of life with dignity and grace, making the best of the circumstances.
ARISTOTLE

If thou art master of thyself, circumstances shall harm thee little.
MARTIN FARQUHAR TUPPER

Superiority to circumstances is one of the most prominent characteristics of great men.

HORACE MANN

It always remains true that if we had been greater, circumstance would have been less strong against us.

GEORGE ELIOT

What is the matter with the world that it is so out of joint? Simply that men do not rule themselves but let circumstances rule them.

RALPH WALDO EMERSON

Watch and profit by every circumstance.

HENRI DE JOMINI

Good is the enemy of great. Greatness is not a function of circumstance. Greatness, it turns out, is largely a matter of conscious choice and discipline.

JAMES CHURTON COLLINS

Extraordinary people survive under the most terrible circumstances and they become more extraordinary because of it.

ROBERTSON DAVIES

You must take personal responsibility. You cannot change the circumstances, the seasons, or the wind, but you can change yourself. That is something you have charge of.

JIM ROHN

We cannot choose our external circumstances, but we can always choose how we respond to them.

EPICTETUS

I am not a product of my circumstances. I am a product of my decisions.

STEPHEN COVEY

Wise men put their trust in ideas and not in circumstances.

RALPH WALDO EMERSON

Happiness depends more on the inward disposition of mind than on outward circumstances.

BENJAMIN FRANKLIN

The truly good and wise man will bear all kinds of fortune in a seemly way, and will always act in the noblest manner that the circumstances allow.

ARISTOTLE

No change of circumstances can repair a defect of character.

RALPH WALDO EMERSON

We can let circumstances rule us, or we can take charge and rule our lives from within.

EARL NIGHTINGALE

Stop blaming outside circumstances for your inside chaos.

STEVE MARABOLI

Who does the best that circumstances allows, Does well, acts nobly, angels could no more.

EDWARD YOUNG

Man is buffeted by circumstances so long as he believes himself to be the creature of outside conditions, but when he realizes that he is a creative power, and that he may command the hidden soil and seeds of his being out of which circumstances grow, he then becomes the rightful master of himself.

JAMES ALLEN

Success is to be had by those who make things happen despite their circumstances. Failures are those who quit because they believed chance played a more important role than choice.

J. S. FELTS

Shallow men believe in luck, believe in circumstances - it was somebody's name, or he happened to be there at the time, or it was so then, and another day would have been otherwise. Strong men believe in cause and effect.

RALPH WALDO EMERSON

Man is not the creature of circumstances, circumstances are the creatures of men. We are free agents, and man is more powerful than matter.

BENJAMIN DISRAELI

When the best things are not possible, the best may be made of those that are.

RICHARD HOOKER

The greater part of our happiness or misery depends upon our dispositions, and not upon our circumstances.

MARTHA WASHINGTON

People are always blaming their circumstances for what they are. I don't believe in circumstances. The people who get on in this world are the people who get up and look for the circumstances they want, and if they can't find them, make them.

GEORGE BERNARD SHAW

Circumstances are the rulers of the weak; they are but the instruments of the wise.

SAMUEL LOVER

CLEANLINESS

People who wash much have a high mind about it, and talk down to those who wash little.
RALPH WALDO EMERSON

Hygiene is the corruption of medicine by morality.
H. L. MENCKEN

What separates two people most profoundly is a different sense and degree of cleanliness.
FRIEDRICH NIETZSCHE

Cleanliness is indeed next to godliness.
JOHN WESLEY

Neatness and cleanliness is not a function of how rich or poor you are but that of mentality and principle.
IKECHUKWU IZUAKOR

Cleanliness may be defined to be the emblem of purity of mind.
JOSEPH ADDISON

The body is your temple. Keep it pure and clean for the soul to reside in.
B. K. S. IYENGAR

If you go long enough without a bath, even the fleas will let you alone.
ERNIE PYLE

Cleanliness has a powerful influence on the health and preservation of the body.
W. ASPINWALL

Nothing inspires cleanliness more than an unexpected guest.
RADHIKA MUNDRA

Cleanliness and order are not matters of instinct; they are matters of education, and like most great things, you must cultivate a taste for them.
BENJAMIN DISRAELI

Cleanliness is a state of purity, clarity, and precision.
SUZE ORMAN

Cleanliness is a mindset – a positive habit that keeps the body, mind, and environment happy, healthy, simple, neat, and delightful.
AMIT RAY

This house is clean enough to be healthy, and dirty enough to be happy.
ANONYMOUS

Cleaning and organizing is a practice, not a project.
MEAGAN FRANCIS

When your environment is clean you feel happy motivated and healthy.
LAILAH GIFTY AKITA

COMPASSION

Compassion is the desire that moves the individual self to widen the scope of its self-concern to embrace the whole of the universal self.
ARNOLD J. TOYNBEE

It is the experience of touching the pain of others that is the key to change ... compassion is a sign of transformation.
JIM WALLIS

He who hath compassion upon others receives compassion from Heaven.
TALMUD

If you want others to be happy, practice compassion. If you want to be happy, practice compassion.
DALAI LAMA

Compassion is the greatest form of love humans have to offer.
RACHAEL JOY SCOTT

We can't heal the world today, but we can begin with a voice of compassion, a heart of love, an act of kindness.
MARY DAVIS

There is no exercise better for the heart than reaching down and lifting people up.
JOHN HOLMES

Sometimes it takes only one act of kindness and caring to change a person's life.
JACKIE CHAN

A kind and compassionate act is often its own reward.
WILLIAM JOHN BENNETT

In compassion, when we feel with the other, we dethrone ourselves from the center of our world, and we put another person there.
KAREN ARMSTRONG

Compassion is the wish to see others free from suffering.
DALAI LAMA

Let our hearts be stretched out in compassion toward others, for everyone is walking his or her own difficult path.
DIETER F. UCHTDORF

Compassion is to look beyond your own pain, to see the pain of others.
YASMIN MOGAHED

More smiling, less worrying. More compassion, less judgment. More blessed, less stressed. More love, less hate.
ROY T. BENNETT

Compassion for others begins with kindness to ourselves.
PEMA CHODRON

Humanity's collective mission in the cosmos lies in the practice of compassion.
DAISAKU IKEDA

Compassion is all about giving all the love that you've got.
CHERYL STRAYED

Look for a way to lift someone up. And if that's all you do, that's enough.
ELIZABETH LESSER

A stranger's compassion can make a world of difference.
OPRAH WINFREY

True compassion means not only feeling another's pain but also being moved to help relieve it.
DANIEL GOLEMAN

Have compassion for all beings, rich and poor alike; each has their suffering. Some suffer too much, others too little.
BUDDHA

Compassion will cure more sins than condemnation.
HENRY WARD BEECHER

Having compassion for yourself means that you honor and accept your humanness.
KRISTEN NEFF

Compassion and tolerance are not a sign of weakness, but a sign of strength.
DALAI LAMA

We are all different. Don't judge, understand instead.
ROY T. BENNETT

A kind gesture can reach a wound that only compassion can heal.
STEVE MARABOLI

Walk with me for a while, my friend – you in my shoes, I in yours – and then let us talk.
RICHELLE E. GOODRICH

The fundamental human experience is that of compassion.
JOSEPH CAMPBELL

The purpose of life is to serve, and to show compassion and the will to help others.
ALBERT SCHWEITZER

The greatness of man is measured by the way he treats the little man. Compassion for the weak is a sign of greatness.
MYLES MUNROE

There never was any heart truly great and generous, that was not also tender and compassionate.

BISHOP ROBERT SOUTH

The value of compassion cannot be over-emphasized. Anyone can criticize. It takes a true believer to be compassionate. No greater burden can be born by an individual than to know no one cares or understands.

ARTHUR H. STAINBACK

CONDUCT

The superior man is slow in his words and earnest in his conduct.
CONFUCIUS

The heart has no secret which our conduct does not reveal.
FRENCH PROVERB

CONDUCT is life: in the long run happiness and prosperity depend upon it. External circumstances are of comparatively little importance; it does not so much matter what surrounds us, as what we are. Watch yourself then day by day.
JOHN LUBBOCK

A man is known by his conduct to his wife, to his family, and to those under him.
NAPOLEON BONAPARTE

Every human being has a right to be respected as a human being unless he forfeits that right by his own conduct.
MANLY HALL

The conduct of our lives is the true mirror of our doctrine.
MICHEL DE MONTAIGNE

Conduct is three-fourths of our life and its largest concern.
MATTHEW ARNOLD

Behave toward everyone as if receiving a great guest.
CONFUCIUS

Confront improper conduct, not by retaliation, but by example.
JOHN FOSTER

Be so that thy conduct can become law universal.
IMMANUEL KANT

The virtue of man ought to be measured, not by his extraordinary exertions, but by his everyday conduct.
BLAISE PASCAL

Depend not on fortune, but on conduct.
PUBLILIUS SYRUS

Laws control the lesser man...Right conduct controls the greater one.
MARK TWAIN

I desire so to conduct the affairs of this administration that if at the end... I have lost every other friend on earth, I shall at least have one friend left, and that friend shall be down inside of me.
ABRAHAM LINCOLN

Purity of mind and conduct is the first glory of a woman.
MADAME DE STAEL

Conduct is the best proof of character.
ANONYMOUS

Remember upon the conduct of each depends the fate of all.
ALEXANDER THE GREAT

A reputation for a thousand years may depend upon the conduct of a single moment.
ERNEST BRAMAH

Let them hate me, provided they respect my conduct.
TIBERIUS

The integrity of men is to be measured by their conduct, not by their professions.
JUNIUS

The world sees in our conduct, in our behavior, the proof that we are the real children of God.
POPE SHENOUDA III

You see a lot of talented people, but you usually don't see talented people who, behind the scenes, know how to conduct themselves on a higher level.
ROMEO SANTOS

Everyone ought to bear patiently the results of his own conduct.
PHAEDRUS

Respect for right conduct is felt by everybody.
JANE AUSTEN

He is not well-bred, that cannot bear ill-breeding in others.
BENJAMIN FRANKLIN

Whenever you are to do a thing, though it can never be known but to yourself, ask yourself how you would act were all the world looking at you, and act accordingly.
THOMAS JEFFERSON

Every man is valued in this world as he shows by his conduct that he wishes to be values.
JEAN DE LA BRUYERE

In every activity do your best and let the world make its own appraisement. You are what you are. Explanations seldom explain. Cultivate a fine sense of independence, based upon the assurance that you are loyal to a high standard conduct.
GRENVILLE KLEISER

CONFIDENCE

Confidence imparts a wonderful inspiration to its possessor.
JOHN MILTON

Confidence is that feeling by which the mind embarks in great and honorable courses
with a sure hope and trust in itself.
MARCUS TULLIUS CICERO

No man has a right to expect others to display confidence in him if he has no
confidence in himself.
ROY L. SMITH

Mutual confidence is the pillar of friendship.
GEORGE HERBERT

All history makes clear that an indispensable quality of any man or class that wishes
to lead, to hold power and privilege in society, is boundless self-confidence.
JAMES BURNHAM

With self-confidence fulfilled, you'll find that folk have confidence in you.
JOHANN WOLFGANG VON GOETHE

Confidence gives the fool the advantage over a wise man.
WILLIAM HAZLITT

Nothing so bolsters our self-confidence and reconciles us with ourselves as the continuous ability to create; to see things grow and develop under our hand, day in, day out.

ERIC HOFFER

It generally happens that assurance keeps an even pace with ability.

SAMUEL JOHNSON

Accept who you are, and revel in it.

MITCH ALBOM

Self-confidence is at the root of most of our confidence in others.

FRANCOIS DE LA ROCHEFOUGAULD

A man may be too confident.

WILLIAM SHAKESPEARE

Fired by success – they could do it because they believed they could do it.

VIRGIL

Self-confidence is the first requisite to great undertakings.

SAMUEL JOHNSON

If I have lost confidence in myself, I have the Universe against me.

RALPH WALDO EMERSON

Look out world, here I come!

SAYING

It is best to act with confidence, no matter how little right you have to it.

LILLIAN HELLMAN

There's one blessing only, the source and cornerstone of beatitude: confidence in self.

LUCIUS ANNAEUS SENECA

Only so far as a man believes strongly, mightily, can he act cheerfully, or do anything worth doing.
FREDERICK W. ROBERTSON

Your success depends mainly upon what you think of yourself and whether you believe in yourself.
WILLIAM J. H. BOETCKER

The man who cannot believe in himself cannot believe in anything else.
ROY L. SMITH

A man cannot be comfortable without his own approval.
MARK TWAIN

Believe that you can whip the enemy, and you have won half of the battle.
GENERAL J. E. B. STUART

Our doubts are traitors, and make us lose the good we oft might win, by fearing to attempt.
WILLIAM SHAKESPEARE

Doubt whom you will, but never yourself.
CHRISTIAN NESTELL BOVEE

They are able because they think they are able.
VIRGIL

Nothing splendid has ever been achieved except by those who dared believe that something inside them was superior to circumstances.
BRUCE BARTON

If you think you can win, you can win. Faith is necessary to victory.
WILLIAM HAZLITT

He can inspire a group only if he himself is filled with confidence and hope of success.
FLOYD V. FILSON

They can do all because they think they can.
VERGIL

The way to develop self-confidence is to do things you fear and get a record of successful experiences behind you.
WILLIAM JENNINGS BRYAN

The gain in self-confidence of having accomplished a tiresome labor is immense.
ARNOLD BENNETT

Confidence is contagious. So is lack of confidence.
VINCE LOMBARDI

Skill and confidence are an unconquered army.
GEORGE HERBERT

The only limit to our realization of tomorrow will be our doubts of today.
FRANKLIN D. ROOSEVELT

The only person you are destined to become is the person you decide to be.
RALPH WALDO EMERSON

We can accomplish almost anything within our ability if we but think that we can!
GEORGE MATTHEW ADAMS

Our belief at the beginning of a doubtful undertaking is the one thing that ensures the successful outcome of our venture.
WILLIAM JAMES

There is little that can withstand a man who can conquer himself.
LOUIS XIV

It is difficult to make a man miserable while he feels he is worthy of himself and claims kindred to the great God who made him.

ABRAHAM LINCOLN

Confidence placed in another often compels confidence in return.

LIVY

He who has lost confidence can lose nothing more.

BOISTE

Self-confidence is that state of being that makes a person feel sure and comfortable so that he is at ease everywhere, under any conditions, and all of the time.

RHODA LACHAR

Self-confidence carries conviction; it makes other people believe in us.

ORISON SWETT MARDEN

The proper development of self-confidence will be one of your most valuable assets. It will influence everything you do, whether you are in business or professional life. A full degree of self-confidence will enable you to occupy an important place, the place to which your talents entitle you.

GRENVILLE KLEISER

CONSCIENCE

A good conscience is a mine of wealth. And in truth what greater riches can there be, what thing more sweet than a good conscience.

ST. BERNARD

Conscience in the soul is the root of all courage. If a man would be brave, let him learn to obey his conscience.

JAMES FREEMAN CLARKE

I am more afraid of my own heart than of the Pope and all his cardinals. I have within me the great Pope, self.

MARTIN LUTHER

Fear is the tax that conscience pays to guilt.

GEORGE SEWALL

A good conscience is to the soul what health is to the body; it preserves a constant ease and serenity within us, and more than countervails all the calamities and afflictions that can possibly befall us.

JOSEPH ADDISON

A peace above all earthly dignities, a still and quiet conscience.

WILLIAM SHAKESPEARE

The foundation of true joy is in the conscience.

LUCIUS ANNAEUS SENECA

Conscience is God's presence in man.

EMANUEL SWEDENBORG

Conscience is the voice of the soul, the passions are the voice of the body.
JEAN-JACQUES ROUSSEAU

My conscience is my crown, contented thoughts my rest; my heart is happy in itself; my bliss is in my breast.
ROBERT SOUTHWELL

There are many luxuries that we may legitimately prefer to it, such as a grateful conscience, a country life, or the woman of our inclination.
ROBERT LOUIS STEVENSON

He will easily be content and at peace, whose conscience is pure.
THOMAS a' KEMPIS

It is easier to fight the world than to wrestle with your conscience.
MATSHONA DHLIWAYO

Wealth and power aren't the most important things in life. What is truly important is have a clear conscience.
ERALDO BANOVAC

Man cannot suffer more than from a guilty conscience.
ERALDO BANOVAC

Follow your conscience. Sleep well.
FRANK SONNENBERG

Fear nothing but your conscience.
SUZY KASSEM

Give me the liberty to know, to utter, and to urge accordingly to conscience, above all liberties.
JOHN MILTON

Conscience is the inner voice that warns us somebody may be looking.
H. L. MENCKEN

The torture of a bad conscience is the hell of a living soul.
JOHN CALVIN

In matters of conscience, the law of the majority has no place.
MAHTMA GANDHI

It is neither right nor safe to go against my conscience.
MARTIN LUTHER

Conscience is a great ledger book in which all our offenses are written and registered, and which time reveals to the sense and feeling of the offender.
SIR RICHARD BURTON

A good conscience is a continual Christmas.
BENJAMIN FRANKLIN

There is no witness so dreadful, no accuser so terrible as the conscience that dwells in the heart of every man.
POLYBUS

Conscience is thus explained only as the voice of God in the soul.
PETER KREEFT

The best tranquilizer is a clear conscience.
BENJAMIN FRANKLIN

He who stands by his heart has God in him. Our conscience is what unites us with God.
SUZY KASSEM

It is a sin only if conscience confirmed it.
NKWACHUKWU BETA

The scientific name of the fear of God is conscience.
NKWACHU OGBUAGU

Conscience is the light by which we interpret the will of God in own lives.
THOMAS MERTON

A clear conscience is a good pillow.
FRENCH PROVERB

Good friends, good books, and a sleepy conscience: this is the ideal life.
MARK TWAIN

Wrong does not cease to be wrong because the majority share in it.
LEO TOLSTOY

Keep conscience clear, then never fear.
BENJAMIN FRANKLIN

A man's first duty is to his own conscience and honor, the party and country come second to that, and never first.
MARK TWAIN

A quiet conscience makes one so serene.
LORD BYRON

Reason often makes mistakes, but conscience never does.
JOSH BILLINGS

Conscience and reputation are two things. Conscience is due to yourself, reputation to your neighbor.
SAINT AUGUSTINE

The testimony of a good conscience is the glory of a good man; have a good conscience and thou shalt ever have gladness. A good conscience may bear right many things and rejoices among adversities.
THOMAS A' KEMPIS

The great beacon light God sets in all, the conscience of each bosom.
ROBERT BROWNING

The conscience is a thousand witnesses.
RICHARD TAVERNER

The only tyrant I accept in this world is the "still, small voice" within me.
MOHANDAS GANDHI

I will stay in jail to the end of my days before I make a butchery of my conscience.
JOHN BUNYAN

A good conscience is a continual feast.
LUCIUS ANNAEUS SENECA

There is one thing alone that stands the brunt of life throughout its course, a quiet conscience.
EURIPIDES

A guilty conscience needs no accuser.
ENGLISH PROVERB

Even when there is no law, there is conscience.
PUBLILIUS SYRUS

Conscience is a sacred sanctuary where God alone may enter as judge.
LAMENNAIS

The real man lies in the depths of the subconscious.
H. L. MENCKEN

CONTENTMENT

Sweet are the thoughts that savor of content; the quiet mind is richer than a crown.
ROBERT GREENE

Then be content, poor heart! God's plans, like lilies pure and white, unfold; we must not tear the close-shut leaves apart. Time will reveal the calyxes of gold!
MARY LOUISE R. SMITH

'Tis better to be lowly born, and range with humble livers in content, than to be perk'd up in a glistening grief, and wear a golden sorrow.
WILLIAM SHAKESPEARE

When the world trembles I'm unmoved, when cloudy, I'm serene; when darkness covers all without I'm always bright within.
DANIEL DEFOE

With only plain rice to eat, with only water to drink, and with only an arm for a pillow, I am still content.
CONFUCIUS

It is better to want what you have than to have what you want.
PHILEMON PROVERB

The secret of contentment is knowing how to enjoy what you have, and be able to lose all desire for things beyond your reach.
LIN YUTANG

He is not rich that possesses much, but he that is content with what he has.
ANONYMOUS

He who has fewest wants, and is most able to live within himself, is not only the happiest, but the richest man, and if he does not abound in what the world calls wealth, he does in independence.

ANONYMOUS

True contentment depends not upon what we have; a tub was large enough for Diogenes, but a world was too little for Alexander.

CHARLES CALEB COLTON

Contentment consists not in adding more fuel, but in taking away some of the fire.

THOMAS FULLER

Contentment is the philosopher's stone, which turns all it toucheth into gold; the poor man is rich with it, and the rich man is poor without it.

ELBERT HUBBARD

Enjoy your own life without comparing it with that of another.

MARIE-JEAN-ANTOINE-NICHOLAS DE CARITAT

The happiest people are usually those who have learned to be contented with less.

ROY L. SMITH

Happy the man, of mortals happiest he, whose quiet mind from vain desires is free; whom neither hopes to deceive, nor fears torment, but lives at peace, within himself content; in thought, or act, accountable to none but to himself, and to the gods alone.

GEORGE LANDSDOWNE

My crown is in my heart, not on my head; not deck's with diamonds and Indian stones, nor to be seen: my crown is called content; a crown it is that seldom kings enjoy.

WILLIAM SHAKESPEARE

A man whose heart is not content is like a snake which tries to swallow an elephant.

CHINESE PROVERB

Let us endeavor to be contented with small things, and to make ourselves happy in the pleasantness of simple pleasures.

HOLME LEE

Let him who has enough ask for nothing more.
HORACE

I am quite my own master, agreeably lodged, perfectly easy in my circumstances. I am contented with my situation and happy because I think myself so.
ALAIN RENE LE SAGE

Sad will be the day for any man when he becomes contented with the thoughts he is thinking and the deeds he is doing – where there is not forever beating at his soul some great desire to do something larger, which he knows that he was meant and made to do.
PHILLIPS BROOKS

Not what we have, but what we enjoy, constitutes our abundance.
JEAN ANTOINE PETIT-SENN

O contentment, make me rich! For without thee there is no wealth.
MOSLIH EDDIN SAADI

I swear, 'tis better to be lowly born, and range with humble livers in content, than to be perk'd up in a glistering grief, and wear a golden sorrow.
WILLIAM SHAKESPEARE

Someone is happy with less than what you have.
ANONYMOUS

And Freedom, leaning on her spear, laughs louder than the laughing giant; some good bank-stock, some note of hand, or trifling railroad share, I only ask that fortune send a little more than I shall spend.
OLIVER WENDELL HOLMES

Content destroys all inordinate ambition; gives sweetness to the conversation, and serenity to all the thoughts; and if does not bring riches, it does the same thing by banishing the desire of them.
JAMES ADDISON

Content makes poor men rich; discontent makes rich men poor.
BENJAMIN FRANKLIN

Do not spoil what you have by desiring what you have not; but remember that what you now have was once among the things only hoped for.
EPICTETUS

Contentment is a pearl of great price, and whoever procures it at the expense of ten thousand desires makes a wise and happy choice.
JOHN BALGUY

Contentment with the divine will is the best remedy we can apply to misfortunes.
SIR WILLIAM TEMPLE

The rarity of happiness among those who achieved much is evidence that achievement is not in itself the assurance of a happy life. The great, like the humble, may have to find their satisfaction in the same plain things.
EDGAR ANDREW COLLARD

An ounce of contentment is worth a pound of sadness to serve God with.
THOMAS FULLER

Content is the philosopher's stone, which turns all it touches into gold.
THOMAS FULLER

A harvest of peace is produced from a seed of contentment.
ANONYMOUS

I have learned, in whatsoever state I am, therewith to be content.
BIBLE

There is no end of craving. Hence contentment alone is the best way to happiness. Therefore, acquire contentment.
SWAMI SIVANANDA

A contented mind is the greatest blessing a man can enjoy in this world.
JOSEPH ADDISON

While we pursue happiness, we flee from contentment.
HASIDIC PROVERB

When you can think of yesterday without regret and tomorrow without fear, you are near contentment.
ANONYMOUS

I am easily satisfied with the very best.
WINSTON CHURCHILL

Contentment is not the fulfillment of what you want, but the realization of how much you already have.
ANONYMOUS

To be content with little is difficult; to be content with much impossible.
MARIE VON EBNER-ESCHENBACH

Fortify yourself with contentment, for this is an impregnable fortress.
EPICTETUS

Those who want much, are always much in need; happy the man to whom God gives with a sparing hand what is sufficient for his wants.
HORACE

Yes! In the poor man's garden grow, far more than herbs and flowers, kind thoughts, contentment, peace of mind, and joy for weary hours.
MARY HOWITT

Few things are needed to make a wise man happy; nothing can make a fool content; that is why most men are miserable.
FRANCOIS DE LA ROCHEFOUCAULD

To be content doesn't mean you don't desire more, it means you're thankful for what you have and patient for what's to come.
TONY GASKINS

Happiness will never come to those who fail to appreciate what they already have.
BILAL ZAOOR

When you are discontent, you always want more, more, more. Your desire can never be satisfied. But when you practice contentment, you can say to yourself, 'Oh yes – I already have everything that I really need.
DALAI LAMA

The world is full of people looking for spectacular happiness while they snub contentment.
DOUG LARSON

Greed yields only sorrow; contentment is best.
BABA QUOTES

I don't look for bliss, just contentment.
ALISON KRAUSS

I moaned because I had no shoes, until I met a man who had no feet.
ANONYMOUS

Contentment is natural wealth, luxury is artificial poverty.
SOCRATES

A man's well being depends upon his degree of contentment.
BABA QUOTES

Contentment gives a crown where fortune hath denied it.
JOHN FORD

He is rich that is satisfied.
THOMAS FULLER

When we cannot find contentment in ourselves, it is useless to seek elsewhere.
FRANCOIS DE LA ROCHEFOUCAULD

A man who is contented with what he has done will never become famous for what he will do.
FRED ESTABROOK

It is right to be contented with what we have, never with what we are.
MACKINTOSH

I am content; that is a blessing greater than riches; and he whom that is given need ask no more.
HENRY FIELDING

Be content with what you have; rejoice in the way things are. When you realize there is nothing lacking, the whole world belongs to you.
LAO TZU

He who is not contented with what he has, would not be contented with what he would like to have.
SOCRATES

Wealth consists not in having great possessions, but in having few wants.
EPICTETUS

Contentment is the only real wealth.
ALFRED NOBEL

Contentment does not come from achievement.
PAUL HENDERSON

Nothing in excess.
SOLON

We don't need to increase our goods nearly as much as we need to scale down are wants. Not wanting something is as good as possessing it.
DONALD HORBAN

The hardest thing is to take less when you can get more.
KIN HUBBARD

Whoever does not regard what he has as most ample wealth is unhappy, though he is master of the world.
EPICURUS

How few are our real wants, and how easy is it to satisfy them! Our imaginary ones are boundless and insatiable.
JULIUS CHARLES HARE

If you desire many things, many things will seem but a few.
BENJAMIN FRANKLIN

How many things there are which I do not want.
SOCRATES

Moderate desires constitute a character fitted to acquire all the good which the world can yield. He who has this character is prepared, in whatever situation he is, therewith to be content and learned the science of being happy.
TIMOTHY DWIGHT

He is poor who does not feel content.
JAPANESE PROVERB

Nothing will content him who is not content with a little.
GREEK PROVERB

Contentment is worth more than riches.
GERMAN PROVERB

Try to live the life of the good man who is more than content with what is allocated to him.

MARCUS AURELIUS

If all misfortunes were laid in one common heap whence everyone must take an equal portion, most people would be contented to take their own and depart.

SOCRATES

To be satisfied with a little, is the greatest wisdom; and he that increaseth his riches, increaseth his cares; but a contented mind is a hidden treasure, and trouble findeth it not.

AKHENATON

If you are content, you have enough to live comfortably.

TITUS M. PLAUTUS

Riches are not from an abundance of worldly goods, but from a contented mind.

MHAMMAND

He that is not content in poverty would not be so neither in plenty; for the fault is not in the thing, but in the mind.

LUCIUS ANNAEUS SENECA

Content has a kindly influence on the soul of man, in respect of every being to whom he stands related. It extinguishes all murmuring, repining, and ingratitude toward the Being who has allotted us our part to act in the world. It destroys all inordinate ambition; gives sweetness to the conversation, and serenity to all thoughts; and if it does not bring riches, it does the same thing by banishing the desire of them.

JOSEPH ADDISON

Joy is indeed a precious quality which very few experience in their lives. The person who knows how to enjoy life will never grow old no matter how many years he can call his own. It is easy to be happy at specific times, but there is a certain art in being happy and contented every day.

ORA CAPELLI

With a few flowers in my garden, half a dozen pictures and some books, I live without envy.

LOPE DE VEGA

Test by a trial how excellent is the life of the good man - the man who rejoices at the portion given hm in the universal lot and abides therein content; just in all his ways and kindly minded toward all men.

MARCUS AURELIUS

One contented with what he has done will never become famous for what he will do. He has lain down to die.

CHRISTIAN NESTELL BOVEE

We are all of us richer than we think we are.

MICHEL DE MONTAIGNE

He that is discontented in one place will seldom be happy in another.

AESOP

To be satisfied with what one has; that is wealth. As long as one sorely needs a certain additional amount, that man isn't rich.

MARK TWAIN

Our desires always increase with our possessions; the knowledge that something remains yet unenjoyed, impairs our enjoyment of the good before us.

SAMUEL JOHNSON

I am always content with that which happens; for I know that what God chooses is better than what I choose.

EPICTETUS

He who is content can never be ruined.

CHINESE PROVERB

To be content with what we possess is the greatest and most secure of riches.

MARCUS TULLIUS CICER

He is richest who is content with the least, for content is the wealth of nature.

SOCRATES

COOPERATION

Men are judged to a large degree by their ability to work with other men.
ROBERT F. BLACK

All your strength is in union. All your danger is in discord.
HENRY WADSWORTH LONGFELLOW

The strength of an organization is not I. It is we.
E. B. ZU TAVERN

The successful man cooperates: we live in an age of cooperation when men succeed as they work together – team work. The organization that cannot cooperate cannot succeed. In the future, it will be difficult for any employee to stay on the payroll very long who is unable to mix agreeably with his co-workers. One of the qualities of increasing importance that makes for success is the ability to cooperate with people.
A. B. ZU TAVERN

Light is the task when many share the load.
HOMER

Cooperation is spelled with two letters – we.
H. M. VERITY

One hand washes the other; give and take.
EPICHARMUS

Many hands make light work.
ENGLISH PROVERB

We live very close together. So, our prime purpose in this life is to help others. And if you can't help them, at least don't hurt them.

DALAI LAMA

Teamwork divides the task and multiplies the success.

ANONYMOUS

Together ordinary people can achieve extraordinary results.

BECKA SCHOETTLE

Cooperation doesn't mean agreement, it means working together to advance the greater good.

SIMON SINEK

Nothing truly valuable can be achieved except by the unselfish cooperation of many individuals.

ALBERT EINSTEIN

Two heads are better than one.

POLISH PROVERB

There is immense power when a group of people with similar interests gets together to work toward the same goals.

IDOWU KOYENIKAN

Cooperation is willing collaboration by free individuals in a collective effort that creates more value than it expends.

JAMES RAYMOND LUCAS

Only when all contribute their firewood can they build up a strong fire.

CHINESE PROVERB

The point that most needs to be borne in mind is that the welfare of every business is dependent upon cooperation and team-work on the part of its personnel. Proper cooperation cannot be secured between groups of men who are constantly quarreling among themselves over petty grievances.

CHARLES GOW

If everyone is moving forward together, then success takes care of itself.
HENRY FORD

Alone we can do so little; together we can do so much.
HELEN KELLER

Teamwork is the ability to work together toward a common vision. The ability to direct individual accomplishments toward organizational objectives. It is the fuel that allows common people to attain uncommon results.
ANDREW CARNEGIE

Cooperation is the thorough conviction that nobody can get there unless everybody gets there.
VIRGINIA BURDEN

It takes two flints to make a fire.
LOUISA ALCOTT

It is amazing what you can accomplish if you do not care who gets the credit.
HARRY S. TRUMAN

No matter how much work a man can do, no matter how engaging his personality may be, he will not advance far in business if he cannot work through others.
JOHN CRAIG

The difference between a pile of bricks and a skyscraper, a shack and a city, a piece of steel and the Brooklyn Bridge, is cooperation. The measure of the strength of an organization is its ability to say we; to think, plan and work together.
A. B. ZU TAVERN

COURAGE

A high heart ought to bear calamities and not flee them, since in bearing them appears the grandeur of the mind and in fleeing them the cowardice of the heart.

PIETRO ARETINO

A ship in harbor is safe, but that is not what ships are built for.

WILLIAM G. SHEDD

To bear other people's afflictions, everyone has courage and enough to spare.

BENJAMIN FRANKLIN

Courage is doing what you're afraid to do. There can be no courage unless you're scared.

EDDIE VERNON RICKENBACKER

Do not pray for easy lives; pray to be stronger men. Do not pray for tasks equal to your powers; pray for powers equal to your tasks.

PHILLIPS BROOKS

Courage starts with showing up and letting ourselves be seen.

BRENE BROWN

Fight on, my merry men all, I'm a little wounded, but I am not slain; I will lay me down for a bleed a while, then I'll rise and fight with you again.

JOHN DRYDEN

Life shrinks or expands in proportion to one's courage.

ANAIS NIN

I do not ask to walk smooth paths nor bear an easy load. I pray for strength and fortitude to climb the rock-strewn road. Give me such courage I can scale the hardest peaks alone, and transform every stumbling block into a steppingstone.

GAIL BROOK BURKET

In Chinese, the word for crisis is wei ji, composed of the character wei, which means danger, and ji, which means opportunity.

JAN WONG

Never let the fear of striking out keep you from playing the game.

BABE RUTH

One ought never to turn one's back on a threatened danger and try to run away from it. If you do that, you will double the danger. But if you meet it promptly and without flinching, you will reduce the danger by half. Never run away from anything. Never!

WINSTON CHURCHILL

Only when we are no longer afraid do we begin to live.

DOROTHY THOMPSON

You gain strength, courage, and confidence by every experience in which you really stop to look fear in the face. You must do the thing which you think you cannot do.

ELEANOR ROOSEVELT

It takes a lot of courage to release the familiar and seemingly secure, to embrace the new. But there is no real security in what is no longer meaningful. There is more security in the adventurous and exciting, for in movement, there is life, and in change, there is power.

ALLEN COHEN

A man of courage is also full of faith.

MARCUS TULLIUS CICERO

Moral excellence comes about as a result of habit. We become just by doing just acts, temperance by doing temperance acts, brave by doing brave acts.

ARISTOTLE

Without courage, wisdom bears no fruit.
BALTASAR GRACIAN

To see what is right and not to do it, is want of courage.
CONFUCIUS

Successful leaders have the courage to take action while others hesitate.
JOHN MAXWELL

Have courage for the great sorrows of life and patience for the small ones; and when you have laboriously accomplished your daily task, go to sleep in peace. God is awake.
VICTOR HUGO

We must have courage to bet on our ideas, to take the calculated risk, and to act. Everyday living requires courage if life is to be effective and bring happiness.
MAXWELL MALTZ

Be strong and of a good courage; be not afraid, neither be thou dismayed; for the Lord thy God is with thee withersoever thou goest.
BIBLE

Nothing is more valuable to a man than courage.
TERENCE

Courage is the first of human qualities because it is the quality which guarantees all others.
WINSTON CHURCHILL

Courage, it would seem, is nothing less than the power to overcome danger, misfortune, fear, injustice, while continuing to affirm inwardly that life with all its sorrows is good; that everything is meaningful even if in a sense beyond our understanding; and that there is always tomorrow.
DOROTHY THOMPSON

Half of a man's wisdom goes with his courage.
RALPH WALDO EMERSON

We could never learn to be brave and patient if there were only joy in the world.
HELEN KELLER

Conscience is the root of all true courage; if a man would be brave let him obey his conscience.
JAME FREEMAN CLARKE

Abraham Lincoln did not go to Gettysburg, having commissioned a poll to find out what would sell in Gettysburg. There were no people with percentages for him, cautioning him about this group or that group or what they found in exit polls a year earlier. When will we have the courage of Lincoln?
ROBERT COLES

Courage is fear holding on a minute longer.
GEORGE SMITH PATTON

God places the heaviest burden on those who can carry its weight.
REGGIE WHITE

If we're growing, we're always going to be out of our comfort zone.
JOHN MAXWELL

Courage is resistance to fear, mastery of fear – not absence of fear.
MARK TWAIN

Some people believe holding on and hanging in there are signs of great strength. However, there are times when it takes much more strength to know when to let go and then do it.
ANN LANDERS

Real courage is doing the right thing when nobody's looking. Doing the unpopular thing because it's what you believe, and the heck with everybody.
JUSTIN CRONIN

However mean your life is, meet it and live it; do not shun it and call it hard names.
HENRY DAVID THOREAU

He's truly valiant, that can wisely suffer the worst that man can breathe.
WILLIAM SHAKESPEARE

What would life be if we had no courage to attempt anything?
VINCENT VAN GOGH

He who is brave is free.
SOCRATES

Have the courage to say no. Have the courage to face the truth. Do the right thing because it is right. These are the magic keys to living your life with integrity.
W. CLEMENT STONE

Wealth lost, something lost; honor lost, much lost; courage lost, all lost.
JOHANN WOLFGANG VON GOETHE

Fear and courage are brothers.
PROVERB

You cannot swim for new horizons until you have courage to lose sight of the shore.
WILLIAM FAULKNER

You don't develop courage by being happy in your relationships everyday. You develop it by surviving difficult times and challenging adversity.
EPICURUS

He who is brave is free.
SENECA

Be the kind of person who dares to face life's challenges and overcome them rather than dodging them.
ROY T. BENNETT

Being terrified but going ahead and doing what must be done – that's courage. The one who feels no fear is a fool, and the one who lets fear rule him is a coward.
PIERS ANTHONY

Never bend your head. Always hold it high. Look the world straight in the eye.
HELEN KELLER

Each mistake teaches you something new about yourself. There is no failure, remember, except in no longer trying. It is the courage to continue that counts.
CHRIS BRADFORD

He who is not courageous enough to take risks will accomplish nothing in life.
MUHAMMAD ALI

Nothing in life is to be feared, it is only to be understood. Now is the time to understand more, so that we may fear less.
MARIE CURIE

The greatest test of courage on the earth is to bear defeat without losing heart.
R. G. INGERSOLL

If you are going through hell, keep going.
WINSTON CHURCHILL

It is not the critic who counts, not the man who points out how the strong stumbled, or where the doer of deeds could have done better. The credit belongs to the man who is actually in the arena, whose face is marred by dust and sweat and blood, who strives valiantly, who errs and comes short again and again, who knows the great enthusiasms, the great devotions, and spends himself in a worthy cause, who at best knows achievement and who at worst if he fails while daring greatly so that his place shall never be with those cold and timid souls who know neither victory or defeat.

THEODORE ROOSEVELT

Anyone can hide. Facing up to things, working through them, that's what makes you strong.
SARAH DRESSEN

Courage is the main quality of leadership, in my opinion, no matter where it is experienced.
WALT DISNEY

The only thing we have to fear is fear itself.
FRANKLIN D. ROOSEVELT

The greatest glory in living lies not in never failing, but in rising every time we fail.
NELSON MANDELA

Courage is the most important of all virtues, because without it we can't practice any other virtue with consistency.
MAYA ANGELOU

It is better by noble boldness to run the risk of being subject to half of the evils we anticipate than to remain in cowardly listlessness for fear of what might happen.
HERODOTUS

Fortune helps the brave.
VIRGIL

He who loses wealth loses much; he who loses a friend loses more; but he who loses his courage loses all.
MIGUEL DE CERVANTES

Let us be brave in the face of adversity.
LUCIUS ANNAEUS SENECA

It is courage, courage, courage, that raises the blood of life to crimson splendor. Live bravely and present a brave front to adversity.
HORACE

Greatness, in the last analysis, is largely bravery – courage in escaping from old ideas and old standards.
JAMES HARVEY ROBINSON

God grant me the courage not to give up what I think is right, even though I think it is hopeless.
ADMIRAL CHESTER W. NIMITZ

Courage is the power to let go of the familiar.
RAYMOND LINDQUIST

One man with courage makes a majority.
ANDREW JACKSON

No great thing comes to any man unless he has courage.
CARDINAL JAMES GIBBONS

Great things are done more through courage than through wisdom.
GERMAN PROVERB

Courage is the thing. All goes if courage goes.
JAMES M. BARRIE

Courage is sustained by calling up anew the vision of the goal.
B. G. SERTILLANGES

We learn courageous action by going forward whenever fear urges us back.
DAVID SEABURY

Courage is the price that life exacts for granting peace.
AMELIA EARHART

Courage is the virtue which champions the cause of right.
MARCUS TULLIUS CICERO

This is courage...to bear unflinchingly what heaven sends.
EURIPIDES

Great men, great nations, have not been boasters and buffoons, but perceivers of the terror of life, and have manned themselves to face it.
RALPH WALDO EMERSON

Courage conquers more within than any foes without, never needs to boast or blame or raise his voice and shout. Courage is a quietness - not martial music made - born of facing up to life even when afraid.
EMILY SARGENT COUNCILMAN

True bravery is shown by performing without witness what one might be capable of doing before all the world.
FRANCOIS DE LA ROCHEFOUCAULD

Heroes may not be braver than anyone else. They're just braver five minutes longer.
RONALD REAGON

Courage is very important. Like a muscle, it is strengthened by use.
RUTH GORDON

Courage in danger is half the battle.
TITUS M. PLAUTUS

Whether you be man or woman you will never do anything in this world without courage. It is the greatest quality of the mind next to honor.
JAMES ALLEN

Always do what you are afraid to do.
RALPH WALDO EMERSON

Facing it, always facing it, that's the way to get through. Face it.
JOSEPH CONRAD

A single feat of daring can alter the whole conception of what is possible.
GRAHAM GREENE

Bravery never goes out of fashion.
WILLIAM MAKEPEACE THACKERAY

Of all the qualities of character which provoke the admiration of men, there are few which do so with such spontaneity and universality as that of courage. It makes an appeal to something deep in human nature which neither friend nor foe can resist. Regardless of the changes in fashion in human conduct, courage is never outmoded. Its appeal is timeless, changeless and universal. If moderation may be said to be the silken thread running through all the virtues, courage may be said to be the foundation of all.

JOHN A. O'BRIEN

All goes if courage goes.

JAMES M. BARRIE

God planted fear in the soul as truly as he planted hope or courage. It is a kind of bell or gong which rings the mind into quick life and avoidance on the approach of danger. It is the soul's signal for rallying.

HENRY WARD BEECHER

Moral courage is a virtue of highest cast and nobler origin than physical. It springs from a consciousness of virtue, and renders a man, in the pursuit of defence of right, superior to the fear of reproach, opposition, or contempt.

S. G. GOODRICH

Our greatest enemies are not wild beasts or deadly germs but fears that paralise thought, poison the mind, and destroy character. Our only protection against fear is faith.

RYLLIS G. LYNIP

The best way to deal with adversity, afflictions and handicaps is to face them frankly, calmly, realistically. Study them carefully and see how they can be overcome, borne with patience, or transmuted into occasions for growth in mind, heart and soul. The fatal mistake is to seek to ignore them, to bury one's head in the sand. What matters is not what happens to an individual but how he reacts to those happenings. It is what he does to them that counts. The frank facing of a menacing situation is the first step in removing its fangs. Thinking pays its richest dividends when done in the face of impending danger, adversity, or actual affliction. Though facing the tribulation with clarity of vision, adherence to ideals and trust in God, the individual secures the courage to transmute adversity into a stairs on which to scale the heights.

JOHN A. O'BRIEN

True courage is cool and calm. The bravest of men have the least of a brutal, bullying insolence, and in the very time of danger are found the most serene and free.

ANTHONY A. SHAFTSBURY

For fourteen years I have not had a day of real health. I have wakened sick and gone to bed weary, yet I have done my work unflinchingly. I have written in bed and out of bed, written in hemorrhages, written in sickness, written torn by coughing, written when my head swam for weakness, and I have it done all for so long that it seems to me I have won my wager and recovered my glove. Yet the battle still goes on: ill or well is a trifle so long as it goes. I was made for a contest, and the Power-That-Be have willed that my battlefield shall be the dingy, inglorious one of the bed and the medicine-bottle.

ROBERT LOUIS STEVENSON

Courage is the best gift of all; courage stands before everything. It is what preserves our liberty, safety, life, and our homes and patents, our country and children. Courage comprises all things: a man with courage has every blessing.

TITUS M. PLAUTUS

The brave man is not he who feels no fear, for that were stupid and irrational; but he whose noble soul subdues its fear, and bravely dares the danger nature shrinks from.

JOANNA BAILLIE

For who gets wealth, that puts not from the shore? Danger hath honour; great designs, their fame; glory doth follow, courage goes before.

SAMUEL DANIEL

If we take the generally accepted definition of bravery as a quality which knows not fear, I have never seen a brave man. All men are frightened. The more intelligent they are, the more they are frightened. The courageous man is the man who forces himself, in spite of fear, to carry on. Discipline, pride, self-respect, self-confidence, and the love of glory are attributes which will make a man courageous even when he is afraid.

GEORGE S. PATTON

I love the man who can smile in trouble, who can gather strength from distress, and grow brave by reaction. 'Tis the business of little minds to shrink, but he whose heart is firm, and whose conscience approves his conduct, will pursue his principles unto death.

THOMAS PAINE

What a new face courage puts on everything!
RALPH WALDO EMERSON

I beg you take courage; the brave soul can mend even disaster.
CATHERINE OF RUSSIA

No man can answer for his courage who has never been in danger.
FRANCOIS DE LA ROCHEFOUCAULD

Courage is the armed sentinel that guards liberty, innocence and right.
JAMES BALDWIN

Fear always springs from ignorance.
RALPH WALDO EMERSON

There is a great beauty in going through life fearlessly. Half our fears are baseless – the other half discreditable.
CHRISTIAN NESTELL BOVEE

He who fears something gives it power over him.
MOORISH PROVERB

Fear makes the wolf bigger than he is.
GERMAN PROVERB

No passion so effectively robs the mind of all its powers of acting and reasoning as fear.
EDMUND BURKE

The most drastic and usually the most effective remedy for fear is direct action.
WILLIAM HENRY BURNHAM

He who fears he shall suffer, already suffers what he fears.
MICHEL DE MONTAIGNE

We are more often frightened than hurt: our troubles spring more often from fancy than reality.
LUCIUS ANNAEUS SENECA

Knowledge is the antidote to fear.
RALPH WALDO EMERSON

For God hath not given us the spirit of fear; but of power, and of love, and of a sound mind.
BIBLE

He who fears to suffer, suffers from fear.
FRENCH PROVERB

Cowards die many times before their deaths; the valiant never taste of death but once.
WILLIAM SHAKESPEARE

The world has no room for cowards. We must all be ready somehow to toil, to suffer, to die. And yours is not the less noble because no drum beats before you when you go out into your daily battlefields, and no crowds shout about your coming when you return from your daily victory or defeat.
ROBERT LOUIS STEVENSON

It requires more courage to suffer than to die.
NAPOLEON BONAPARTE

One doesn't discover new lands without consenting to lose sight of shore for a very long time.
ANDRE GIDE

It is easy to be brave from a safe distance.
AESOP

Without justice, courage is weak.
BENJAMIN FRANKLIN

Courage doesn't mean you don't get afraid. Courage means you don't let fear stop you.
BETHANY HAMILTON

A hero is no braver than an ordinary man, but he is braver five minutes longer.
RALPH WALDO EMERSON

Courage is never to let your actions be influenced by your fears.
ARTHUR KOESTLER

Courage is what you find lacking in most people because courage is constantly limited by fear, and fear is possessed by most people and possibly by all people.
DAVID SARNOFF

This is the way to cultivate courage: first by standing firm on some conscientious principle, some law of duty. Next, by being faithful to truth and right on small occasions and common events. Third, by trusting God for help and power.
JAMES FREEMAN CLARKE

COURTESY

Be courteous to all, but intimate with few, and let those few be well-tried before you give them your confidence.

GEORGE WASHINGTON

Courtesy is the keynote of success with the general public.

R. W. DALE

Really big people are, above everything else, courteous, considerate and generous – not just to some people in some circumstances – but to everyone all the time.

THOMAS J. WATSON

Acquire the reputation of courtesy; for it is enough to make you liked. Politeness is the main ingredient of culture.

BALTASAR GRACIAN

Courteous speaking gets friendly answers.

ROY L. SMITH

Life is not so short but that there is always time for courtesy.

RALPH WALDO EMERSON

If a man be gracious and courteous to strangers, it shows he is a citizen of the world.

FRANCIS BACON

Many men fail because they do not see the importance of being kind and courteous to the men under them. Kindness to everybody always pays for itself. And besides, it is a pleasure to be kind.

CHARLES M. SCHWAB

Nothing is gained by not being kind and courteous.
NEAL ADAMS

You can't live your life trying to please people. You be courteous, and you be respectful, but you've got to do things in the way that you want to do them.
KIP MOORE

If you will be cherished when you are old, be courteous while you be young.
JOHN LYLY

A wise man in his house should find a wife gentle and courteous, or no wife at all.
EURIPIDES

Nothing is ever lost by courtesy. It is the cheapest of the pleasures, costs nothing and conveys much. It pleases him who gives and him who receives, and thus, like mercy, it is twice blessed.
ERASTUS WIMAN

Lack of courtesy is an extreme form of disrespect.
KHALEEL DATAY

He who sows courtesy reaps friendship.
SAINT BASIL

The greater person is one of courtesy.
ALFRED TENNYSON

Courtesy is a small act, but it packs a mighty wallop.
LEWIS CARROLL

To be humble to superiors is duty, to equals courtesy, to inferiors nobleness.
BENJAMIN FRANKLIN

The small courtesies sweeten life, the greater ennoble it.
CHRISTIAN NESTELL BOVEE

The habit of attending to small things and of appreciating small courtesies is one of the important marks of a good person.

NELSON MANDELA

All doors open to courtesy.

THOMAS FULLER

Courtesy is a smile in action.

JOHN A. O'BRIEN

A gentleman never heard a story before.

AUSTIN O'MALLEY

How sweet and gracious, even in common speech, is that fine sense which men call courtesy! Wholesome as air and genial as the light, welcome in every clime as breath of flowers, it transmutes aliens into trusting friends, and gives its owner a passport round the globe.

JAMES T. FIELDS

Hail! Ye small sweet courtesies of life; for smooth do ye make the road of it, like grace and beauty, which beget inclinations to love at first sight; it is ye who open the door and let the stranger in.

LAURENCE STERNE

A man's own good-breeding is his best security against other people's ill manners.

EARL OF CHESTERFIELD

Courtesy on one side only lasts not long.

GEORGE HERBERT

Shepherd, I take thy word, and trust thy honest offer'd courtesy, which oft is sooner found in lowly sheds with smoky rafters, than in tap'stry halls, and courts of princes.

JOHN MILTON

Small kindnesses, small courtesies, small considerations, habitually practiced in our social intercourse, give a greater charm to the character than the display of great talents and accomplishments.

M. A. KELTY

In all the affairs of life, social as well as political, courtesies of a small and trivial character are the ones which strike deepest to the grateful and appreciating heart.

HENRY CLAY

As charity covers a multitude of sins begore God, so does politeness before men.

LORD GREVILLE

There is no outward sign of true courtesy that does not rest on a deep moral foundation.

JOHANN WOLFGANG VON GOETHE

Courtesy is as much a mark of a gentleman as courage.

THEODORE ROOSEVELT

Courtesies of a small and trivial character are the ones which strike deepest in the grateful and appreciating heart.

HENRY CLAY

Courtesy is itself a form of service. By gentleness of manner, by an unobstructive sympathy, by thoughtfulness for others in little things we may smooth the roughness of life.

R. W. DALE

CREATION

Man unites himself with the world in the process of creation.
ERICH FROMM

For good and evil, man is a free creative spirit. This produces the very queer world we live in, a world in continuous creation and, therefore, continuous change and insecurity.
JOYCE CARY

It's wise to learn - tis Godlike to create.
B. G. SAXE

Proximity to the crowd, to the majority view, spells the death of creativity. For a soul can create only when alone, and some are chosen for the flowering that takes place in the dark avenues of the night.
ABRAHAM JOSHUA HESCHEL

A master needs quiet. Calm and quiet are his most imperative needs. Isolation and complete loneliness are my only consolation, and my salvation.
RICHARD WAGNER

Everything vanishes around me, and works are born as if out of the void. Ripe, graphic fruits fall off. My hand has become the obedient instrument of a remote will.
PAUL KLEE

Whatever creativity is, it is, in part, a solution to a problem.
BRIAN ALDISS

Like every writer, I am asked where my work originates, and if I knew I would go there more often to find more.
ARTHUR MILLER

Nothing will change the fact that I cannot produce the least thing without absolute solitude.
JOHANN WOLFGANG VON GOETHE

Creativity is seeing what others see and thinking what no one else ever thought.
ALBERT EINSTEIN

A creative life is an amplified life. It's a bigger life, a happier life, an expanded life, and a hell of a lot more interesting life.
ELIZABETH GILBERT

Don't wait for inspiration. It comes while working.
HENRI MATISSE

The worst enemy to creativity is self-doubt.
SYLVIA PLATH

You can't use up creativity. The more you use, the more you have.
MAYA ANGELOU

There is no innovation and creativity without failure.
BRENE BROWN

If you want to live your life in a creative way, as an artist, you have to not look back too much.
STEVE JOBS

Imagination is the beginning of creation. You imagine what you desire, you will what you imagine, and at last, you create what you will.
GEORGE BERNARD SHAW

Creativity requires the courage to let go of certainties.
ERICH FROMM

The comfort zone is the great enemy to creativity.
DAN STEVENS

You never have to change anything you got up in the middle of the night to write.
SAUL BELLOW

I dwell in possibility.
EMILY DICKINSON

Imagination rules the world.
NAPOLEON BONAPARTE

Curiosity about life in all aspects, I think, is still the secret of great creative people.
LEO BURNETT

Everything you can imagine is real.
PABLO PICASSO

The desire to create is one of the deepest yearnings of the human soul.
DIETER F. UCHTDORF

Create with the heart; build with the mind.
CRISS JAMI

I've always loved the night, when everyone else is asleep and the world is mine. It's quiet and dark – the perfect time for creativity.
JONATHON HARNISCH

Man's most valuable faculty is his imagination.
ANONYMOUS

The power of imagination makes us infinite.

JOHN MUIR

Thank God for the creative ideas that enrich life by adding your own creative contributions to human progress.

WILFERD PETERSON

CURIOSITY

Curiosity is one of the permanent and certain characteristics of a vigorous mind.
SAMUEL JOHNSON

A man should live if only to satisfy his curiosity.
YIDDISH PROVERBS

Curiosity is ill manners in another's house.
THOMAS FULLER

Curiosity is the thirst of the soul.
SAMUEL JOHNSON

Friendly concern is often simple curiosity.
BARON MCKAY

Satisfaction of one's curiosity is one of the greatest sources of happiness in life.
LINUS PAULING

One of the secrets of life is to keep our intellectual curiosity acute.
WILLIAM LYON PHELPS

The important thing is not to stop questioning. Curiosity has its own reason for existing.
ALBERT EINSTEIN

Research is formalized curiosity. It is poking and prying with a purpose.
ZORA NEALE HURSTON

I'm naturally curious, and I've always been driven by my curiosity. Curiosity gets people excited. Curiosity leads to new ideas, new jobs, new industries.
ANNE SWEENEY

Basically, I have been compelled by curiosity.
MARY LEAKEY

Knowing the answers will help you in school. Knowing how to question will help you in life.
WARREN BERGER

I have no special talents. I am only passionately curious.
ALBERT EINSTEIN

The future belongs to the curious.
ANONYMOUS

Curiosity is the engine of achievement.
KEN ROBINSON

Curiosity keeps leading us down new paths.
WALT DISNEY

Life must be lived, and curiosity kept alive.
ELEANOR ROOSEVELT

Much of what I stumbled into by following my curiosity an intuition turned out to be priceless later on.
STEVE JOBS

Curiosity is the lust of the mind.
THOMAS HOBBES

Learning is by nature, curiosity.
PLATO

Blessed are the curious, for they shall have adventures.
ANONYMOUS

Ideas come from curiosity.
WALT DISNEY

The best in business have boundless curiosity and open minds.
ROBIN SHARMA

There was no telling what people might find out once they felt free to ask whatever questions they wanted to do.
JOSEPH HELLER

DEATH

Death is no respector of persons whether you are king or peasant. The greatest oak must fall.
MARCUS AURELIUS

He that lives to live forever, never fears dying.
WILLIAM PENN

If you would not be forgotten as soon as you are dead, either write things worth reading or do things worth writing.
BENJAMIN FRANKLIN

It is not death that a man should fear, but he should fear never beginning to live.
MARCUS AURELIUS

As a well-spent day brings happy sleep, so a life well spent brings happy death.
LEONARDO DA VINCI

The presence of death makes more meaningful all of the values of life.
JOSHUA LIEBMAN

Then shall the dust return to the earth as it was; and the spirit shall return unto God who gave it.
BIBLE

Live a trustful, tranquil, God-centered life, meeting storm with calm, adversity with fortitude, defeat with faith and – Death can only mean immortality.
RHODA LACHAR

Life's race well run, Life's work well done, Life's victory won, Now cometh rest.
E. H. PARKER

I often feel that death is not the enemy of life, but its friend, for knowledge that our years are limited which makes them so precious.
JOSHUA LIEBMAN

It matters not how a man dies, but how he lives. The act of dying is not of importance, it lasts so short of time.
SAMUEL JOHNSON

After the game, the king and pawn go into the same box.
ITALIAN SAYING

It hath often been said, that it is not death, but dying, which is terrible.
HENRY FIELDING

To die is poignantly bitter, but the idea of having to die without having lived is unbearable.
ERICH FROMM

He hath lived ill that knows not know how to die well.
THOMAS FULLER

Flowers and buds fall, and the old and ripe fall.
MALAY PROVERB

A man's dying is more the survivor's affair than his own.
THOMAS MANN

He that dies pays all his debts.
WILLIAM SHAKESPEARE

Nobody knows, in fact, what death is, nor whether to man it is not perchance the greatest of all blessings; yet people fear it as if they surely knew it to be worst of evils.
SOCRATES

Let us endeavor so to live that when we come to die even the undertaker will be sorry.
MARK TWAIN

A death, those heirs that seem the saddest, behind their masks may be the gladdest.
ART BUCK

To live in hearts we leave behind is not to die.
CLYDE CAMPBELL

Fortunate people often have very favorable beginnings and very tragic endings. What matters isn't being applauded when you arrive – for that is common – but being missed when you leave.
BALTASAR GRACIAN

When it's time to die, let us not discover that we have never lived.
HENRY DAVID THOREAU

If you're afraid to die, you will not be able to live.
JAMES BALDWIN

People living deeply have no fear of death.
ANAIS NIN

The dead have no rights. They are nothing; and nothing cannot own something.
THOMAS JEFFERSON

For a man who has done his natural duty, death is as natural and welcome as sleep.
GEORGE SANTAYANA

When good men die, their goodness does not perish.
EURIPIDES

Only those are fit to live who are not afraid to die.
DOUGLAS MACARTHUR

Live as you will wish to have lived when you are dying.
CHRISTIAN FURCHTEGOTT GELLERT

I have fought the good fight, I have finished the race, I have kept the faith.
BIBLE

The call of death is a call of love. Death can be sweet if we answer it in the affirmative, if we accept it as one of the great eternal forms of life and transformation.
HERMANN HESSE

Death is not the greatest loss in life. The greatest loss is what dies inside us while we live.
NORMAN COUSINS

Death is not the opposite of life, but part of it.
HARUKI MURAKAMI

When man dies his spirit returns to God who gave it.
WILLIAM SHAKESPEARE

DECISION

Nothing is more difficult, and therefore more precious, than to be able to decide.
NAPOLEON BONAPARTE

It is the characteristic excellence of the strong man that he can bring momentous issues to the fore and make a decision about them. The weak are always forced to decide between alternatives they have not chosen themselves.
DIETRICH BONHOEFFER

The mark of an educated man is the ability to make a reasoned guess on the basis of insufficient information.
E. L. LOWELL

When once a decision is reached and execution is the order of the day, dismiss absolutely all responsibility and care about the outcome.
WILLIAM JAMES

He who considers too much will perform little.
FRIEDRICH SCHILLER

More decisions are dictated by human feelings than are made by logic and reason.
DR. PAUL PARKER

Your capacity to say "NO" determines your capacity to say "YES" to greater things.
E. STANLEY JONES

Of a truth, he was a wise man who said, "thou shouldst not decide till thou hast heard what both have to say."
ARISTOPHANES

It does not take much strength to do things, but it requires great strength to decide on what to do.

ELBERT HUBBARD

The man who insists upon seeing with perfect clearness before he decides, never decides.

HENRI FREDERIC AMIEL

We make our decisions, and then our decisions turn around and make us.

F. W. BOREHAM

It doesn't make any difference who says a thing or what the position of the man may be, the great question is: "is he right or is he wrong?"

BERNARD M. BARUCH

I have to be wrong a certain number of times in order to be right a certain number of times. However, in order to be either, I must first make a decision.

FRANK N. GIAMPIETRO

When confronted with two courses of action, I jot down on a piece of paper all the arguments in favor of each one - then, on the opposite side, I write the arguments against each one. Then by weighing the arguments, pro and con, and canceling them out, one against the other, I take the course indicated by what remains.

BENJAMIN FRANKLIN

A wise man makes his own decisions, an ignorant man follows the public opinion.

CHINESE PROVERB

To be constantly changing one's plans isn't decision at all - it's indecision.

RABINDRANATH TAGORE

In many lines of work, it isn't how much you do that counts, but how much you do well and how often you decide right.

WILLIAM FEATHER

An executive is a man who decides; sometimes, he decides right, but always he decides.

JOHN HENRY PATTERSON

Quick decisions are unsafe decisions.
SOPHOCLES

To choose, it is first necessary to know.
HERMAN FINER

I have accustomed myself to receive with respect the opinions of others but always take the responsibility of deciding for myself.
ANDREW JACKSON

The decision – maker must not be distracted by problems his subordinates should resolve for themselves.
GEORGE C. MARSHALL

Choose always the way that seems the best, however rough it may be; custom will soon render it easy and agreeable.
PYTHAGORAS

Not all of your decisions will be correct. None of us is perfect. But if you get into the habit of making decisions, experience will develop your judgment to a point where more and more of your decisions will be right. After all, it is better to be right 51 percent of the time and get something done, than it is get nothing done because you fear to reach a decision.
H. W. ANDREWS

I think we should follow a simple rule: if we can take the worst, take the risk.
DR. JOYCE BROTHERS

The best we can do is size up the chances, calculate the risks involved, estimate our ability to deal with them, and then make our plans with confidence.
HENRY FORD

When one bases his life on principle, 99 percent of his decisions are already made.
ANONYMOUS

Decide on what you think is right, and stick to it.
GEORGE ELIOT

Reason with most people, means their own opinions.
WILLIAM HAZLITT

Statistics are no substitute for judgment.
HENRY CLAY

It is the heart always that sees before the head can see.
THOMAS CARLYLE

Deliberation often loses a good chance.
LATIN PROVERB

He who has a choice has trouble.
DUTCH PROVERB

Once a decision was made, I did not worry about it afterward.
HARRY S. TRUMAN

Man does not simply exist, but always decides what his existence will be, what he will become in the next moment.
VIKTOR FRANKL

A true history of human events would show that a far larger proportion of our acts are the result of sudden impulse and accident than of that reason of which we so much boast.
PETER COOPER

Conditions are never just right. People who delay action until all factors are favorable do nothing.
WILLIAM FEATHER

If you wait for inspirations you'll be standing on the corner after the parade is a mile down the street.
BEN NICHOLAS

A man without decision can never be said to belong to himself; he is as a wave of the sea, or a feather in the air which ever breeze blows about.

JOHN FOSTER

Nothing is so exhausting as indecision, and nothing is so futile.

BERTRAND RUSSELL

Not to decide is to decide.

HARVEY COX

In making our decisions, we must use the brains that God has given us. But we must also use our hearts, which He also gave us.

FULTON OURSLER

There is no more miserable human being than one in whom nothing is habitual but indecision.

WILLIAM JAMES

There is a time when we must firmly choose the course we will follow, or the relentless drift of events will make the decision for us.

HERBERT V. PROCHNOW

Be willing to make decisions. That's the most important quality in a good leader. Don't fall victim to what I call the "ready-aim-aim-aim-aim syndrome." You must be willing to fire.

T. BOONE PICKENS

When a person tells you "I'll let you know" – you know.

OLIN MILLER

Through indecision opportunity is often lost.

LATIN PROVERB

When, against one's will, one is pressured into making a hurried decision, the best answer is always "no," because "no" is more easily changed to "yes," than "yes," than "yes" is changed to "no."

CHARLES E. NIELSON

DEPENDABILITY

Ability is important in our quest for success, but dependability is critical.
ZIG ZIGLAR

The greatest ability is dependability.
BOB JONES, SR.

In adults, dependability is the fruit of maturity; in a child, it is the seed.
RICHARD M. EYRE

If you are a man of dependability, you are worth more than if you were clever.
ROY L. SMITH

Gain a modest reputation for being unreliable, and you will never be asked to do a thing.
PAUL THEROUX

Dependability is more important than talent. Dependability is a talent, and it is a talent all can have. It makes no difference how much ability we possess if we are not responsible and dependable.
FLOY L. BENNETT

There is nothing dependable that is not backed by character.
ROY L. SMITH

One does not need to be brilliant to be dependable.
ROY L. SMITH

Dependability is the base upon which all confidence rests in full security. Confidence may be termed the active result of basic dependability.

ROBERT E. HICKS

Dependability is built over time. When people see that you keep your word, make careful promises, and work to correct mistakes, their trust and ability to depend on you will grow.

CHARACTER FIRST EDUCATION

It is worth everything to be dependable.

TODD W. VAN BECK

The more dependable and resourceful we are, the more respect we command and deserve from our superiors and fellow employees alike.

TODD W. VAN BECK

Not every person with ability is dependable, and not every dependable person has ability.

BILLY MCCONNEL

Dependability has a much more satisfactory market than cleverness.

ROY L. SMITH

We often have to put up with most from those on whom we most depend.

BALTASAR GRACIAN

Build for your team a feeling of oneness, of dependence on one another and of strength to be derived by unity.

VINCE LOMBARDI

Depend on no man, or no friend but him who can depend on himself. He only who acts conscientiously toward himself, will act so toward others.

JOHANN KASPAR LAVATER

I learned that you get your first job on your ability and every other after that on your dependability.

MIKE ROYER

Ability is a wonderful thing, but its value is greatly enhanced by dependability. Ability implies repeatability and accountability.

ROBERT A. HEINLEIN

DETERMINATION

Failure will never overtake me, if my determination to succeed is strong enough.

OG MANDINO

If you set goals and go after them with all the determination you muster, your gifts will take you places that will amaze you.

LES BROWN

You've done it before, and you can do it now. See the positive possibilities. Redirect the substantial energy of your frustration and turn it into positive, effective, unstoppable determination.

RALPH MARSTON

The price of success is hard work, dedication to the job at hand, and the determination that we win or lose, we have applied the best of ourselves to the task at hand.

VINCE LOMBARDI

Desire is the key to motivation, but it's determination and commitment to an unrelenting pursuit of your goal – a commitment to excellence – that will enable you to attain the success you seek.

MARIO ANDRETTI

Whatever you do, do it with determination. You have one life to live; do your work with passion and give your best. Whether you want to be a chef, doctor, actor, or a mother, be passionate to get the best result.

ALIA BHATT

In all human affairs, there are efforts, and there are results, and the strength of the effort is the measure of the result.

JAMES ALLEN

The difference between the impossible and possible lies in a man's determination.

TOMMY LASORDA

A determination to succeed is the only way to succeed that I know anything about.

WILLIAM FEATHER

To him that is determined it remains only to act.

ITALIAN PROVRB

If you learn to try again you will never be whipped.

ROY L. SMITH

Most men fail, not through lack of education, but from lack of dogged determination, from lack of dauntless will.

ORISON SWETT MARDEN

Determination and gumption will carry a man far.

E. F. GIRARD

America was not built on fear. America was built on courage, on imagination and an unbeatable determination to do the job at hand.

HARRY S. TRUMAN

Determination gives you the resolve to keep going in spite of all the roadblocks that lay before you.

DENIS WAITLEY

He who walks in the eightfold noble path with unswerving determination is sure to reach Nirvana.

BUDDHA

You've got to get up every morning with determination if you're going to go to bed with satisfaction.
GEORGE HORACE LORIMER

Pursue one great decisive aim with force and determination.
CARL VON CLAUSEWITZ

The truest wisdom is a resolute determination.
NAPOLEON BONAPARTE

The determination to win is the better part of winning.
DAISAKU IKEDA

Stay focused and stay determined. Don't look to anyone else to be your determination – have self-determination. It will take you very far.
JUSTICE SMITH

Do not underestimate the determination of a quiet man.
IAIN DUCAN SMITH

Nothing is impossible in this world. Firm determination, it is said, can move heaven and earth. Things appear far beyond one's power, because one cannot set his heart on any arduous project due to want of strong will.
YAMAMOTO TSUNETOMO

Victory is the child of preparation and determination.
SEAN HAMPTON

Never go backward. Attempt, and do it with all your might. Determination is power.
CHARLES SIMMONS

Determination Over Negativity is a belief that anything is possible no matter who you are or where you come from.
DONOVAN MITCHELL

Determination becomes obsession, and then it becomes all that matters.

JEREMY IRVINE

The only good luck many great men ever had was being born with the ability and determination to overcome bad luck.

CHANNING POLLOCK

An invincible determination can accomplish almost anything, and this lies the great distinction between great and little men.

THOMAS FULLER

You can have all the talent in the world, but without determination, you won't get very far.

MALORIE BLACKMAN

Our greatest glory is not in never failing but in rising every time we fall.

CONFUCIUS

I have willpower and determination. I am very resilient, like a rock.

CARNIE WILSON

I just hate losing, and that gives you an extra determination to work harder.

WAYNE ROONEY

I think the key is basically just your determination. As far an artist is concerned, it's just about your drive and your dream.

CHRIS BROWN

Lack of will power has caused more failure than lack of intelligence or ability.

FLOWER A. NEWHOUSE

The real difference between man is energy. A strong will, a settled purpose, an invincible determination, can accomplish almost anything; and in this lies the distinction between great men and little men.

THOMAS FULLER

Everyone has a dream, but those whose dreams become reality lies in determination.
J. S. FELTS

If you have made mistakes, even serious ones, there is always another chance for you. What we call failure is not the falling down, but the staying down.
MARY PICKFORD

Most people who fail in their dream fail not from lack of ability, but from lack of commitment.
ZIG ZIGLAR

If you really want something, you'll find a way. If you don't, you'll find an excuse.
ANONYMOUS

A determined soul will do more with a rusty monkey wrench than a loafer will accomplish with all the tools in a machine shop.
RUPERT HUGHES

People do not lack strength; they lack will.
VICTOR HUGO

Determine that the thing can and shall be done, and then we shall find the way.
ABRAHAM LINCOLN

The truest wisdom, in general, is a resolute determination.
NAPOLEON

He is a well made man who has a good determination.
RALPH WALDO EMERSON

DISCIPLINE

A soldier is not developed on a feather bed.

HENRY WARD BEECHER

If men live decently, it is because discipline save their very lives for them.

SOPHOCLES

No horse gets anywhere until he is harnessed. No steam or gas ever drives anything until it is confined. No Niagara is ever turned into light and power until it is tunneled. No life ever grows great until it is focused, dedicated, disciplined.

HARRY EMERSON FOSDICK

It is the bridle and the spur that makes a good horse.

THOMAS FULLER

Life is always a discipline, for the lower animals as well as for men; it is so dangerous that only by submitting to some sort of discipline can we become equipped to live in any true sense at all.

HENRY ELLIS

Man must be disciplined, for he is by nature raw and wild.

IMMANUEL KANT

Your disciplines today will govern you tomorrow.

THOMAS BLANDI

No discipline seems pleasant at the time, but painful. Later on, however, it produces a harvest of righteousness and peace for those who have been trained by it.

BIBLE

That aim in life is highest, which requires the highest and finest discipline.
HENRY DAVID THOREAU

There is no man that lives who does not need to be drilled, disciplined, and developed into something higher and nobler and better than he is by nature.
HENRY WARD BEECHER

We do today what they won't do tomorrow so we can accomplish what they can't.
DWAYNE JOHNSON

Winners embrace hard work. They love the discipline of it, the trade-off they're making to win. Losers, on the other hand, see it as a punishment.
And that's the difference.
LOU HOLTZ

We must suffer one of two things the pain of discipline or the pain of regret and disappointment.
JIM ROHN

Personal discipline, when it becomes a way of life in our personal, family, and career lives, will enable us to do some incredible things.
ZIG ZIGLAR

Self-discipline is doing what needs to be done when it needs to be done when you don't feel like doing it.
ANONYMOUS

Discipline is just choosing between what you want now and what you want most.
ANONYMOUS

A person without discipline is like a ship without a rudder in the storm of life.
ROBERT NAJEMY

Discipline is the refining fire by which talent becomes ability.
ROY L. SMITH

Power comes by discipline, and by discipline alone.
E. STANLEY JONES

Self-respect is the fruit of discipline; the sense of dignity grows with the ability to say no to oneself.
ABRAHAM JOSHUA HESCHEL

A disciplined mind leads to happiness, and an undisciplined mind leads to suffering.
DALAI LAMA

With self-discipline, most anything is possible.
THEODORE ROOSEVELT

Discipline yourself, and others won't have to.
JOHN WOODEN

Of the great lessons I've learned is that you've got to discipline your life. No matter how good you may be you've got to be willing to cut out of your life those things that keep you from going to the top.
BOB RICHARDS

Without self-discipline, success is impossible period.
LOU HOLTZ

Self-discipline is the magic power that makes you virtually unstoppable.
ANONYMOUS

Develop self-discipline. Do what needs to be done, even if you don't want to do it.
ANONYMOUS

There is no luck except where there is discipline.
IRISH PROVERB

We don't have to be smarter than the rest; we have to be more disciplined than the rest.
WARREN BUFFETT

By constant self-discipline and self-control you can develop greatness of character.
GRENVILLE KLEISER

Discipline is the bridge between goals and accomplishments.
JIM ROHN

The ability to discipline yourself to delay gratification in the short term in order to enjoy greater rewards in the long term is the indispensable prerequisite to success.
MAXWELL MALTZ

The pain of self-discipline will never be as great as the pain of regret.
ANONYMOUS

Discipline not desire determines your destiny.
ANONYMOUS

I think self-discipline is something, it's like a muscle. The more you exercise it, the stronger it gets.
DANIEL GOLDSTEIN

Through self-discipline comes freedom.
ARISTOTLE

Your ability to discipline yourself to set clear goals, and then to work toward them every day, will do more to guarantee your success than any other single factor.
BRIAN TRACY

Self-discipline is doing what needs to be done, even if you don't want to.
ANONYMOUS

Everything we want to do in life requires discipline. And like strength, flexibility, and endurance, it can be built over time.
LAIRD HAMILTON

Discipline is what you must have to resist the lure of excuses.
BRIAN TRACY

For whatever goal you want to achieve, there is discomfort along that path. Self-discipline drives you through this discomfort and allows you to achieve and attain. It's an essential component of mastery, and nothing great was ever accomplished without it.

PETER HOLLINS

Only disciplined ones are purely free in life and undisciplined are slaves to their moods and passions.

ELIUD KIPCHOGE

The foundation of a strong self comes from small acts of daily discipline.

OPHELIA FILEK

You cannot aim yourself at anything if you are completely undisciplined and untutored.

JORDAN PETERSON

He who lives without discipline dies without honor.

ICELANDIC PROVERB

I cannot conceive of a good life which isn't, in some sense, a self-disciplined life.

PHILIP TOYNBEE

No man ever became great doing as he pleased. Little men do as they please – little nobodies. Great men submit themselves to the laws governing the realm of their greatness.

R. C. HALVERSON

EDUCATION

A man's mind, stretched by new ideas, may never return to its original dimensions.
OLIVER WENDELL HOLMES JR.

Only the educated are free.
EPICTETUS

If you think education is expensive, try ignorance.
ANDY MCINTYRE

Education is not learning; it is the exercise and development of the powers of the mind. There are two great methods by which this end may be accomplished: it may be done in the halls of learning, or in the conflicts of life.
DONALD LAIRD

It is impossible for a man to learn what he thinks he already knows.
EPICTETUS

The direction in which education starts a man will determine his future life.
PLATO

The only person who is educated is the one who has learned how to learn...
and change.
CARL ROGERS

If a man empties his purse into his head, no man can take it away from him. An investment in knowledge always pays the best interest.
BENJAMIN FRANKLIN

To teach is to learn twice.
JOSEPH JOUBERT

Apply yourself. Get all the education you can, but then, by God, do something. Don't just stand there, make it happen.
LEE IACOCCA

Children must be taught how to think, not what to think.
MARGARET MEAD

Educating the mind without educating the heart is no education at all.
ARISTOTLE

Education is the most powerful weapon which you can use to change the world.
NELSON MANDELA

They cannot stop me. I will get my education, if it is in the home, school, or anyplace.
MALALA YOUSAFZAI

The purpose of education, finally, is to create in a person the ability to look at the world for himself, to make his own decisions.
JAMES BALDWIN

Knowledge is power. Information is liberating. Education is the premise of progress, in every society, in every family.
KOFI ANNAN

One child, one teacher, one book, one pen can change the world.
MALALA YOUSAFZAI

Develop a passion for learning. If you do, you will never cease to grow.
ANTHONY J. D'ANGELO

Education is the key to unlocking the world, a passport to freedom.
OPRAH WINFREY

Give a man a fish and you feed him for a day, teach a man to fish and you feed him for a lifetime.
MAIMONIDES

The foundation of every state is the education of its youth.
DIOGENES

A person who won't read has no advantage over one who can't read.
MARK TWAIN

To educate a man in mind and not in morals is to educate a menace to society.
THEODORE ROOSEVELT

I tell students that the opportunities I had were a result of having a good educational background. Education is what allows you to stand out.
ELLEN OCHOA

To read without reflecting is like eating without digesting.
EDMUND BURKE

An expert is one who knows more and more about less and less.
NICHOLAS M. BUTLER

Study without reflection is a waste of time; reflection without study is dangerous.
CONFUCIUS

Seeing much, suffering much and studying much, are the three pillars of learning.
BENJAMIN DISRAELI

All of have meditated on the art of governing mankind have been convinced that the fate of empires depends on the education of youth.
ARISTOTLE

Tell me and I forget, teach me and I may remember, involve me and I learn.
BENJAMIN FRANKLIN

No matter how busy you may think you are, you must find time for reading or surrender yourself to self-chosen ignorance.

CONFUCIUS

To live for a time close to great minds is the best kind of education.

JOHN BUCHAN

Learning is not attained by chance. It must be sought for with ardor and attended to with diligence.

ABIGAIL ADAMS

Learning is the best of all wealth; it is easy to carry, thieves cannot steal it, and tyrants cannot seize it; neither fire nor water can destroy it; and far from decreasing, it increases by giving.

NALADIYAR

The aim of education should be to teach us rather how to think, than what to think.

JAMES BEATTIE

Every now and then a man's mind is stretched by a new idea or sensation, and never shrinks back to its former dimensions.

OLIVER WENDELL HOLMES

He who asks a question is a fool for five minutes; he who does not ask a question remains a fool forever.

CHINESE PROVERB

The greatest education to be had can be found in a library full of books. There, we can meet with those who are no longer alive, visit faraway places, relive history from a front row seat, listen to many of the greatest minds who have ever lived, take advice from the greatest of counselors, and learn from many of the world's greatest teachers; all in a lonely aisle flanked with some dusty old books.

J. S. FELTS

Next in importance to freedom and justice is popular education, without which neither freedom nor justice can be permanently maintained.

JAMES A. GARFIELD

You should have education enough so that you won't have to look up to people; and then more education so that you will be wise enough not to look down on people.

M. L. BOREN

Education is the mother of leadership.

WENDELL WILLKIE

Education makes people easy to lead, but difficult to drive; easy to govern, but impossible to enslave.

HENRY PETER BROUGHAM

A learned man has always wealth in himself.

LATIN PROVERB

What we learn with pleasure we never forget.

LOUIS MERCIER

EMOTION

Probably one of the most important lessons man has to learn is how to guide by his reason the great driving force of his emotions.
WILLIAM ROSS

Let's not forget that the little emotions are the great captains of our lives and we obey them without realizing.
VINCENT VAN GOGH

All the knowledge I possess everyone else can acquire, but my heart is all my own.
JOHANN WOLFGANG VON GOETHE

The young man who has not wept is a savage, and the old man who will not laugh is a fool.
GEORGE SANTAYANA

The advantage of the emotions is that they lead us astray.
OSCAR WILDE

The energy that actually shapes the world springs from emotions.
GEORGE ORWELL

Man is, and was always, a block-head and dullard; much readier to feel and digest, than to think and consider.
THOMAS CARLYLE

The heart has such an influence over the understanding that it is worthwhile to engage it in our interest.
EARL OF CHESTERFIELD

Let my heart be wise. It is the god's best gift.
EURIPIDES

Seeing's believing, but feeling's the truth.
THOMAS FULLER

Time cools, time clarifies, no mood can be maintained quite unaltered through the course of hours.
THOMAS MANN

Reason guides but a small part of man, and that the least interesting. The rest obeys feeling, true or false, and passion, good or bad.
JOSEPH ROUX

Whatever makes an impression on the heart seems lovely in the eye.
SA'DI

It is only with the heart that one can see rightly; what is essential is invisible to the eye.
ANTOINE DE SAINT-EXUPERY

The secret to life is never to have an emotion that is unbecoming.
OSCAR WILDE

The heart is half a prophet.
YIDDISH PROVERB

Nothing vivifies, and nothing kills, like the emotions.
JOSEPH ROUX

The degree of one's emotion varies inversely with one's knowledge of the facts – the less you know the hotter you get.
BERTRAND RUSSELL

Swift instinct leaps; slow reason feebly climbs.
EDWARD YOUNG

When dealing with people remember you are not dealing with creatures of logic, but with creatures of emotion, creatures bristling with prejudice, and motivated by pride and vanity.
DALE CARNEGIE

Half our mistakes in life arise from feeling where we ought to think, and thinking where we ought to feel.
JAMES CHURTON COLLINS

He who reigns himself and rules his passions, desires and fears is more than a king.
JOHN MILTON

My faith helps me overcome such negative emotions and find my equilibrium.
DALAI LAMA

Negative emotions like loneliness, envy, and guilt have an important role to play in a happy life; they're big, flashing signs that something needs to change.
GRETCHEN RUBIN

The sign of an intelligent people is their ability to control their emotions by the application of reason.
MARYA MANNES

If you don't control your emotions, your emotions will control your acts, and that's not good.
MARIANO RIVERA

Emotions are contagious. We've all know it experientially. You know after you have a really fun coffee with a friend, you feel good. When you have a rude clerk in a store, you walk away feeling bad.
DANIEL GOLEMAN

Your emotions are the slaves to your thoughts, and you are the slave to your emotions.
ELIZABETH GILBERT

The emotions are not always subject to reason...but they are always subject to action. When thoughts do not neutralize and undesirable emotion, action will.
WILLIAM JAMES

Action and feeling go together and by regulating the action which is under the more direct control of the will, we can regulate the feeling, which is not.
WILLIAM JAMES

If you can command yourself, you can command the world.
CHINESE PROVERB

Man who man would be must rule the empire of himself.
PERCY BYSSHE SHELLEY

Until you learn to control your emotions, you will never control your life.
J. S. FELTS

Men, as well as women, are much oftener led by their hearts than by their understandings.
EARL OF CHESTERFIELD

No emotion, any more than a wave, can long retain its own individual form.
HENRY WARD BEECHER

Emotion, without knowledge, is dangerous.
J. S. FELTS

We have lost confidence in reason because we have learned that man is chiefly a creature of habit and emotion.
JOHN DEWEY

I don't want to be at the mercy of my emotions. I want to use them, to enjoy them, and to dominate them.
OSCAR WILDE

Our emotions are, without doubt, the driving forces that make us act as we do, and they often make us do things on the impulse of the moment, before we have attempted to use reason to determine whether the results of our act will be good or bad.
WILLIAM ROSS

ENTHUSIASM

Nothing was ever achieved without enthusiasm.
RALPH WALDO EMERSON

Enthusiasm is the mother of effort, and without it nothing great was ever accomplished.
RALPH WALDO EMERSON

Greet the dawn with enthusiasm, and you may expect satisfaction at sunset.
BRUCE BARTON

Without enthusiasm, there is no progress in the world.
WOODROW WILSON

You cannot kindle a fire in any other heart until it is burning in your own.
COLEMAN COX

Some kind of widespread enthusiasm or excitement is apparently needed for the realization of vast and rapid change.
ERIC HOFFER

Enthusiasm is the element of success in everything. It is the light that leads and the strength that lifts men on and up in the great struggles of scientific pursuits and of professional labor. It robs endurance of difficulty, and makes pleasure of duty.
BISHOP DOANE

The successful man has enthusiasm: Good work is never done in cold blood, heat is needed to forge anything. Every great achievement is the story of a flaming heart.
E. B. ZU TAVERN

A man can succeed at almost anything for which he has unlimited enthusiasm.

CHARLES M. SCHWAB

Enthusiasm is the great hill-climber.

ELBERT HUBBARD

The sense of this word among the Greeks affords the noblest definition of it: enthusiasm signifies God in us.

MADAME DE STAEL

Enthusiasm moves the world.

B. BALFOUR

Most great men and women are not perfectly rounded in their personalities, but are instead people whose one driving enthusiasm is so great it makes their faults seem insignificant.

CHARLES A. CERAMI

All we need to make us happy is something to be enthusiastic about.

CHARLES KINGSLEY

Every great and commanding movement in the annals of the world is the triumph of enthusiasm. Nothing great was ever achieved without it.

RALPH WALDO EMERSON

The world belongs to the enthusiast who keeps cool.

WILLIAM MCFEE

Flaming enthusiasm, backed up by horse sense and persistence, is the quality that most frequently makes for success.

DALE CARNEGIE

Knowledge is power, but enthusiasm pulls the switch.

IVERN BALL

None are so old as those who have outlived enthusiasm.
HENRY DAVID THOREAU

Years wrinkle the face, but to give up enthusiasm wrinkles the soul.
WATTERSON LOWE

The secret of genius is to carry the spirit of the child into old age, which means never losing your enthusiasm.
ALDOUS HUXLEY

Enthusiasm is the yeast that makes your hopes shine to the stars. Enthusiasm is the sparkle in your gait. The grip of your hand, the irresistible surge of will and energy to execute your ideas.
HENRY FORD

Enthusiasm is the energy and force that builds literal momentum of the human soul and mind.
BRYANT H. MCGILL

It's faith in something and enthusiasm for something that makes a life worth living.
OLIVER WENDELL HOLMES

Every production of genius must be the production of enthusiasm,
BENJAMIN DISRAELI

Every man is enthusiastic at times. One man has enthusiasm for thirty minutes, another man has it for thirty days. But it is the man who has it for thirty years who makes a success in life.
EDWARD B. BUTLER

If you're not happy every morning when you get up, leave for work, or start to work at home, if you're not enthusiastic about doing that, you're not going to be successful.
DOANLD M. KENDALL

In order to do great things, one must be enthusiastic.
LOUIS DE ROUVROY

Enthusiasm is of the greatest value, so long as we are not carried away by it.

JOHANN WOLFGANG VON GOETHE

Experience sows that success is due less to ability than to zeal. The winner is he who gives himself to his work, body and soul.

CHARLES BUXTON

Enthusiasm is the greatest asset in the world. It beats money and power and influence.

HENRY CHESTER

Enthusiasm is the highest paid quality on earth.

FRANK BETTGER

No person who is enthusiastic about his work has anything to fear from life.

SAMUEL GOLDWYN

EQUALITY

We believe, as asserted in the Declaration of Independence, that all men are created equal; but that does not mean that all men are or can be equal in possessions, in ability, or in merit; it simply means that all shall stand equal in the court of law.

WILLIAM JENNINGS BRYAN

Wherever there is a human being, I see God-given rights inherent in that being, whatever may be the sex or complexion.

WILLIAM LLOYD GARRISON

The struggle for equal opportunity in America is the struggle for America's soul. The ugliness of bigotry stands in direct contradiction to the very meaning of America.

HUBERT H. HUMPHREY

No one can make you feel inferior without your consent.

ELEANOR ROOSEVELT

They who say all men are equal speak an undoubted truth, if they mean all that have an equal right to liberty, to their property, and to their protection of the laws. But they are mistaken if they think men are equal in their station and employments, since they are not so by their talents.

VOLTAIRE

All of us do not have equal talent, but all of us should have an equal opportunity to develop our talents.

JOHN F. KENNEDY

We will never have true civilization until we have learned to recognize the rights of others.

WILL ROGERS

Equality is the soul of liberty; there is, in fact, no liberty without it.
FRANCES WRIGHT

The word 'equality' shows up too much in our founding documents for anyone to pretend it's not the American way.
MARTHA PLIMPTON

All men are created equal, it is only men themselves who place themselves above equality.
DAVID ALLAN COE

If you want to see the true measure of a man, watch how he treats his inferiors, not his equals.
B. K. ROWLING

In order to be great, you just have to care. You have to care about your world, community, and equality.
KATORI HALL

A lot of different flowers make a bouquet.
ISLAMIC PROVERB

There's nothing complicated about equality.
ALICE PAUL

Race, gender, religion, sexuality, we are all people and that's it.
CONNOR FRANTA

I hope that we always have diversity and that we have equality and representation every step of the way.
MARSAI MARTIN

Equal rights for all, special privileges for none.
THOMAS JEFFERSON

No man is above the law, and no man is below the law.
THEODORE ROOSEVELT

All the citizens of a state cannot be equally powerful, but they may be equally free.
VOLTAIRE

We are all equal because we are all the property of God.
JOHN LOCKE

No poor, rural, weak or black person should ever again have to bear the additional burden of being deprived of the opportunity for an education, a job, or simply justice.
JIMMY CARTER

ETHICS

Ethical behavior is concerned, above all, with human values, not with legalisms.
E. M. SULLIVAN

I have yet to meet a man as fond of high moral conduct as he is of outward appearances.
CONFUCIUS

A man without ethics is a wild beast loosed upon this world.
MANLY HALL

Ethical life and service are an aid, but they are not an end in themselves. The end is to be one with God.
SWAMI PRABHAVANANDA

A man may not transgress the bounds of major morals, but may make errors in minor morals.
CONFUCIUS

Ethics is the science of human duty.
DAVID SWING

True morality consists not in following the beaten track, but in finding out the true path for ourselves and in fearlessly following it.
MOHANDAS GANDHI

Ethics is about what is right, not who is right.
ANONYMOUS

I pledge myself as follows: To realize that I am a business or professional man ambitious to succeed, but that I am first an ethical man and wish no success that is not founded on the highest justice and morality. To use my greatest endeavor to elevate the standard of the calling in which I am engaged and to conduct myself in such a way that others may find it wise, profitable, and conductive to happiness to follow my example.

CODE OF ETHICS, SERTOMA INTERNATIONAL

A gentleman takes as much trouble to discover what is right as the lesser men take to discover what will pay.

CONFUCIUS

Most people are willing to take the Sermon on the Mount as a flag to sail under; but few will use is as a rudder by which to steer.

OLIVER WENDELL HOLMES

Ethics is knowing the difference between what you have a right to do and what is right to do.

POTTER STEWART

In law, a man is guilty when he violates the rights of others. In ethics, he is guilty if he only thinks of doing so.

IMMANUEL KANT

The first step in the evolution of ethics is a sense of solidarity with other human beings.

ALBERT SCHWEITZER

Great people have great values and great ethics.

JEFFREY GITOMER

I am fully aware that everybody has a right to succeed, and success should be with ethics.

SHARAD PAWAR

In just about every area of society, there's nothing more important than ethics.

HENRY PAULSON

About morals, I know only that what is moral is what you feel good after, and what is immoral is what you feel bad after.

ERNEST HEMINGWAY

Wrong is wrong, even if everyone is doing it. Right is right, even if no one is doing it.

WILLIAM PENN

Ethical decisions ensure that everyone's best interests are protected. When in doubt, don't.

HARVEY MACKAY

Ethics is about how we meet the challenge of doing the right thing, when that will cost more than we want to pay.

THE JOSEPH INSTITUTE OF ETHICS

To starve to death is a small thing, but to lose one's integrity is a great one.

CHINESE PROVERB

EXERCISE

The only way for a rich man to be healthy is by exercise and abstinence, to live as if he were poor.

SIR WILLIAM TEMPLE

Warm your body by healthful exercise, not by cowering over a stove.

HENRY DAVID THOREAU

Exercise is the chief source of improvement in our faculties.

HUGH BLAIR

The chief desire of the human race is to attain happiness. True happiness is impossible without true health. And true health is impossible without exercise.

VIC TANNY

Use legs and have legs.

JOHN CLARKE

Give about two hours, every day, to exercise; for health must not be sacrificed to learning. A strong body makes the mind strong.

THOMAS JEFFERSON

An early morning walk is a blessing for the whole day.

HENRY DAVID THOREAU

It is remarkable how one's wits are sharpened by physical exercise.

PLINY THE YOUNGER

Without a proper amount of daily exercise no one can remain healthy.
ARTHUR SCHOPENHAUER

Exercise not only changes your body, it changes your mind, your attitude and your mood.
ANONYMOUS

Exercise should be regarded as a tribute to the heart.
GENE TUNNEY

Physical fitness is not only one of the most important keys to a healthy body, it is the basis of dynamic and creative intellectual activity.
JOHN F. KENNEDY

Walking is the best possible exercise. Habituate yourself to walk very far.
THOMAS JEFFERSON

If we could give every individual the right amount of nourishment and exercise, not too little and too much, we would have found the safest way to health.
HIPPOCRATES

Exercise is amazing, from the inside out. I feel so alive and have more energy.
VANESSA HUDGENS

A vigorous five-mile walk will do more good for an unhappy but otherwise healthy adult than all the medicine and psychology in the world.
PAUL DUDLEY WHITE

Those who think they have not time for bodily exercise will sooner or later have to find time for illness.
EDWARD STANLEY

Exercise is king. Nutrition is queen. Put them together and you've got a kingdom.
JACK LALANNE

The hardest thing about exercise is to start doing it. Once you are doing exercise regularly, the hardest thing is to stop it.

ERIN GRAY

Good things come to those who sweat.

ANONYMOUS

When it comes to health and well-being, regular exercise is about as close to a magic potion as you can get.

THICH NHAT HANH

A one-hour workout is 4% of your day. No excuses.

ANONYMOUS

If you are in a bad mood go for a walk. If you are still in a bad mood go for another walk.

HIPPOCRATES

After dinner, rest a while, after supper walk a mile.

ARABIAN PROVERB

EXPERIENCE

Human beings, who are almost unique in having the ability to learn from others, are also remarkable for their apparent disinclination to do so.
DOUGLAS ADAMS

Experience keeps a dear school, but fools will learn in no other.
BENJAMIN FRANKLIN

One thorn of experience is worth a whole wilderness of warning.
JAMES RUSSELL LOWELL

Is there anyone so wise as to learn by the experience of others?
VOLTAIRE

Experience is a good school. But the fees are high.
HEINRICH HEINE

Experience is the best teacher.
PROVERB

There are some things you have to experience to understand.
ANONYMOUS

Never regret. If it's good, it's wonderful. If it's bad, it's experience.
VICTORIA HOLT

Some things cannot be taught; they must be experienced. You never learn the most valuable lessons in life until you go through your own journey.

ROY T. BENNETT

If at first you don't succeed, you're doing it wrong. Learn from the experience. Try again, but with a different approach.

STEVE MARABOLI

A brain was only capable of what it could conceive, and it couldn't conceive what it had never experienced.

GRAHAM GREENE

The spectacles of experience; through them you will see clearly a second time.

HENRIK IBSEN

Most of the images of reality on which we base our actions are really based on vicarious experience.

ALBERT BANDURA

Nothing ever becomes real until experienced. Even a proverb is no proverb until your life has illustrated it.

JOHN KEATS

Experience is the teacher of all things.

JULIUS CAESAR

What one has not experienced, one will never understand in print.

ISADORA DUNCAN

Good judgement comes from experience, and experience comes from bad judgement.

RITA MAE BROWN

The more you do, the more experience you have and the next time it will be easier to choose the right thing.

ANDY LAU

Nothing which has entered into our experience is ever lost.
WILLIAM ELLERY CHANNING

No one ever got good at anything by just reading a book about it. Real skill and improvement come from experience.
JUSTIN HAMMOND

Judgement comes from experience and great judgement comes from bad experience.
ROBERT PACKWOOD

It is the true nature of mankind to learn from mistakes, not from example.
FRED HOYLE

Experience has been a stern but excellent teacher.
OG MANDINO

There are many truths of which the full meaning cannot be realized until personal experience has brought it home.
JOHN STEWART MILL

If we could sell our experiences for what they cost us, we'd all be millionaires.
PAULINE PHILLIPS

Life is a series of experiences, each one of which makes us bigger, even though sometimes it is hard to realize this. For the world was built to develop character, and we must learn that the setbacks and griefs which we endure help us in our marching onward.
HENRY FORD

Experience is what you get when you didn't get what you wanted.
RANDY PAUSCH

Turn your wounds into wisdom.
OPRAH WINFREY

Every experience, good or bad, is a priceless collector's item.
ISAAC MARION

Experience is a lesson of the past to lessen the burden of the future.
MICHAEL SAGE

Employ your time in improving yourself by other men's writings so that you shall come easily by what others have labored hard for.
SOCRATES

Be thankful for everything that happens in your life; it's all an experience.
ROY T. BENNETT

Every experience makes you grow.
ELIZABETH SHUE

Every experience is a positive experience if I view it as an opportunity for growth and self-mastery.
BRIAN TRACY

We learn from failure, not from success.
BRAM STOKER

Experience teaches only the teachable.
ALDOUS HUXLEY

View life as a continuous learning experience.
DENNIS WAITLEY

The mind once enlightened cannot again become darkened.
THOMAS PAINE

Experience is a private, very largely speechless affair.
JAMES BALDWIN

Every experience, however bitter, has its lesson, and to focus one's attention on the lesson helps one overcome the bitterness.
EDWARD HOWARD GRIGGS

It is from the level of calamities...that we learn impressive and useful lessons.
WILLIAM MAKEPEACE THACKERAY

When I have listened to my mistakes, I have grown.
HUGH PRATHER

Experience is simply the name we give our mistakes.
OSCAR WILDE

Nothing is a waste of time if you use the experience wisely.
AUGUSTE RODIN

Experience is a great teacher.
JOHN LEGEND

Judgement comes from experience – and experience comes from bad judgement.
WALTER WRISTON

Information's pretty thin stuff unless mixed with experience.
CLARENCE DAY

Experience is the name every one gives his mistakes.
ELBERT HUBBARD

What we have to learn to do, we learn by doing.
ARISTOTLE

All genuine knowledge originates in direct experience.
MAO TSE-TUNG

A little experience often upsets a lot of theory.
CADMAN

Men must try and try again. They must suffer the consequences of their own mistakes and learn by their own failures and their own successes.
LAWSON PURDY

Education is what you get when you read the fine print; experience is what you get when you don't.
PETE SEEGER

I have but one lamp by which my feet are guided, and that is the lamp of experience. I know no way of judging of the future but by the past.
PATRICK HENRY

If you will call your "troubles" "experiences," and remember that every experience develops latent force within you, you will grow vigorous and happy, however, adverse your circumstances may seem to be.
J. R. MILLER

A prudent person profits from personal experience, a wise one from the experience of others.
DR. JOSEPH COLLINS

There is no gold mine so rich in possibilities as your own experience. Buried in your memory, ready to be dug out, evaluated and applied to present problems, is a record of all your mistakes and failures, all your triumphs and successes. You have only to select what you feel will be of aid to you, in the form of some wisdom or judgment or skill you have gained through some past experience – and you have a power at hand to serve your current need. The most successful men and women are those who have learned to make the best use of the talents and knowledge acquired throughout life.
HAROLD SHERMAN

Experience is not what happens to man; it is what a man does with what happens to him.
ALDOUS HUXLEY

FAIRNESS

Who says life is fair, where is that written?
WILLIAM GOLDMAN

Life is never fair, so keep your faith firm.
LAILAH GIFTY AKITA

Life isn't easy, or even fair.
DIPA SANATANI

An honorable man is fair even to his enemies; a dishonorable man is unfair even to his friends.
MEHMET MURAT ILDAN

Fair-minded people never twist rules for personal gain.
FRANK SONNENBERG

Stand up for what is fair against the unfair.
SUZY KASSEM

Play fair, be prepared for others to play dirty, and don't let them drag you into the mud.
RICHARD BRANSON

Lacking of fairness to an opponent is essentially a sign of weakness.
EMMA GOLDMAN

Win or lose, do it fairly.
KNUTE ROCKNE

Fairness is what justice really is.
POTTER STEWART

In our hearts and in our laws, we must treat all our people with fairness and dignity, regardless of their race, religion, gender or sexual orientation...
WILLIAM J. CLINTON

The only stable state is the one in which all men are equal before the law.
ARISTOTLE

Fair and softly goes far.
MIGUEL DE CERVANTES

Fair thoughts and happy hours attend on you.
WILLIAM SHAKESPEARE

You shall not be partial in judgment; you shall hear the small and the great alike.
BIBLE

These men ask for just the same thing, fairness, and fairness only. This, so far as in my power, they, and all others, shall have.
ABRAHAM LINCOLN

A fair-minded person tries to see both sides of an argument.
AESOP

Fairness is not an attitude. It's a professional skill that must be developed and exercised.
BRIT HUME

It is not fair to ask of others what you are not willing to do yourself.
ELEANOR ROOSEVELT

Fairness is man's ability to rise above his prejudices.
WES FESLER

Fairness is an across-the-board requirement for all our interactions with each other... Fairness treats everybody the same.
BARBARA JORDAN

No matter who or what you support, I believe in supporting fairness first.
JENNETTE MCCURDY

Fairness means not to use fraud and trickery in the exchange of commodities and services and the exchange of feelings.
ERICH FROMM

FAITH

Frequently remind yourself that God is with you, that He will never fail you, that you can count upon him. Say these words, "God is with me, helping me."

NORMAN VINCENT PEALE

Cast your cares on the Lord for He cares.

ANONYMOUS

Fear knocked at the door and faith answered. No one was there.

OLD ENGLISH PROVERB

The only way to learn strong faith is to endure strong trials.

GEORGE MUELLER

There are only two ways to live...one is as though nothing is a miracle...the other is as if everything is.

ALBERT EINSTEIN

As you practice counting your blessings, you will find that your faith is being suddenly revitalized.

ROBERT SCHULLER

Faith is staying focused on the positive and being grateful for what you have. Faith is trusting that the right answer to a problem will come to you – it's waiting patiently until things get resolved – knowing that prayer can be answered in many ways. All I have seen teaches me to trust the Creator for all I have not seen.

ANONYMOUS

Faith is reason grown courageous.
SHERWOOD EDDY

The principal part of faith is patience.
GEORGE MACDONALD

Faith is no irresponsible shot in the dark. It is a responsible trust in God, who knows the desires of your hearts, the dreams you are given, and the goals you have set. He will guide your paths right.
ROBERT SCHULLER

He who has faith has...an inward reservoir of courage, hope, confidence, calmness, and assuring trust that all will come out well - even though to the world, it may appear to come out most badly.
B. C. FORBES

Keep faith. The most amazing things in life tend to happen right at the moment you're about to give up hope.
ANONYMOUS

Your faith can move mountains, and your doubt can create them.
ANONYMOUS

Your hardest times often lead to the greatest moments of your life. Keep the faith. It will all be worth it in the end.
ANONYMOUS

For we walk by faith, not by sight.
BIBLE

In God's hands, nothing you go through gets wasted. Keep persevering, you have a purpose.
STEVEN FURTICK

Skepticism has not founded empires, established principles, or changed the world's heart. The great doers of history have always been men of faith.
EDWIN HUBBEL CHAPIN

There are no tricks in plain and simple faith.
WILLIAM SHAKESPEARE

Let us have faith that right makes might, and in that faith, let us to the end, dare to do our duty, as we understand it.
ABRAHAM LINCOLN

Without faith, we are as stained glass windows in the dark.
ANONYMOUS

If ye have faith as a grain of mustard seed, ye shall say unto this mountain, remove hence to yonder place; and it shall remove; and nothing shall be impossible unto you.
BIBLE

A simple, childlike faith in a divine friend solves all problems that come to us by land or sea.
HELEN KELLER

Faith is the substance of things hoped for, the evidence of things unseen.
BIBLE

I believe every one of us is born with a purpose. No matter who you are, what you do, or how far you think you have to go, you have been tapped by a force greater than yourself to step into your God-given calling.
OPRAH WINFREY

True peace comes from knowing God is in control.
ANONYMOUS

Faith does not make things easy, it makes them possible.
ANONYMOUS

Now faith is confidence in what we hope for and assurance about what we do not see.
BIBLE

God will not look you over for medals, degrees or diplomas but for scars.
ELBERT HUBBARD

When you have faith in God, you don't have to worry about the future. You just know it's all in his hands. You just go and do your best.
ELDER BYRAN MATHISON

And now these three remain: faith, hope and love. But the greatest of these is love.
BIBLE

You must not lose faith in humanity. Humanity is like an ocean; if a few drops of the ocean are dirty, the ocean does not become dirty.
MAHATMA GANDHI

Do not be afraid; our fate cannot be taken from us; it is a gift.
DANTE ALIGHIERI

My faith didn't remove the pain, but it got me through the pain. Trusting God didn't diminish or vanquish the anguish, but it enabled me to endure it.
ROBERT ROGERS

Faith is unquestioning belief.
RONALD HOPFER

Send a drop of faith, with a single prayer. And God will show the way, as faith is always there.
JULIE HEBERT

Who is so of little faith that, in a moment of great disaster or heartbreak, has not called to his God?
OG MANDINO

If you will believe and stay in faith, and expect good things, you too can defy the odds.
JOEL OSTEEN

Faith is not the power of positive thinking; it is believing in God and trusting that His will is always the best, even when you cannot understand why.

SHARI HOWERTON

Faith means to have trust or confidence in something, such as having faith that the sun will rise and set each day.

CHRIS JOHNSTON

A man's steps are directed by the Lord – how then can anyone understand his own way?

BIBLE

Faith. It does not make things easy, it makes them possible.

ANONYMOUS

It is the heart which experiences God, not the reason.

BLAISE PASCAL

Faith is believing what we cannot prove.

ALFRED TENNYSON

Faith is believing when it is beyond the power of reason to believe.

VOLTAIRE

You're not free until you've been made captive by supreme belief.

MARIANNE MOORE

Our faith triumphant o'er our fears.

HENRY WADSWORTH LONGFELLOW

As your faith is strengthened, you will find that there is no longer the need to have a sense of control, that things will flow as they will, and that you will flow with them, to your great delight and benefit.

EMMANUEL

Be faithful in small things because it is them your strength lies.
MOTHER TERESA

All who call on God in true faith, earnestly from the heart, will certainly be heard, and will receive what they have asked and desired.
MARTIN LUTHER

Faith is to believe what you do not see; the reward of this faith is to see what you believe.
SAINT AUGUSTINE

That deep emotional conviction od the presence of a superior reasoning power, which is revealed in the incomprehensible universe, forms my idea of God.
ALBERT EINSTEIN

We need not be afraid of the future, for the future will be in our own hands. We shall need courage, energy and determination, but above all, we shall need faith – faith in ourselves, in our communities and in our country.
THOMAS E. DEWEY

Prayer should be the key of the morning and the lock of the night.
OWEN FELTHAM

Faith is the acknowledgement of God's supreme dominion over us and our dependence upon him. Since we are indebted to God for the faculties of our minds and bodies, we must give him the worship of both. In other words, we must worship our Creator with both our intellects and our bodies. Otherwise we are shortchanging him.
JOHN A. O'BRIEN

When you pray, you must not be like the hypocrites; for they love to stand and pray in the synagogues and at the street corners, that they may be seen by men. Truly, I say to you, they have their reward. But when you pray, go into your room and shut the door and pray to your Father who is in secret; and your Father who sees in secret will reward you.
BIBLE

Ask, and it shall be given to you; seek, and you shall find; knock, and it shall be opened unto you.

BIBLE

Pray as if everything depended on God, and work as if everything depended upon man.

SAINT AUGUSTINE

Prayer is the most powerful form of energy one can generate. The influence of prayer on the human mind and body is as demonstrable as that of secreting glands. Prayer is a force as real as terrestrial gravity. It supplies us with a steady flow of sustaining power in our daily lives.

ALEXIS CARREL

I have been driven many times to my knees by the overwhelming conviction that I had nowhere else to go. My own wisdom, and that of all about me, seemed insufficient for the day.

ABRAHAM LINCOLN

Prayer is the very soul and essence of religion and therefore prayer must be the very core of the life of man, for no man can live without religion.

MOHANDAS K. GANDHI

Prayer is the soul getting into contact with the God in whom it believes.

HARRY EMERSON FOSDICK

Here is my creed. I believe in one God, creator of the universe. That he governs it by his providence. That he ought to be worshipped. That the most acceptable service we render him is doing good to his other children. Hat the soul of man is immortal, and will be treated with justice in another life respecting its conduct in this.

BENJAMIN FRANKLIN

Cast all your cares on God; that anchor holds.

ALFRED TENNYSON

All things proclaim the existence of a God.

NAPOLEON

The most important thought I ever had was that of my individual responsibility to God.

DANIEL WEBSTER

I am fully assured that God does not, and therefore that men ought not to require any more of any man than this, to believe the scripture to be God's word, and to endeavor to find the true sense of it, and to live according to it.

CHILLINGWORTH

The beauty of the world and the orderly arrangement of everything celestial makes us confess that there is an excellent and eternal nature, which ought to be worshipped and admired by all mankind.

MARCUS TULLIUS CICERO

I believe in the sun even when it isn't shining. I believe in love even when I feel it not. I believe in God even when he is silent.

ANONYMOUS

There comes a time when you've used your brains, your training, your technical skill, and the die is cast and the events are in the hands of God, and there you have to leave them.

DWIGHT D. EISENHOWER

The things which are impossible with men are possible with God.

BIBLE

Without the assistance of the Divine Being … I cannot succeed. With that assistance, I cannot fail.

ABRAHAM LINCOLN

Faith without works is like a bird without wings; though she may hop about on earth, she will never fly to heaven. But when both are joined together, then doth the soul mount up to her eternal rest.

BEAUMONT

We walk by faith, not by sight.

BIBLE

Thou shalt love thy Lord thy God with all thy heart, and with all thy soul, and with all thy mind.

BIBLE

Faith is an important foundation for accomplishment.

A. M. NELSON

Faith is a dynamo of power: it is the backbone of all great accomplishments. It is the flaming inner core of self-confidence, optimism and enthusiasm.

E. F. GIRARD

You must have faith! Supreme faith in God! Unwavering faith in yourself.

E. F. GIRARD

Faith, mighty faith, the promise sees and looks to God alone. Laughs at impossibilities, and cries, "it shall be done."

CHARLES WESLEY

FAMILY

Happiness is having a large, loving, caring, close-knit family in another city.
GEORGE BURNS

Woman is the salvation or the destruction of the family. She carries its destiny in the folds of the mantle.
HENRI FREDERICK AMIEL

A happy family is just an earlier heaven.
SIR JOHN BOWRING

Family and friendships are two of the greatest facilitators of happiness.
JOHN MAXWELL

Home should be an anchor, a port in a storm, a refuge, a happy place in which to dwell, a place where we are loved and where we can love.
MARVIN J. ASHTON

Families are like branches on a tree. We grow in different directions yet our roots remain as one.
ANONYMOUS

Nothing is better than going home to family and eating good food and relaxing.
IRINA SHAYK

Having somewhere to go is home. Having someone to love is family. Having both is blessing.
ANONYMOUS

If you would have a happy family life, remember two things: in matters of principle, stand like a rock; in matters of taste, swim with the current.
THOMAS JEFFERSON

Families are like fudge – mostly sweet with a few nuts.
ANONYMOUS

Husband, wife and children form the world's greatest team. Whether that team wins or loses depends upon whether husband and wife practice human love.
RHODA LACHAR

We may have our differences, but nothing's more important than family.
COCO

To us, family means putting your arms around each other and being there.
BARBARA BUSH

Family gives you the roots to stand tall and strong.
ANONYMOUS

The most important thing in the world is family and love.
JOHN WOODEN

When everything goes to hell, the people who stand by you without flinching – they are your family.
JIM BUTCHER

An ounce of blood is worth more than a pound of friendship.
SPANISH PROVERB

Family means nobody gets left behind or forgotten.
DAVID OGDEN STIERS

Few men have been admired by their own households.
MICHEL DE MONTAIGNE

One father is more than a hundred schoolmasters.
GEORGE HERBERT

The happiest moments of my life have been the few which I have passed at home in the bosom of my family.
THOMAS JEFFERSON

FORGIVENESS

Never does the human soul appear so strong as when it forgoes revenge.
EDWIN HUBBEL CHAPIN

It's one of the greatest gifts you can give yourself, to forgive. Forgive everybody.
MAYA ANGELOU

The weak can never forgive. Forgiveness is the attribute of the strong.
MAHATMA GANDHI

Always forgive your enemies; nothing annoys them so much.
OSCAR WILDE

He that cannot forgive others breaks the bridge over which he must pass himself; for every man has need to be forgiven.
EDWARD HERBERT

It's not an easy journey, to get to a place where you forgive people. But it is such a powerful place, because it frees you.
TYLER PERRY

Forgiveness is above all, a personal choice, a decision of the heart to go against natural instinct to pay back evil with evil.
POPE JOHN PAUL II

Forgiveness does not mean ignoring what has been done or putting a false label on an evil act. It means, rather, that the evil act no longer remains as a barrier to the relationship. Forgiveness is a catalyst creating the atmosphere necessary for a fresh start and a new beginning.
MARTIN LUTHER KING, JR.

As I walked out the door toward the gate that would lead to my freedom, I knew if I didn't leave my bitterness and hatred behind, I'd still be in prison.

NELSON MANDELA

Forgiveness is the needle that knows how to mend.

JEWEL

I believe forgiveness is the best form of love in any relationship. It takes a strong person to say they're sorry and an even stronger person to forgive.

YOLANDA HADID

Forgiveness does not change the past, but it does enlarge the future.

PAUL LEWIS BOESE

When someone wrongs you, you don't forgive them for them, you forgive them for you.

CHRISTINE LAKIN

Forgive your enemies, but never forget their names.

JOHN F. KENNEDY

Forgiveness is not always easy. At times, it feels more painful than the wound we suffered, to forgive the one that inflicted it. And yet, there is no peace without forgiveness.

MARIANNE WILLIAMSON

The stupid neither forgive nor forget; the naïve forgive and forget; the wise forgive but do not forget.

THOMAS SZASZ

There is no revenge so complete as forgiveness.

JOSH BILLINGS

Never forget the three powerful resources you always have available to you: love, prayer, and forgiveness.

H. JACKSON BROWN, JR.

Forgiveness is a virtue of the brave.
INDIRA GANDHI

Forgiveness days you are given another chance to make a new beginning.
DESMOND TUTU

Forgiveness is a gift you give yourself.
SUZANNE SOMERS

Forgive yourself for your faults and your mistakes, and move on.
LES BROWN

It is easier to forgive an enemy than to forgive a friend.
WILLIAM BLAKE

When a deep injury is done us, we never recover until we forgive.
ALAN PATON

Sins cannot be undone, only forgiven.
IGOR STRAVINSKY

Forgiveness is the sweetest revenge.
ISAAC FRIEDMANN

Forgiveness is all-powerful. Forgiveness heals all ills.
CATHERINE PONDER

To forgive is the highest, most beautiful form of love. In return, you will receive untold peace and happiness.
ROBERT MULLER

A forgiveness ought to be like a cancelled note, torn in two and burned up, so that it never can be shown against the man.
HENRY WARD BEECHER

The more a man knows, the more he forgives.
ANONYMOUS

Humanity is never so beautiful as when praying for forgiveness, or else forgiving another.
JEAN PAUL RICHTER

To understand is to forgive.
FRENCH PROVERB

Only the brave know how to forgive; it is the most refined and generous pitch of virtue human nature can arrive at.
LAURENCE STERNE

FREEDOM

For everything that is really great and inspiring is created by the individual who can labour in freedom.

ALBERT EINSTEIN

Is freedom anything else than the right to live as we wish? Nothing else.

EPICTETUS

No one outside ourselves can rule us inwardly. When we know this, we become free.

BUDDHA

For what avail the plough or sail, or land or life, if freedom fail?

RALPH WALDO EMERSON

What do you suppose will satisfy the Soul, except to walk free, and own no superior.

WALT WHITMAN

No person is your friend (or kin) who demands your silence, or denies your right to

E. PHILIP RANDOLPH

The secret of freedom lies in educating people, whereas the secret of tyranny is in keeping them ignorant.

MAXIMILIEN ROBESPIERRE

I prefer liberty with danger than peace with slavery.

JEAN-JACQUES ROUSSEAU

When we lose the right to be different, we lose the privilege to be free.
CHARLES EVANS

People demand freedom of speech as a compensation for the freedom of thought which they seldom use.
SOREN KIERKEGAARD

Expose yourself to your deepest fear; after that, fear has no power, and the fear of freedom shrinks and vanishes. You are free.
JIM MORRISON

While we are free to choose our actions, we are not free to choose the consequences of our actions.
STEPHEN COVEY

From every mountainside, let freedom ring.
MARTIN LUTHER KING, JR.

All men are born free and equal, and have certain natural, essential, and unalienable rights.
JOHN QUINCY ADAMS

The secret of happiness is freedom and the secret of freedom is courage.
LOUIS BRANDEIS

Those who deny freedom to others deserve it not for themselves.
ABRAHAM LINCOLN

I may not agree with a word you say, but I shall defend unto my death your right to say it.
VOLTAIRE

Better to starve free than be a fat slave.
AESOP

A right is not what someone gives you; it's what no one can take from you.
RAMSEY CLARK

Liberty is one of the most valuable blessings that heaven has bestowed upon mankind.
MIGUEL DE CERVANTES

God grants liberty only to those who love it, and are always ready to guard and defend it.
DANIEL WEBSTER

Those who expect to reap the blessings of freedom, must, like men, undergo the fatigue of supporting it.
THOMAS PAINE

Personal liberty is the paramount essential to human dignity and human happiness.
EDWARD BULWER-LYTTON

It is my certain conviction that no man loses his freedom except through his own weakness.
MAHATMA GANDHI

FRIEND

You cannot be friends upon any other terms than upon the terms of equality.
WOODROW WILSON

A friend is a person with whom I may be sincere. Before him, I may think aloud.
RALPH WALDO EMERSON

A true friend is the greatest of all blessings, and that which we take the least of all to acquire.
FRANCOIS DE LA ROCHEFOUCAULD

Be civil to all; sociable to many; familiar with few; friend to one; enemy to none.
BENJAMIN FRANKLIN

Don't walk in front of me, I may not follow; Don't walk behind, I may not lead; Walk beside me, and just be my friend.
ALBERT CAMUS

Friendship is a strong and habitual inclination in two persons to promote the good and happiness of another.
EUSTANCE BUDGELL

Friendship makes prosperity more brilliant, and lightens adversity by dividing and sharing it.
MARCUS TULLIUS CICERO

I keep my friends as misers do their treasures, because, of all the things granted us by wisdom, none is greater or better than friendship.
PIETRO ARETINO

If a man does not make new acquaintances as he advances through life, he will soon find himself alone. A man, sir, must keep his friendships in constant repair.

SAMUEL JOHNSON

It's no good trying to keep up friendships. It's painful for both sides. The fact is, one grows out of people, and the only thing is to face it.

WILLIAM SOMERSET MAUGHAM

One friend in a lifetime is much; two are many; three are hardly possible.

HENRY ADAMS

One loyal friend is worth ten thousand relatives.

EURIPIDES

The firmest friendships have been formed in mutual adversity, as iron is most strongly united by the fiercest flame.

CHARLES CALEB COLTON

True friendship is like sound health, the value of it is seldom known until it be lost.

CHARLES CALEB COLTON

True happiness consists not in the multitude of friends, but in the worth and choice.

BENJAMIN JONSON

What wealth it is to have such friends that we cannot think of them without elevation.

HENRY DAVID THOREAU

My friend is that one whom I can associate with my choicest thought.

HENRY DAVID THOREAU

A friend in the market is better than money in the chest.

THOMAS FULLER

Because of you, I laugh a little harder, cry a little less, and smile a lot more.

ANONYMOUS

A true friend accepts who you are, but also helps you become who you should be.
ANONYMOUS

You meet a person and you just click – you're comfortable with them, like you've know them your whole life, and you don't have to pretend to be anyone or anything.
ANONYMOUS

Rare as is true love, true friendship is rarer.
JEAN DE LA FONTAINE

Truly great friends are hard to find, difficult to leave and impossible to forget.
ANONYMOUS

Things are never quite as scary when you've got a best friend.
BILL WATTERSON

The great thing about new friends is that they bring new energy to your soul.
SHANNA RODRIGUEZ

A friendship can weather most things and thrive in thin soil; but it needs a little mulch of letters and phone calls and small, silly presents every so often – just to save it from drying out completely.
PAM BROWN

If you have one true friend you have more than your share.
THOMAS FULLER

A good friend is like a four-leaf clover: hard to find and lucky to have.
IRISH PROVERB

There is nothing I would not do for those who are really my friends.
JANE AUSTEN

There's nothing like a really loyal, dependable, good friend. Nothing.
JENNIFER ANISTON

It is one of the blessings of old friends that you can afford to be stupid with them.
RALPH WALDO EMERSON

The greatest healing therapy is friendship and love.
HUBERT H. HUMPHREY

True friendship ought never to conceal what it thinks.
ST. JEROME

Life without a friend is death without a witness.
SPANISH PROVERB

I feel the need of relations and friendship, of affection, of friendly intercourse... I cannot miss these things without feeling, as does any intelligent man, a void and a deep need.
VINCENT VAN GOGH

Friendships are fragile things, and require as much care in handling as any other fragile and precious thing.
RANDOLPH S. BOURNE

Your wealth is where your friends are.
TITUS M. PLAUTUS

Friendship is a sheltering tree.
SAMUEL TAYLOR COLERIDGE

A man cannot speak to his son but as a father, to his wife but as a husband, to his enemy but upon terms; whereas a friend may speak as the case requires, and not as it sorteth with the person.
FRANCIS BACON

Friendship is love without his wings.
LORD BYRON

A true friend is one soul in two bodies.
ARISTOTLE

There is no wilderness like a life without friends; friendship multiplies blessings and minimizes misfortunes; it is a unique remedy against adversity, and it soothes the soul.
BALTASAR GRACIAN

There is nothing on this earth more to be prized than true friendship.
SAINT THOMAS AQUINAS

Man's best support is a very dear friend.
MARCUS TULLIUS CICERO

No medicine is more valuable, none more efficacious, none better suited to the cure of all our temporal ills than a friend to whom we may turn for consolation in time of trouble, and with whom we may share our happiness in time of joy.
SAINT AILREDOF RIEVAULX

One thing everybody in the world wants and needs is friendliness.
WILLIAM E. HELLER

A man cannot be said to succeed in this life who does not satisfy one friend.
HENRY DAVID THOREAU

We take care of our health, we lay up money, we make our roof tight and our clothing sufficient, but who provides wisely that he shall not be wanting in the best property of all - friends?
RALPH WALDO EMERSON

There is no physician like a true friend.
ANONYMOUS

True happiness ... arises, in the first place, from the enjoyment of one's self, and in the next from the friendship and conversation of a few select companions.
JOSEPH ADDISON

Of all the things which wisdom provides to make life entirely happy, much the greatest is the possession of friendship.

EPICURUS

True friendship is a plant of slow growth, and must undergo and withstand the shocks of adversity, before it is entitled to the appellation.

GEORGE WASHINGTON

O friendship! Of all things the most rare, and therefore most rare because most excellent, whose comfort in misery is always sweet, and whose counsels in prosperity are ever fortunate.

JOHN LYLY

From quiet homes and first beginning out to the undiscovered ends there's nothing worth the wear of winning but laughter and the love of friends.

HILLAIRE BELLOC

Friends are needed both for joy and for sorrow.

YIDDISH PROVERB

What a great blessing is a friend with a heart so trusty you may safely bury your secrets in it, whose conscience you may fear less than your own, who can relieve your cares by his conversation, your doubts by his counsels, your sadness by his good humor, and whose very looks give you comfort.

LUCIUS ANNAEUS SENECA

We are all travellers in the wilderness of this world, and the best that we find in our travels is an honest friend.

ROBERT LOUIS STEVENSON

Forsake not an old friend, for the new is not comparable unto him.

BIBLE

I have loved my friends as I do virtue, my soul, my God.

THOMAS BROWNE

Friendship is the gift of the gods, and the most precious boon to man.

BENJAMIN D'ISRAELI

Cherish friendship in your breast, new is good, but old is best; make new friends, but keep the old; those are silver, these are gold.

JOSEPH PARRY

The loss of a friend is like that of a limb; time may heal the anguish of the wound, but the loss cannot be repaired.

ROBERT SOUTHEY

There is a magnet in your heart that will attract true friends. That magnet is unselfishness, thinking of others first … when you learn to live for others, they will live for you.

PARAMAHANSA YOGANANDA

The only way to have a friend is to be one.

RALPH WALDO EMERSON

Blessed are they who have the gift of making friends, for it is one of God's best gifts. It involves many things, but above all, the power of getting out of one's self, and appreciating whatever is noble and loving in another.

THOMAS HUGHES

Loyalty is what we seek in friendship.

MARCUS TULLIUS CICERO

Friendship … is born at the moment when one man says to another "What! You too? I thought that no one but myself …

C. S. LEWIS

A friend is someone who knows all about you and still loves you.

ELBERT HUBBARD

There is nothing we like to see so much as the gleam of pleasure in a person's eye when he feels that we have sympathized with him, understood him, interested ourself in his welfare. At these moments something fine and spiritual passes between two friends. These moments are the moments worth living.

DON MARQUIS

The essence of friendship is entireness, a total magnanimity and trust.
RALPH WALDO EMERSON

True friendship comes when silence between two people is comfortable.
DAVE TYSON GENTRY

There can be no friendship when there is no freedom. Friendship loves the free air, and will not be fenced up in straight and narrow enclosures.
WILLIAM PENN

Wear a smile and have friends; wear a scowl and have wrinkles.
GEORGE ELIOT

Give and take makes good friends.
SCOTTISH PROVERB

In time of prosperity friends will be plenty; in time of adversity not one in twenty.
JAMES HOWELL

No man is much pleased with a companion who does not increase, in some respect, his fondness of himself.
SAMUEL JOHNSON

The condition which high friendship demands is the ability to do without it.
RALPH WALDO EMERSON

A friend may well be reckoned the masterpiece of nature.
RALPH WALDO EMERSON

Friendship is the pleasing game of interchanging praise.
OLIVER WENDELL HOLMES

The most called-upon prerequisite of a friend is an accessible ear.
MAYA ANGELOU

A loyal friend laughs at your jokes when they're not so good, and sympathizes with your problems when they're not so bad.
ARNOLD H. GLASOW

Politeness is an inexpensive way of making friends.
WILLIAM FEATHER

You can make more friends in two months by becoming more interested in other people than you can in two years by trying to get people interested in you.
ANONYMOUS

We secure our friends not by accepting favors but by doing them.
THUCYDIDES

Friendship multiplies the good of life and divides the evil. 'Tis the sole remedy against misfortune, the very ventilation of the soul.
BALTASAR GRACIAN

The chain of friendship, however bright, does not stand the attrition of constant close contact.
SIR WALTER SCOTT

Friendship increases in visiting friends, but not in visiting them too often.
ANONYMOUS

I am learning to live close to the lives of my friends without ever seeing them. No miles of any measurement can separate your soul from mine.
JOHN MUIR

Friends are lost by calling often and calling seldom.
SCOTTISH PROVERB

A cheerful friend is like a sunny day, which sheds its brightness on all around.
JOHN LUBBOCK

Laugh, and the world laughs with you; weep and you weep alone.
ELLA WHEELER WILCOX

The richest man in the world is not the one who still has the first dollar he ever earned. It's the man who still has his best friend.
MARTHA MASON

Life has no pleasure nobler than that of friendship.
ABRAHAM LINCOLN

They are rich who have true friends.
THOMAS FULLER

The rich know not who is a friend.
ANONYMOUS

Grief can take care of itself, but to get the full value of a joy you must have somebody to divide it with.
MARK TWAIN

There is no man that imparteth his joys to his friends, but he joyeth the more; and no man that imparteth his griefs to his friends, but he grieveth the less.
FRANCIS BACON

No man can be happy without a friend, nor be sure of his friend till he is unhappy.
THOMAS FULLER

The friend of my adversity I shall always cherish most. I can better trust those who helped to relieve the gloom of my dark hours than those who are so ready to enjoy with me the sunshine of my prosperity.
ULYSSES S. GRANT

Chance makes our parents, but choice makes our friends.
JACQUES DELILLE

Friendship is the source of the greatest pleasures, and without friends even the most agreeable pursuits become tedious.

SAINT THOMAS AQUINAS

The worst solitude is to be destitute of sincere friendship.

FRANCIS BACON

There is a definite process by which one made people into friends, and it involved talking to them and listening to them for hours at a time.

REBECCA WEST

He does good to himself who does good to his friend.

ERASMUS

Don't flatter yourself that friendship authorizes you to say disagreeable things to you intimates. The nearer you come into relation with a person, the more necessary do tact and courtesy become.

OLIVER WENDELL HOLMES

I always felt that the great high privilege, relief and comfort of friendship was that one had to explain nothing.

KATHERINE MANSFIELD

Nobody who is afraid of laughing, and heartily too, at his friend can be said to have a true and thorough love for him.

JULIUS CHARLES HARE

When good cheer is lacking, our friends will be packing.

ANONYMOUS

Friendship is like money, easier made than kept.

SAMUEL BUTLER

In prosperity our friends know us; in adversity we know our friends.

JOHN CHURTON COLLINS

Friends are relatives you make for yourself.
EUSTACHE DESCHAMPS

God gave us our relatives; thank God we can choose our friends.
ETHEL WATTS MUMFORD

Ah, how good it feels! The hand of an old friend.
HENRY WADSWORTH LONGFELLOW

As in the case of wines that improve with age, the oldest friendships ought to be the most delightful.
MARCUS TULLIUS CICERO

Be slow to fall into friendship; but when thou art in, continue firm and constant.
SOCRATES

Be slow in choosing a friend, slower in changing.
BENJAMIN FRANKLIN

To like and dislike the same things, this is what makes a solid friendship.
SALLUST

Friendship is one mind in two bodies.
MENCLUS

A single rose can be my garden...a single friend, my world.
LEO BUSCAGLIA

Friendship is a single soul dwelling in two bodies.
ARISTOTLE

Friends and good manners will carry you where money won't go.
MARGARET WALKER

Nothing but heaven itself is better than a friend who is really a friend.
TITUS M. PLAUTUS

It takes a long time to grow an old friend.
JOHN LEONARD

Wishing to be friends is quick work, but friendship is a slow ripening fruit.
ARISTOTLE

Since there is nothing so well worth having as friends, never lose a chance to make them.
FRANCESCO GUICCIARDINI

Life has no blessing like a prudent friend.
EURIPIDES

Friendship increases by visiting friends, but by visiting seldom.
BENJAMIN FRANKLIN

Wherever you are it is your own friends who make your world.
WILLIAM JAMES

The most I can do for my friend is simply to be his friend.
HENRY DAVID THOREAU

What a pity that so many people are living with so few friends when the world is full of lonesome strangers who would give anything just to be somebody's friend.
MILO L. ARNOLD

'Tis the human touch in the world that counts – the touch of your hand and mine – which means far more to the sinking heart than shelter or bread or wine. For shelter is gone when the night is o'er and bread lasts only a day. But the touch of the hand and the sound of the voice live on in the soul alway.
SPENCER M. FREE

Five years from now you will be pretty much the same as you are today except for two things: the books you read and the people you get close to.
CHARLES E. JONES

To have a good friend is one of the highest delights of life; to be a good friend is one of the noblest and most difficult undertakings.
GEORGE WASHINGTON

My best friend is the one who brings out the best in me.
HENRY FORD

A faithful friend is a strong defense: and he that hath found such a one hath found a treasure.
BIBLE

A true friend is the best possession.
BENJAMIN FRANKLIN

Much certainty of the happiness and purity of our lives depends on our making a wise choice of our companions and friends.
JOHN LUBBOCK

It is great to have friends when one is young, but indeed it is still more so when you are getting old. When we are young, friends are, like everything else, a matter of course. In the old days we know what it means to have them.
EDWARD GRIEG

The making of friends who are real friends, is the best token we have of a man's success in life.
EDWARD E. HALE

Reprove thy friend privately; commend him publicly.
SOLON

There should be no inferiors and no superiors for true world friendship.
CARLOS P. ROMULA

A friend is a present you give yourself.
ROBERT LOUIS STEVENSON

A slender acquaintance with the world must convince every man that actions, not words, are the true criterion of the attachment of friends.
GEORGE WASHINGTON

A faithful friend is a sturdy shelter: he that has found one has found a treasure. There is nothing so precious as a faithful friend, and no scales can measure his excellence.
APOCRYPHA

Friends are God's apology for relations.
HUGH KINGSMILL

The friendship that can cease has never been real.
SAINT JEROME

"A friend is the one who comes in when the whole world has gone out." Even as David thanked God for Jonathan and praised him in well-remembered lines, so have we abundant reasons to thank God today for friends and to resolve to keep these friendships in constant repair.
EDGAR DEWITT JONES

Friendship is the allay of our sorrows, the ease of our passions, the discharge of our oppressions, the sanctuary to our calamities, the counsellor of our doubts, the clarity of our minds, the emission of our thoughts, the exercise and improvement of what we meditate.
JEREMY TAYLOR

For friendship, of itself a holy tie, is made more sacred by adversity.
JOHN DRYDEN

A friend is, as it were, a second half.
MARCUS TULLIUS CICERO

Fame is the scentless sunflower, with gaudy crown of gold; but friendship is the breathing rose, with sweets in every fold.
OLIVER WENDELL HOLMES

A true friend unbosoms freely, advises justly, assists readily, adventures boldly, takes all patiently, defends courageously, and continues a friend unchangeably.
WILLIAM PENN

By friendship you mean the greatest love, the greatest usefulness, the most open communication, the noblest sufferings, the severest truth, the heartiest counsel, and the greatest union of minds of which brave men and women are capable.
JEREMY TAYLOR

Friendship, gift of Heaven, delight of great souls; friendship, which kings, so distinguished for ingratitude, are unhappy enough not to know.
VOLTAIRE

Do not keep the alabaster box of your love and tenderness sealed up until your friends are dead. Filll their lives with sweetness. Speak approving, cheering words while their ears can hear them and while hearts can be thrilled by them.
HENRY DAVID BEECHER

If you have a friend worth loving, love him! Yes, and let him know that you love him, ere life's evening tinge his brow with sunset glow, why should good words ne'er be said of a friend – till he is dead? Scatter thus your seeds of kindness all enriching as you go leave them! Trust the harvest-giver; he will make each seed to grow. And until the happy end, your life shall never lack a friend.
ANONYMOUS

Honest men esteem and value nothing so much in this world as a real friend. Such a one is as it were another self, to whom we impart our most secret thoughts, who partakes of our joy, and comforts us in our affliction; add to this, that his company is an everlasting pleasure to us.
BIDPAI

A true friend is forever a friend.
GEORGE MACDONALD

Treat your friends for what you know them to be. Regard no surfaces. Consider not what they did, but what they intended.
HENRY DAVID THOREAU

True friends thou hast, and their adoption tried, grapple them to thy soul with hoops of steel.
WILLIAM SHAKESPEARE

Love your friend with his faults.
ANONYMOUS

A friend is the half of my life.
ANONYMOUS

Spend in all things else, but of old friends be most miserly.
JAMES RUSSELL LOWELL

In friendship we find nothing false or insincere; everything is straightforward, and springs from the heart.
MARCUS TULLIUS CICERO

Friendship is the highest degree of perfection in society.
MICHEL DE MONTAIGNE

A good man is the best friend, and therefore soonest to be chosen, longer to be retained; and indeed, never to be parted with.
JEREMY TAYLOR

We cannot tell the precise moment when friendship is formed. As in filling a vessel drop by drop, there is at last a drop which makes it run over; so in a series of kindnesses there is, at last, one which makes the heart run over.
JAMES BOSWELL

Flatterers look like friends, as wolves like dogs.
GEORGE CHAPMAN

Whether you recognize it or not, you tend to become like those you surround yourself with.

J. S. FELTS

The same man cannot be both friend and flatterer.

BENJAMIN FRANKLIN

Friends are good, - good, if well chosen.

DANIEL DEFOE

Misfortune shows those who are not really friends.

ARISTOTLE

I am wealthy in my friends.

WILLIAM SHAKESPEARE

Life is to be fortified by many friendships. To love, and to be loved, is the greatest happiness of existence.

SYDNEY SMITH

So long as we are loved by others I should say that we are almost indispensable; and no man is useless while he has a friend.

ROBERTLOUIS STEVENSON

Be very careful in the selection of your friends: "the most valuable and fairest furniture of life."

MARCUS TULLIUS CICERO

To give counsel as well as take it is a feature of true friendship.

MARCUS TULLIUS CICERO

The better part of one's life consists of his friendships.

ABRAHAM LINCOLN

FRUGALITY

There is no dignity quite so impressive, and no independence quite so important, as living within your means.

CALVIN COOLIDGE

He who will not economize will have to agonize.

CONFUCIUS

Frugality is one of the most beautiful and joyful words in the English language, and yet one that we are culturally cut off from understanding and enjoying. The consumption society has made us feel that happiness lies in having things, and has failed to teach us the happiness of not having things.

ELISE BOULDING

The way to wealth is as plain as the way to market. It depends on two words, industry and frugality: that is, waste neither time nor money, but make the best use of both. Without industry and frugality, nothing will do, and with them, everything.

BENJAMIN FRANKLIN

Can anything be so elegant as to have few wants, and to serve them one's self?

RALPH WALDO EMERSON

He that will not stoop for a pin will never be worth a pound.

SAMUEL PEPYS

Only buy what you need. Think function, not fashion.

HARKEN HEADERS

Being frugal doesn't mean slashing your spending or depriving yourself of things that you enjoy. It means knowing the value of the dollar and making every effort to spend it wisely.

FRANK SONNENBERG

Living a frugal lifestyle gives you the opportunity to invest more money towards your future.

JOHN RAMPTON

I have learned to seek my happiness by limiting my desires, rather than in attempting to satisfy them.

JOHN STUART MILL

By sowing frugality, we reap liberty, a golden harvest.

AGESILAUS

We make ourselves rich by making our wants few.

HENRY DAVID THOREAU

Beware of little expenses. A small leak will sink a great ship.

BENJAMIN FRANKLIN

The greatest wealth is to live content with little.

PLATO

First gain all you can, and, secondly save all you can, then give all you can.

JOHN WESLEY

Life can be beautiful. It doesn't have to be expensive.

CHRISTINE LOUISE HOHLBAUM

I'd like to live as a poor man with lots of money.

PABLO PICASSO

The Bible warns us against greed and selfishness, it does encourage frugality and thrift.
BILLY GRAHAM

Great wealth is a gift from heaven; moderate wealth results from frugality.
CHINESE PROVERB

You can never get enough of what you don't need to make you happy.
ERIC HOFFER

Frugality is a handsome income.
DESIDERIUS ERASMUS

Do not save what is left after spending, but spend what is left after saving.
WARREN BUFFETT

If you buy things you do not need, soon you will have to sell things you need.
WARREN BUFFETT

You understand a whole lot about money when there isn't any. What you learn is that money is hard to come by, and it is important not to waste it.
JACK BOGLE

One of the most difficult things in the world is to convince a woman that even a bargain costs money.
EDGAR WATSON HOWE

FUTURE

I expect to spend the rest of my life in the future, so I want to be reasonably sure of what kind of future it's going to be. That is my reason for planning.
CHARLES F. KETTERING

I know no way of judging the future but by the past.
PATRICK HENRY

Let him who would enjoy a good future waste none of the present.
ROGER BABSON

The future hides in it gladness and sorrow.
JOHANN WOLFGANG VON GOETHE

There is a past which is gone forever, but there is a future which is still our own.
FREDERICK. W. ROBERTSON

If you do the very best you can, the future will take care of itself.
GEORGE MITCHELL

The future belongs to those who earn it.
ANONYMOUS

The man least dependent upon the morrow goes to meet the morrow most cheerfully.
EPICURUS

He that fears not the future may enjoy the present.
THOMAS FULLER

The only way to predict the future is to have power to shape the future.
ERIC HOFFER

Yesterday is not ours to recover, but tomorrow is ours to win or lose.
LYNDON B. JOHNSON

Never let the future disturb you. You will meet it, if you have to, with the same weapons of reason which today arm you against the present.
MARCUS AURELIUS

Work for your future as if you are going to live forever, for your afterlife as if you are going to die tomorrow.
ARABIAN PROVERB

Nobody can really guarantee the future. The best we can do is size up the chances, calculate the risks involved, estimate our ability to deal with them and then make our plans with confidence.
HENRY FORD II

What the future holds for us, depends on what we hold for the future. Hard working todays make high-winning tomorrows.
WILLIAM E. HOLLER

He who can see three days ahead will be rich for three thousand years.
JAPANESE PROVERB

I neither complain of the past, nor do I fear the future.
MICHEL DE MONTAIGNE

Go forth to meet the shadowy future without fear and with a manly heart.
HENRY WADSWORTH LONGFELLOW

The future belongs to those who believe in the beauty of their dreams.
ELEANOR ROOSEVELT

What we do today will determine your future.
CATHERINE PULSIFER

May the happiest days of your past, be the saddest days of your future.
IRISH SAYING

Your past, present and future are moulded by your thoughts. Remember – your thinking is your autobiography.
JAMES BORG

When all is lost, the future still remains.
CHRISTIAN BOVEE

Everyone has it within his power to say, this I am today, that I shall be tomorrow.
LOUIS L'AMOUR

Only man clogs his happiness with care, destroying what is with thoughts of what may be.
JOHN DRYDEN

Tomorrow is the day when idlers work, and fools reform, and mortal men lay hold on heaven.
EDWARD YOUNG

Tomorrow is the only day in the year that appeals to a lazy man.
JIMMY LYONS

I never think of the future. It comes soon enough.
ALBERT EINSTEIN

The best way of predicting the future is to invent it.
ALAN KAY

The future always holds something for the man who keeps his faith in it.
H. L. HOLLIS

When no new thoughts fill the mind – when no horizons beckon – when life is in the past, not in the future - you are on the way to uselessness.
DR. FREDERICK K. STAMM

GENEROSITY

The most truly generous persons are those who give silently without hope of praise or reward.
CAROL RYRIE BRINK

For it is in giving that we receive.
ST. FRANCIS OF ASSISI

Give what you have. To someone, it may be better than you dare to think.
HENRY WADSWORTH LONGFELLOW

But I give best when I give from that deeper place; when I give simply, freely and generously, and sometimes for no particular reason. I give best when I give from my heart.
STEVE GOODIER

The wise man does not lay up his own treasures. The more he gives to others, the more he has for his own.
LAO TZU

If truth doesn't set you free, generosity of spirit will.
KATERINA STOYKOVO KLEMER

Generosity is the most natural outward expression of an inner attitude of compassion and loving-kindness.
DALAI LAMA

Oh! If the good hearts had fat purses, how much better everything would go!
VICTOR HUGO

Taking satisfies you. Giving satisfies two.
MAXIME LAGACE

Your path to greatness starts the moment you find the courage to reach out with generosity.
KEITH FERRAZZI

No one has become poor by giving.
ANNE FRANK

Always give without remembering and always receive without forgetting.
BRIAN TRACY

We make a living by what we get. We make a life by what we give.
WINSTON CHURCHILL

If you're in the luckiest one percent of humanity, you owe it to the rest of humanity to think about the other 99 percent.
WARREN BUFFETT

What does one person give to another? He gives of himself, of the most precious he has, he gives of his life...
ERICH FROMM

Life's persistent and most urgent question is, 'What are you doing for others?'
MARTIN LUTHER KING, JR

Remember that the happiest people are not those getting more, but those giving more.
ROBIN SHARMA

To do more for the world than the world does for you – that is success.
HENRY FORD

Real generosity is doing something nice for someone who'll never find it out.
FRANK A. CLARK

You cannot continue to succeed in the world or have a fulfilling life in the world unless you choose to use your life in the service somehow to others and give back what you have been given. That's how you keep it. That's how you get it. That's how you grow it.

OPRAH WINFREY

I have found that among its other benefits, giving liberates the soul of the giver.

MAYA ANGELOU

Never hesitate when you have an impulse toward charity.

MIKE MANSON

Humanity needs givers, not takers.

MAXIME LEGACE

When you give to the needy, do not let your left hand know what your right hand is doing.

BIBLE

GENTLENESS

Nothing is so strong as gentleness, nothing so gentle as real strength.
FRANCIS DE SALES

In a gentle way, you can shake the world.
MAHATMA GANDHI

In the long run, the sharpest weapon of all is a kind and gentle spirit.
ANNE FRANK

Only the gentle are ever really strong.
JAMES DEAN

Criticism, like rain, should be gentle enough to nourish a man's growth without destroying his roots.
FRANK A. CLARK

It is always a good idea to be good and kind to yourself. Do whatever it takes to treat yourself with love and gentleness. You are a rare gem.
GIFT GUGU MONA

The great mind knows the power of gentleness, only tries force, because persuasion fails.
ROBERT BROWNING

Use a sweet tongue, courtesy, and gentleness, and thou mayst manage to guide an elephant with a hair.
SA'DI

A gentle word, a kind look, a good-natured smile can work wonders and accomplish miracles.
WILLIAM HAZLITT

Gentle persuasion succeeds where force fails.
AESOP

A gentle answer turns away wrath, but a harsh word stirs up anger.
KING SOLOMON

We must be gentle now; we are gentlemen.
WILLIAM SHAKESPEARE

The gentle mind by gentle deeds is known, for a man by nothing is so well betrayed as by his manners.
EDMUND SPENSER

Friends share our pain and touch our wounds with a gentle and tender hand.
HENRI J. M. NOUWEN

Be gentle with your words – you can't take them back.
WILLIE NELSON

An able man shows his spirit by gentle words and resolute actions.
EARL OF CHESTERFIELD

If a man would reap praise, you must sow the seeds, gentle words and useful deeds.
BENJAMIN FRANKLIN

The most gentle people in the world are macho males, people who are confident in their masculinity and have a feeling of well-being in themselves. They don't have to kick in doors, mistreat women, or make fun of gays.
CLINT EASTWOOD

It takes strength to be gentle and kind.
STEVEN MORRISSEY

GRATITUDE

A prudent man will think more important what fate has conceded to him, than what it has denied.

BALTASAR GRACIAN

A single grateful thought toward heaven is the most complete prayer.

GOTTHOLD EPHRAIM LESSING

Blow, blow, thou winter wind, thou are not so unkind as man's ingratitude.

WILLIAM SHAKESPEARE

Blessed is he who has found his work; let him ask no other blessedness.

THOMAS CARLYLE

He enjoys much who is thankful for little; a grateful mind is both a great and a happy mind.

THOMAS SECKER

He is a wise man who does not grieve for the things which he has not, but rejoices for those which he has.

EPICTETUS

Gratitude turns what we have into enough.

ANONYMOUS

How happy a person is depends upon the depth of his gratitude. You will notice at once that the unhappy person has little gratitude toward life, other people, and God.

JOHN MILLER

Ingratitude is always a kind of weakness. I have never known men of ability to be ungrateful.

JOHANN WOLFGANG VON GOETHE

Men are slower to recognize blessings than evils.

LIVY

That is not more pleasing exercise of the mind than gratitude.

JOSEPH ADDISON

Thou hast given so much to me...Give one more thing, a grateful heart.

GEORGE HERBERT

We must find time to stop and thank the people who make a difference in our lives.

JOHN F. KENNEDY

Gratitude is the sign of noble souls.

AESOP

Gratitude looks to the Past and love to the Present; fear, avarice, lust, and ambition look ahead.

C. S. LEWIS

When it comes to life, the critical thing is whether you take things for granted or take them with gratitude.

GILBERT KEITH CHESTERTON

The soul that gives thanks can find comfort in everything; the soul that complains can find comfort in nothing.

HANNAH WHITALL SMITH

Reflect on your present blessings, of which every man has plenty; not on your past misfortunes, of which all men have some.

CHARLES DICKENS

When I started counting my blessings, my whole life turned around.
WILLIE NELSON

Thankfulness is the quickest path to joy.
JEFFERSON BETHKE

O Lord that lends me life, lend me a heart replete with thankfulness.
WILLIAM SHAKESPEARE

The more grateful I am, the more beauty I see.
MARY DAVIS

Gratitude is a powerful catalyst for happiness. It's the spark that lights a fire of joy in your soul.
AMY COLLETTE

Gratitude is not only the greatest of virtues but the parent of all others.
MARCUS TULLIUS CICERO

Let us rise and be thankful, for if we didn't learn a lot today, at least we learned a little, and if we didn't learn a little, at least we didn't get sick, and if we got sick, and we didn't die, let us all be thankful.
BUDDHA

Gratitude helps you to grow and expand; gratitude brings joy and laughter into your life and into the lives of all those around you.
EILEEN CADDY

There is a calmness to a life lived in gratitude, a quiet joy.
RALPH H. BLUM

Gratitude is the sweetest thing in a seeker's life – in all human life. If there is gratitude in your heart, then there will be tremendous sweetness in your eyes.
SRI CHINMOY

The root of joy is gratefulness.
DAVID STEINDL-RAST

Gratitude is the heart's memory.
FRENCH PROVERB

Gratitude unlocks the fullness of life. It turns what we have into enough, and more. It turns denial into acceptance, chaos to order, confusion to clarity. It can turn a meal into a feast, a house into a home, a stranger into a friend.
MELODY BEATTIE

Being thankful is not always experienced as a natural state of existence, we must work at it, akin to a type of strength training for the heart.
LARISSA GOMEZ

Today I choose to live with gratitude for the love that fills my heart, the peace that rests within my spirit, and the voice of hope that says all things are possible.
ANONYMOUS

We can only be said to be alive in those moments when our hearts are conscious of our treasures.
THORTON WILDER

Enough is a feast.
BUDDHIST PROVERB

Nothing is more honorable than a grateful heart.
LUCIUS ANNAEUS SENECA

Gratitude is riches. Complaint is poverty.
DORIS DAY

When you are grateful, fear disappears, and abundance appears.
ANTHONY ROBBINS

Got no checkbooks, got no banks, still I'd like to express my thanks. I got the sun in the morning and the moon at night.
IRVING BERLIN

No duty is more urgent than giving thanks.
JAMES ALLEN

Gratitude and attitude are not challenges; they are choices.
ROBERT BRAATHE

Rest and be thankful.
WILLIAM WORDSWORTH

If a fellow isn't thankful for what he's got, he isn't likely to be thankful for what he's going to get.
FRANK A. CLARK

Be thankful for what you have; you'll end up having more. If you concentrate on what you don't have, you will never, never have enough.
OPRAH WINFREY

Who does not thank for little will not thank for much.
ESTONIAN PROVERB

Seeds of discouragement will not grow in the thankful heart.
ANONYMOUS

The private and personal blessings we enjoy – the blessings of immunity, safeguard, liberty and integrity – deserve the thanksgiving of a whole life.
JEREMY TAYLOR

We don't thank God enough for much that he has given us. Our prayers are too often the beggar's prayer, the prayer that asks for something. We offer too few prayers of thanksgiving and of praise.
ROBERT E. WOODS

We often take for granted the very things that most deserve our gratitude.
CYNTHIA OZICK

A thankful heart is not only the greatest virtue, but the parent of all the virtues.
MARCUS TULLIUS CICERO

God's goodness hath been great to thee; let never day or night unhallowed pass, but still remember what the Lord hath done.
WILLIAM SHAKESPEARE

Consider the superior things which you possess, and in gratitude remember how wonderfully you would long after them, if you had them not.
MARCUS AURELIUS

The grateful heart will always find opportunities to show its gratitude.
AESOP

Be glad of life because it gives you the chance to love and to work and to play and to look at the stars.
HENRY VAN DYKE

HABIT

We become what we repeatedly do.
SEAN COVEY

Motivation is what gets you started. Habit is what keeps you going.
JIM RYUN

Just do it! First you make your habits, then your habits make you.
LUCAS REMMERSWAAL

Let go of your old tired habits and plant new habits in fertile soil.
HARLEY KING

Your little choices become habits that affect the bigger decisions you make in life.
ELIZABETH GEORGE

Get into the habit of asking yourself, "Does this support the life I'm trying to create?"
KRISTI LING SPENCER

95% of everything you do is the result of habit.
ARISTOTLE

It is easier to prevent bad habits than to break them.
BENJAMIN FRANKLIN

Successful people aren't born that way. They become successful by establishing the habits of doing things unsuccessful people don't like to do.
WILLIAM MAKEPEACE THACKERAY

We are what we repeatedly do. Excellence then, is not an act, but a habit.
WILL DURANT

As long as habit and routine dictate the pattern of living, new dimensions of the soul will not emerge.
HENRY VAN DYKE

Each year one vicious habit discarded, in time might make the worst of us good.
BENJAMIN FRANKLIN

You'll never change your life until you change something you do daily. The secret of your success is found in your daily routine.
JOHN MAXWELL

Good habits formed at youth make all the difference.
ARISTOTLE

In essence, if we want to direct our lives, we must take control of our consistent actions. It's not what we do once in a while that shapes our lives, but what we do consistently.
ANTHONY ROBBINS

The common denominator of success - the secret of success of every man who has ever been successful - lies in the fact that he formed the habit of doing things that failures don't like to do.
ALBERT GRAY

Habits are like a cable. We weave a strand of it every day and soon it cannot be broken.
HORACE MANN

The moment we pass out of our habits we lose all sense of permanency and routine.
GEORGE MOORE

Habits are safer than rules; you don't have to watch them. And you don't have to keep them, either; they keep you.
FRANK CRANE

Nothing is more powerful than habit.

OVID

Have a time and place for everything, and do everything in its time and place, and you will not only accomplish more, but have far more leisure than those who are always hurrying.

TRYON EDWARDS

Repeat anything often enough and it will start to become you.

TOM HOPKINS

When we have practiced good actions awhile, they become easy; when they are easy, we take pleasure in them; when they please us, we do them frequently; and then, by frequency of act, they grow into a habit.

JOHN TILLOTSON

Make good habits and they will make you.

PARKS COUSINS

A man's fortune has its form given to it by his habits.

ANONYMOUS

A single bad habit will mar an otherwise faultless character, as an ink drop soileth the pure white page.

HOSEA BALLOU

We naturally like what we have been accustomed to ... This is likewise one of the causes which prevent men from finding truth.

MAIMONIDES

The less of routine, the more of life.

A. BRONSON ALCOTT

Any act often repeated soon forms a habit; and habit allowed, steadily gains in strength. At first it may be but as the spider's web, easily broken through, but if not resisted it soon binds us with chains of steel.

TRYON EDWARDS

The formation of right habits is essential to your permanent security. They diminish your chance of falling when assailed, and they augment your chance of recovery when overthrown.

JOHN TYNDALL

Excellence is an art won by training and habituation. We do not act rightly because we have virtue or excellence, but we rather have those because we have acted rightly. We are what we repeatedly do. Excellence, then, is not an act but a habit.

ARISTOTLE

You lay the foundations for your children's habits in their early childhood. The foundations for habits of poverty or riches, industry or idleness, good or evil. Teach them the right habits then, and their future life is safe.

G. F. FOLSOM

Your life and personality are largely the product of your daily habits. You develop precisely in the way in which you exercise your various powers. Habits repeated long enough become automatic.

GRENVILLE KLEISER

Since habits become power, make them work with you and not against you.

E. STNLEY JONES

HAPPINESS

Happiness is beneficial for the body, but it is grief that develops the powers of the mind.
MARCEL PROUST

A man should always consider how much he has more than he wants, and how much more unhappy he might be than he really is.
JOSEPH ADDISON

Happiness depends, on as nature shows, less on exterior things than most suppose.
WILLIAM COWPER

A happy life must be to a great extent a quiet life, for it is only in an atmosphere of quiet that true joy can live.
BERTRAND RUSSELL

Happiness depends on ourselves.
ARISTOTLE

The greatest happiness you can have is knowing that you do not necessarily require happiness.
WILLIAM SAROYAN

A table, a chair, a bowl of fruit and a violin; what else does a man need to be happy.
ALBERT EINSTEIN

Money can't buy happiness, but it can make you awfully comfortable while you're being miserable.
CLARE BOOTH LUCE

Happiness is mostly a by-product of doing what makes us feel fulfilled.
BENJAMIN SPOCK

Happiness is good health and a bad memory.
INGRID BERGMAN

Happiness grows at our own firesides, and is not to be picked in strangers' gardens.
DOUGLAS WILLIAM JERROLD

The essence of philosophy is that a man should so live that his happiness shall depend as little on external things.
EPICTETUS

Be happy for this moment. This moment is your life.
OMAR KHAYYAM

To watch the corn grow or the blossoms set; to draw hard breath over the ploughshare or spade; to read, to think, to love, to pray, are the things that make men happy.
JOHN RUSKIN

Mankind is the artificer of his own happiness.
HENRY DAVID THOREAU

Happiness in this world, when it comes, comes incidentally. Make it the object of pursuit, and it is never attained.
NATHANIEL HAWTHORNE

Friends, books, a cheerful heart, and conscience clear are the most choice companions we have here.
WILLIAM MATHER

Most folks are as happy as they make up their mind to be.
ABRAHAM LINCOLN

If you want to be happy, be.
LEO TOLSTOY

The supreme happiness of life is the conviction of being loved for yourself, or, more correctly, being loved in spite of yourself.
VICTOR HUGO

When ambition ends, happiness begins.
THOMAS MERTON

Happiness can exist only in acceptance.
GEORGE ORWELL

I, not events, have the power to make me happy or unhappy today. I can choose which it shall be. Yesterday is dead, tomorrow hasn't arrived yet. I have just one day, today, and I'm going to be happy in it.
GROUCHO MARX

Anything you're good at contributes to happiness.
BERTRAND RUSSELL

True happiness is...to enjoy the presence, without anxious dependence upon the future.
LUCIUS ANNAEUS SENECA

The moments of happiness we enjoy take us by surprise. It is not that we seize them, but that they seize us.
ASHLEY MONTAGU

To find happiness, we must search our hearts, for it comes from within, through our own efforts and beliefs.
ALFRED ARMAND MONTAPERT

The person who can live a happy life is the one who believes he can.
LARRY JOHN PHILLIPS

Be happy with what you have and are, be generous with both, and you won't have to hunt for happiness.
WILLIAM E. GLADSTONE

The art of being happy lies in the power of extracting happiness from common things.
HENRY WARD BEECHER

Plenty of people miss their share of happiness, not because they never found it, but because they didn't stop to enjoy it.
WILLIAM FEATHER

Happiness is that pleasure which flows from the sense of virtue and from the consciousness of right deeds.
HENRY MOORE

The purpose of our lives is to be happy.
DALAI LAMA

When a man has lost all happiness, he's not alive. Call him a breathing corpse.
SOPHOCLES

Happiness is the meaning and the purpose of life, the whole aim and end of human existence.
ARISTOTLE

The pursuit of happiness...is the greatest feat man has to accomplish.
ROBERT HENRI

The joyfulness of a man prolengeth his days.
BIBLE

Men are made for happiness, and anyone who is completely happy has a right to say to himself: "I am doing God's will on earth."
ANTON CHEKHOV

To live as fully, as completely as possible, to be happy... is the true aim and end to life.
LLEWELYN POWERS

There is no duty so much underrated as the duty of being happy.
ROBERT LOUIS STEVENSON

Different men seek...happiness in different ways and by different means.
ARISTOTLE

Even the lowliest, provided he is whole, can be happy, and in his own way, perfect.
JOHANN WOLFGANG VON GOETHE

All men have happiness as their object: there are no exceptions. However different the means they employ, they aim as the same end.
BLAISE PASCAL

We all live with the objective of being happy; our lives are all different and yet the same.
ANNE FRANK

One is happy as a result of one's own efforts – once one knows the necessary ingredients of happiness – simple tastes, a certain degree of courage, self-denial to a point, love of work, and, above all, a clear conscience.
GEORGE SAND

No one gives joy or sorrow...We gather the consequences of our deeds.
GARUDA PURANA

Happiness, happiness...the flavor is with you – with you alone, and you can make it as intoxicating as you please.
JOSEPH CONRAD

The man who makes everything that leads to happiness depend upon himself, and not upon other men, has adopted the very best plan for living happily.
PLATO

Learn how to feel joy.
LUCIUS ANNAEUS SENECA

Our greatest happiness does not depend on the condition of life in which chance has placed us, but is always the result of a good conscience, good health, occupation and freedom in all just pursuits.
THOMAS JEFFERSON

I believe the recipe for happiness to be just enough money to pay the monthly bills you acquire, a little surplus to give you confidence, a little too much work each day, enthusiasm for your work, a substantial share of good health, a couple of real friends and a wife and children to share life's beauty with you.

B. KENFIELD MORLEY

What can be added to the happiness of man, who is in health, out of debt, and has a clear conscience.

ADAM SMITH

It is not easy to find happiness in ourselves, and it is not possible to find it elsewhere.

AGNES REPPLIER

Happiness is not in our circumstances, but in ourselves. It is not something we see, like a rainbow, or feel, like the heat of a fire. Happiness is something we are.

JOHN B. SHEERIN

Most true happiness comes from one's inner life, from the disposition of the mind and soul. Admittedly, a good inner life is difficult to achieve, especially in these trying times. It takes reflection and contemplation and self-discipline.

W. L. SHIRER

Happiness is not a goal, it is a by-product.

ELEANOR ROOSEVELT

Our actions are the springs of our happiness or misery.

PHILIP SKELTON

True happiness...is not attained through self-gratification, but through fidelity to a worthy purpose.

HELEN KELLER

We are content to forgo joy when pain is also lost.

LATIN PROVERB

The knowledge that something remains yet unenjoyed impairs our enjoyment of the good before us.

SAMUAEL JOHNSON

The talent for being happy is appreciating and liking what you have, instead of what you don't have.
WOODY ALLEN

Not what we have, but what we use, not what we see, but what we choose – these are the things that mar or bless human happiness.
JOSEPH FORT NEWTON

We always have enough to be happy if we are enjoying what we do have – and not worrying about what we don't have.
KEN KEYES JR.

We are no longer happy so soon as we wish to be happier.
WALTER SAVAGE LANDOR

Man is fond of counting is troubles, but he does not count his joys. If he counted them up as he ought to, he would see that every lot has enough happiness provided for it.
FYODOR DOSTOYEVSKY

I am happy and content because I think I am.
ALAIN-RENE LESAGE

Unhappy is the man, though he rule the world, who doesn't consider himself supremely blessed.
MARCUS ANNAEUS SENECA

I am responsible for my own well-being, my own happiness. The choices and decisions I make regarding my life directly influence the quality if my days.
KATHLEEN ANDRUS

I finally figured out the only reason to be alive is to enjoy it.
RITA MAE BROWN

There is no cure for birth or death save to enjoy the interval.
GEORGE SANTAYANA

That man is happiest who lives from day to day and asks no more, garnering the simple goodness of life.

EURIPIDES

Happiness is produced not so much by great pieces of good fortune that seldom happens, as by little advantages that occur every day.

BENJAMIN FRANKLIN

Happiness is not a state to arrive at, but a manner of traveling.

MARGARET LEE RUNBACK

Unless each day can be looked back upon by an individual as one which he has had some fun, some joy, some real satisfaction, that day is a loss.

ANONYMOUS

Man's real life is happy, chiefly because he is ever expecting that it soon will be so.

EDGAR ALLEN POE

We are never so happy or so unhappy as we think.

FRANCOIS DE LA ROCHEFOUCAULD

The mind is its own place, and in itself can make a heaven of hell, a hell of heaven.

JOHN MILTON

All happiness is in the mind.

ANONYMOUS

A happy life consists in tranquility of mind.

MARCUS TILLIUS CICERO

Half the unhappiness in the world is due to the failure of plans which were never reasonable, and often impossible.

EDGAR WATSON HOWE

The only true happiness comes from squandering ourselves for a purpose.

JOHN MASON BROWN

Happiness lies in the joy of achievement and the thrill of creative effort.
FRANKLIN D. ROOSEVELT

You have to believe in happiness, or happiness never comes.
DOUGLAS MALLOCH

In order to have great happiness, you have to have great pain and unhappiness –
otherwise how would you know when you're happy.
LESLIE CARON

Happiness is not the absence of conflict, but the ability to cope with it.
ANONYMOUS

Happiness does not depend on outward things, but on the way we see them.
LEO TOLSTOY

Riches, like glory or health, have no more beauty or pleasure than their possessor is
pleased to lend them.
MICHEL DE MONTAIGNE

Happiness often sneaks in through a door you didn't know you left open.
JOHN BARRYMORE

Happiness in intelligent people is the rarest thing I know.
ERNEST HEMINGWAY

Happiness doesn't depend on any external conditions, it is governed by our
mental attitude.
DALE CARNEGIE

It is not how much we have, but how much we enjoy, that makes happiness.
CHARLES SPURGEON

Do not speak of your happiness to one less fortunate than yourself.
PLUTARCH

Happiness is like a kiss. You must share it to enjoy it.
BERNARD MELTZER

Happiness is the only good. The time to be happy is now. The place to be happy is here. The way to be happy is to make others so.
ROBERT GREEN INGERSOLL

Just do what must be done. This may not be happiness, but it is greatness.
GEORGE BERNARD SHAW

The two enemies of human happiness are pain and boredom.
ARTHUR SCHOPENHAUER

Happiness is the interval between periods of unhappiness.
DON MARQUIS

It is the chiefest point of happiness that a man is willing to be what he is.
DESIDERIUS ERASMUS

Human felicity is produced not so much by great pieces of good fortune that seldom happen, as by little advantages that occur every day.
BENJAMIN FRANKLIN

Happiness is a way-station between too little and too much.
CHANNING POLLOCK

How to gain, how to keep, how to recover happiness is in fact for most men at all times the secret motive of all they do, and of all they are willing to endure.
WILLIAM JAMES

Man is happy only as he finds a work worth doing – and does it well.
B. MERRILL ROOT

Happiness has many roots, but none more important than security.
B. R. STETTINIUS JR.

Happiness is only a by-product of successful living.
DR. AUSTEN FOX RIGGS

Talk happiness. The world is sad enough without your woe.
ORISON SWETT MARDEN

Real happiness is cheap enough, yet how dearly we pay for its counterfeit.
HOSEA BALLOU

The belief that youth is the happiest time of life is founded on a fallacy. The happiest person is the person who thinks the most interesting thoughts, and we grow happier as we grow older.
WILLIAM LYON PHELPS

Like swimming, riding, writing or playing golf, happiness can be learned.
DR. BORIS SOKOLOFF

One is never as unhappy as one thinks, nor as happy as one hopes.
FRANCOIS DE LA ROCHEFOUCAULD

Having only coarse food to eat, plain water to drink, and a bent arm for a pillow, one can still find happiness therein.
CONFUCIUS

The greatest happiness is to transform one's feelings into actions.
MADAME DE STAEL

O happy who thus liveth! Not caring much for gold; with clothing which sufficeth to keep him from the cold, though poor and plain his diet, yet merry 'tis, and quiet.
ANONYMOUS

A man who finds no satisfaction in himself seeks for it in vain elsewhere.
FRANCOIS DE LA ROCHEFOUCAULD

Above all, let us never forget that an act of goodness is in itself an act of happiness. It is the flower of a long inner life of joy and contentment; it tells of peaceful hours and days on the sunniest heights of our soul.
MAURICE MAETERLINCK

Looking for happiness is like clutching the shadow or chasing the wind.
JAPANESE PROVERB

Happiness is the legitimate fruitage of love and service. Set happiness before you as an end, no matter what guise of wealth, or fame, or oblivion even, and you will not attain it. But renounce it and seek the pleasure of God, and that instant is the birth of your own.
ARTHUR S. HARDY

Few persons realize how much of their happiness is dependent upon their work, upon the fact they are kept busy and not left to feed upon themselves. Happiness comes most to persons who seek her least, and think least about it. It is not an object to be sought; it is a state to be induced. It must follow and not lead. It must overtake you, and not you overtake it.
JOHN BURROUGHS

He who leaves his house in search of happiness pursues a shadow.
S. G. CHAMPION

If you ever find happiness by hunting for it, you will find it as the old woman did her lost spectacles - on her own nose all the time.
JOSH BILLINGS

Happiness and virtue rest upon each other; the best are not only the happiest, but the happiest are usually the best.
EDWARD BULWER-LYTTON

To be happy is easy enough if we give ourselves, forgive others, and live with thanksgiving. No self-centered person, no ungrateful soul can ever be happy, much less make anyone else happy. Life is giving, not getting.
JOSEPH F. NEWTON

The happy people are those who are producing something; the bored people are those who are consuming much and producing nothing.
WILLIAM R. INGE

Only one thing I know. The only ones among you who will be really happy are those who will have sought and found how to serve.
ALBERT SCHWEITZER

No one truly knows happiness who has not suffered, and the redeemed are happier than the elect.
HENRI FREDERICK AMIEL

Happiness comes from striving – doing – loving – achieving – conquering – always something positive and forceful.
DAIVD STARR JORDAN

Remember this, - that very little is needed to make a happy life.
MARCUS AURELIUS

To be of use in the world is the only way to be happy.
HANS CHRISTIAN ANDERSON

Happiness lies in the taste, and not in things; and it is from having what we desire that we are happy – not from having what others think desirable.
FRANCOIS DE LA ROCHEFOUCAULD

A man must seek his happiness and inward peace from objects which cannot be taken away from him.
HUMBOLDT

Give a man health and a course to steer, and he'll never stop to trouble whether he's happy or not.
GEORGE BERNARD SHAW

If you work at that which is before you ... expecting nothing, fearing nothing, but satisfied with your present activity according to nature, and with heroic truth in every word and sound which you speak, you will live happy. And there is no man who is able to prevent this.
MARCUS AURELIUS

We act as though comfort and luxury were the chief requirements of life, when all that we need to make us really happy is something to be enthusiastic about.
ANONYMOUS

This is the true joy in life, the being used for a purpose recognized by yourself as a mighty one; the being thoroughly worn out before you are thrown on the scrap heap; the being a force of nature instead of a feverish selfish little clod of ailments and grievances complaining that the world will not devote itself to making you happy.

GEORGE BERNARD SHAW

I am still determined to be cheerful and happy in whatever situation I may be, for I have also learnt that the greater part of our happiness or misery depends upon our disposition, and not upon our circumstances.

MARTHA WASHINGTON

I look at what I have not and think myself unhappy; others look at what I have and think me happy.

JOSEPH ROUX

Very little is necessary to make a happy life.

MARCUS AURELIUS

The extent, to which you are happy, is in direct proportion to your recognition of what you have to be thankful.

J. S. FELTS

If the chief part of human happiness arises from the consciousness of being loved, as I believe it does, those sudden changes of fortune seldom contribute much to happiness.

ADAM SMITH

A happy person is not a person in a certain set of circumstances, but rather a person with a certain set of attitudes.

HUGH DOWNS

The journey is what brings us happiness not the destination.

DAN MILLMAN

Happiness is not determined by what's happening around you, but rather what's happening inside you. Most people depend on others to gain happiness, but the truth is, it always comes from within.

ANONYMOUS

A multitude of small delights constitutes happiness.
CHARLES BAUDELAIRE

If this world afford true happiness, it is to be found in a home where love and confidence increase with the years., where the necessities of life come without severe strain, where luxuries enter only after their cost has been carefully considered.
A. EDWARD NEWTON

May we never let the things we can't have, or don't have, or shouldn't have, spoil our enjoyment of the things we do have and can have. As we value our happiness let us not forget it, for one of the greatest lessons in life is learning to be happy without the things we cannot or should not have.
RICHARD L. EVANS

There are two ways of being happy: we must either dimmish our wants or augment our means - either may do - the result is the same and it is for each man to decide for himself and to do that which happens to be easier.
BENJAMIN FRANKLIN

Happiness lies, first of all, in health.
GEORGE WILLIAM CURTIS

If a man has important work, and enough leisure and income to enable him to do it properly, he is in possession of as much happiness as is good for any of the children of Adam.
R. H. TAWNEY

Happiness comes fleetingly now and then, to those who have learned to do without it, and to them only.
DON MARQUIS

There is no happiness except in the realization that we have accomplished something.
HENRY FORD

According to Aristotle and others, happiness is not something you can "feel" or experience at a particular moment. It is the quality of a whole life. The happy life is the good life.
MORTIMER ADLER

My creed is this: Happiness is the only good. The place to be happy is here. The time to be happy is now. The way to be happy is to make others so.

ROBERT GREEN INGERSOLL

Whoso trusteth in the Lord, happy is he.

BIBLE

Get your happiness out of your work or you will never know what happiness is.

ELBERT HUBBARD

We must not look outside for our happiness, but in ourselves, in our own minds. "The Kingdom of Heaven is within you." If we cannot be happy here, why should we expect to be so hereafter?

JOHN LUBBOCK

I may not be able to accomplish as much as some others, but I can be just as happy.

CHARLES ALLEN

To be bright and cheerful often requires an effort; there is a certain art in keeping ourselves happy.

JOHN LUBBOCK

Half of the world is on the wrong scent in the pursuit of happiness. They think it consists in having and getting, and in being served by others. It consists in giving and in serving others.

HENRY DRUMMOND

Remember happiness doesn't depend upon who you are or what you have; it depends solely upon what you think.

DALE CARNEGIE

HEALTH

Health is a gift, but you have to work to keep it.

ELBERT HUBBARD

Health is certainly more valuable than money, because it is by health that money is procured.

SAMUEL JOHNSON

Health squandered can never be compensated for by the mere acquisition of money.

ORISON SWETT MARDEN

If you mean to keep as well as possible, the less you think about your health the better.

OLIVER WENDELL HOLMES

More people are killed by overeating and drinking than by the sword.

SIR WILLIAM OSLER

The best physicians are "Dr. Diet" and "Dr. Quiet."

JOSH BILLINGS

If you would live in health, be old early.

SPANISH PROVERB

It is certain that tis easier to preserve Health than to recover it, and to prevent Diseases than to cure them.

DR. GEORGE CHEYNE

Look to your health; and if you have it, praise God, and value it next to a good conscience; for health is the second blessing that we mortals are capable of; a blessing that money cannot buy.

IZAAK WALTON

Nature, time and patience are the three great physicians.

PROVERB

Without health all men are poor.

ANONYMOUS

A healthy outside starts from the inside.

ROBERT URICH

Health is not valued till sickness comes.

THOMAS FULLER

Take care of your body. It's the only place you have to live.

JIM ROHN

You can't expect to look like a million bucks if you eat from the dollar menu.

ANONYMOUS

Heath requires healthy food.

ROGER WILLIAMS

Your body hears everything your mind says.

NAOMI JUDD

The way you think, the way you behave, the way you eat, can influence your life by 30 to 50 years.

DEEPAK CHOPRA

To enjoy the glow of good health, you must exercise.

ANONYMOUS

To keep the body in good health is a duty...otherwise we shall not be able to keep our mind strong and clear.

BUDDHA

It takes more than just a good looking body. You've got to have the heart and soul to go with it.

EPICTETUS

The healthy, the strong individual, is the one who asks for help when he needs it. Whether he's got an abscess on his knee or in his soul.

RONA BARRETT

To lengthen thy life, lessen thy meals.

BENJAMIN FRANKLIN

A man too busy to take care of his health is like a mechanic too busy to take care of his tools.

SPANISH PROVEB

People who cannot find time for recreation are obliged sooner or later to find time for illness.

JOHN WANAMAKER

To insure good health: eat lightly, breathe deeply, live moderately, cultivate cheerfulness, and maintain an interest in life.

WILLIAM LOUDEN

He who has health, has hope; and he who has hope, has everything.

ARABIAN PROVERB

Men dig their graves with their own teeth and die more by those fatal instruments than the weapons of their enemies.

THOMAS MOFFETT

For the bare purpose of preserving ourselves in good health, there needs no better physic than a temperate and regular life.

LOUIS CORNARO

Wholesome food and drink are cheaper than doctors and hospitals.
DR. CARL C. WAHL

The health of the people is really the foundation upon which all their happiness and all their powers as a State depend.
BENJAMIN DISRAELI

To lengthen your life, says an old proverb, shorten your meals. Plain living and high thinking will secure health for most of us.
JOHN LUBBOCK

Health is the second blessing that we mortals are capable of, - a blessing that money cannot buy.
IZAAK WALTON

A good laugh and a long sleep are the best cures in the doctor's book.
IRISH PROVERB

Time is generally the best doctor.
OVID

The groundwork of all happiness is health.
LEIGH HUNT

The greatest wealth is health.
VIRGIL

Any man who leads the regular and temperate life, not swerving from it in the least degree where his nourishment is concerned, can be but little affected by other disorders or incidental mishaps. Whereas, on the other hand, I truly conclude that disorderly habits of living are those which are fatal.
LOUIS CORNARO

The greatest mistake a man can make is to sacrifice health for any other advantage.
ARTHUR SCHOPENHAUER

To the sick, while there is life there is hope.
MARCUS TULLIUS CICERO

Eat to live, and do not live to eat.
BENJAMIN FRANKLIN

Health is better than wealth.
DR. NORMAN BEALS

The requisites of health are plain enough; regular habits, daily exercise, cleanliness, and moderation in all things – in eating as well as in drinking – would keep most people well.
JOHN LUBBOCK

HOME

There is nothing more important than a good, safe, secure home.
ROSALYNN CARTER

Seek home for rest, for home is best.
THOMAS TUSSER

Home sweet home. This is the place to find happiness. If one doesn't find it here, one doesn't find it anywhere.
M. K. SONI

The dog is a lion in his own house.
PERSIAN PROVERB

Where we love is home. Home that our feet may leave, but not our hearts.
OLIVER WENDELL HOLMES

A house is built by human hands, but a home is built by human hearts.
JOHN HOWARD PAYNE

No matter under what circumstances you leave it, home does not cease to be home. No matter how you lived there – well or poorly.
JOSEPH BRADSKY

Home is the most popular, and will be the most enduring of all earthly establishments.
CHANNING POLLOCK

The sun at home warms better than the sun elsewhere.
ALBANIA PROVERB

A house is made of walls and beams; a home is built with love and dreams.
ANONYMOUS

There's nothing half so pleasant as coming home again.
MARGARET ELIZABETH SANGSTER

A house is built of logs and stone, of tiles and posts and piers; a home is built of loving deeds that stand a thousand years.
VICTOR HUGO

Home is where love resides, memories are created, friends and family belong, and laughter ends.
ANONYMOUS

Perhaps you have a mother, likewise a sister too, perhaps you have a sweetheart to weep and mourn for you. If this be your condition I advise you to never roam, I advise you by experience you had better stay at home.
ANONYMOUS

Home, the spot of earth supremely blest, a dearer, sweeter spot than all the rest.
ROBERT MONTGOMERY

A palace without affection is a poor hovel, and the meanest hut with love in it is a palace for the soul.
ROBERT GREEN INGERSOLL

Be it ever so humble, there's no place like home.
JOHN HOWARD PAYNE

Happy the man, whose wish and care a few paternal acres bound, content to breathe his native air, in his own ground.
ALEXANDER POPE

Home is home, be it never so homely.
ENGLISH PROVERB

A hundred men may make an encampment, but it takes a woman to make a home.
CHINESE PROVERB

Home is where you feel at home and are treated well.
DALAI LAMA

There is no place like home.
L. FRANK BAUM

He is happiest, be he king or peasant, who finds peace in his home.
JOHANN WOLFGANG VON GOETHE

A house is not a home unless it contains food and fire for the mind as well as the body.
BENJAMIN FRANKLIN

There is nothing like staying at home for real comfort.
JANE AUSTEN

A man's house is his castle.
JAMES OTIS

A house that does not have one warm, comfy chair in it is useless.
MAY SARTON

A comfortable house is a great source of happiness. It ranks immediately after health and a good conscience.
SYDNEY SMITH

People are usually the happiest at home.
WILLIAM SHAKESPEARE

Winter is the time for comfort, for good food and warmth, for the touch of a friendly hand and for a talk besides the fire; it is the time for home.
EDITH SITWELL

No matter how big you are, when you go back home, your family treats you like a normal person.
AJITH KUMAR

Every bird likes its own nest best.
RANDLE COTGRAVE

Home is where the heart is.
ANONYMOUS

Our home joys are the most delightful earth affords, and the joy of parents in their children is the most holy joy of humanity. It makes their hearts pure and good, it lifts men up to their Father in heaven.
JOHANN PESTALOZZI

There is no home that is not twice as beautiful as the most beautiful city.
AFRICAN PROVERB

If solid happiness we prize, within our breast this jewel lies, and they are fools who roam. The world has nothing to bestow; from our own selves our joys must flow, and that dear hut, our home.
NATHANIEL COTTON

Home is the place where character is built, where sacrifices to contribute to the happiness of others are made, and where love has taken up is abode.
ELIJAH KELLOGG

'Mid pleasures and palaces though we may roam, be it ever so humble, there's no place like home.
JOHN HOWARD PAYNE

And where we love is home, home that our feet may leave, but not our hearts. The chain may lengthen, but it never parts.

OLIVER WENDELL HOLMES

A home is the first necessity of every family; it is a indispensable to the education and qualification of every citizen.

SEWARD

Whoever makes home seem to the young dearer and more happy, is a public benefactor.

HENRY WARD BEECHER

HONESTY

An honest heart possesses a kingdom.
LUCIUS ANNAEUS SENECA

For he who is honest is noble, whatever his fortunes or birth.
CARY

God looks at the clean hands, not the full ones.
PUBILIUS SYRUS

Honesty is, after all, the basic starting point of character. Honesty is the indispensable essential of every worthwhile success.
CHARLES CROW

How happy is he born and taught, that serveth not another's will; whose armor is his honest thought, and simple truth his utmost skill!
HENRY WOTTON

I hope I shall possess firmness and virtue enough to maintain what I consider the most enviable of all titles, the character of an honest man.
GEORGE WASHINGTON

No legacy is so rich as honesty.
WILLIAM SHAKESPEARE

What do I get for being honest? You are getting the consciousness on your own mind that you are right. The best reward that life can bring.
ADOLPH PHILIP GOUTHEY

Whoever can be trusted with very little can also be trusted with much, and whoever is dishonest with very little will also be dishonest with much.
BIBLE

Honesty saves everyone's time.
ANONYMOUS

Being honest may not get you a lot of friends, but it'll always get you the right ones.
JOHN LENNON

A half-truth is a whole lie.
YIDDISH PROVERB

If you tell the truth, you don't need a long memory.
JESSE VENTURA

Honesty is often very hard. The truth is often painful. But the freedom it can bring is worth the trying.
FRED ROGERS

No matter how plain a woman may be, if truth and honesty are written across her face, she will be beautiful.
ELEANOR ROOSEVELT

If it is not right, do not do it; if it is not true, do not say it.
MARCUS AURELIUS

The real source of inner joy is to remain truthful and honest.
DALAI LAMA

Remember, as long as you live, that nothing but strict truth can carry you through the world, with either your conscience or your honor unwounded.
EARL OF CHESTERFIELD

The high minded man must care more for the truth than for what people think.
ARISTOTLE

This above all: to thine own self be true, and it must follow, as the night the day, thou canst not be false to any man.
WILLIAM SHAKESPEARE

Telling the truth and making someone cry is better than telling a lie and making someone smile.
PAULO COELHO

It is not easy to keep silent when silence is a lie.
VICTOR HUGO

To know what is right and not to do it is the worst of cowardice.
CONFUCIUS

The good I stand on is my truth and honesty.
WILLIAM SHAKESPEARE

Honesty is the best, as well as the only right policy.
JOHN LUBBOCK

There is no foundation like the rock of honesty and fairness, and when you begin to build your life on that rock, with the cement of faith in God that you have, then you have a real start.
RONALD REAGAN

No man has a good enough memory to make a successful liar.
ABRAHAM LINCOLN

To seek the truth, for sake of knowing the truth, is one of the noblest objects a man can live for.
DEAN WILLIAM R. INGE

Speak with honesty, think with sincerity and act with integrity.
ANONYMOUS

To thine own self be true, and it must follow, as the night the day, thou canst not then be false to any man.
WILLIAM SHAKESPEARE

Honesty is more than not lying. It is truth telling, truth speaking, truth living, and truth loving.
JAMES FAUST

Make yourself an honest man.
THOMAS CARLYLE

An honest man is the noblest work of God.
ALEXANDER POPE

Honesty has a power that very few people can handle.
STEVEN AITCHISON

Honesty prospers in every condition of life.
FRIEDRICH SCHILLER

Be honest, brutally honest.
LAURYN HILL

If honesty did not exist, we ought to invent it as the best means of getting rich.
MIRABEAU

There is no twilight zone of honesty in business – a thing is right or wrong – it's black or white.
JOHN F. DODGE

He that loseth his honestie hath nothing else to lose.
JOHN LYLY

The first step to greatness is to be honest.
SAMUEL JOHNSON

Honesty is the first chapter of the book of wisdom.
THOMAS JEFFERSON

HONOR

A man who permits his honor to be taken, permits his life to be taken.
PIETRO ARETINO

A man of honor should never forget what he is because he sees what others are.
BALTASAR GRACIAN

He has honor if he holds himself to an ideal of conduct though it is inconvenient,
unprofitable, or dangerous to do so.
WALTER LIPPMANN

My honor is dearer to me than my life.
MIGUEL DE CERVANTES

Honor is easier kept than recovered.
SAYING

It is preferable to die with honor than to live in disgrace.
SA'DI

Let the honor of thy fellow be as dear to thee as thine own.
TALMUD

Either live or die with honor.
JOHN CLARKE

No amount of ability is of the slightest avail without honor.
ANDREW CARNEGIE

I have a lantern. You steal my lantern. What, then, is your honor worth no more to you than the price of my lantern.

EPICTETUS

You can be deprived of your money, your job and your home by someone else, but remember that no one can ever take away your honor.

WILLIAM LYON PHELPS

That nation is worthless that will not, with pleasure, venture all for its honor.

FRIEDRICH SCHILLER

Mine honor is my life; both grow in one; take honor from me, and my life is done.

WILLIAM SHAKESPEARE

Be honorable yourself if you wish to associate with honorable people.

WELSH PROVERB

Let honor be to us as strong an obligation as necessity is to others.

PLINY THE YOUNGER

Honor thy father and mother.

BIBLE

My heart to the ladies, my life to the king, and my soul to God, but my honor is my own.

SAYING

Honor lies in honest toil.

GROVER CLEVELAND

From our ancestors come our names, from our virtues our honors.

ANONYMOUS

Honor has not to be won; it must only not be lost.

ARTHUR SCHOPENHAUER

I would prefer even to fail with honor than win by cheating.
SOPHOCLES

The greatest way to live with honor in this world is to be what we pretend to be.
SOCRATES

Who sows virtue reaps honor.
LEONARDO DA VINCI

What is left when honor is lost?
PUBLILIUS SYRUS

Show me the man you honor, and I will know what kind of man you are.
THOMAS CARLYLE

It is not titles that honor men, but men that honor titles.
NICCOLO MACHIAVELLI

It is better to deserve honors and not have them than to have them and not deserve them.
MARK TWAIN

Live today and every day like a man of honor.
CHARLES ELIOT

The journey of high honor lies not in smooth ways.
PHILIP SIDNEY

Honor is honor, but gold and silver are not honor.
PHERECYDES

Our own heart, and not other men's opinions, form our true honor.
SAMUEL TAYLOR COLERIDGE

Without integrity and honor, having everything means nothing.
ROBIN SHARMA

No person was ever honored for what he received. Honor has been the reward for what he gave.
CALVIN COOLIDGE

Rather fail with honor than succeed by fraud.
SOPHOCLES

HOPE

Hope Is being able to see that there is a light despite all the darkness.
DESMOND TUTU

Hope is outreaching desire with expectancy of good. It is characteristic of all living beings.
EDWARD S. AME

Hope is a lover's staff; walk hence with that, and manage it against despairing thoughts.
WILLIAM SHAKESPEARE

There is no medicine like hope, no incentive so great, and no tonic so powerful as expectation of something better tomorrow.
ORISON SWETT MARDEN

When you say a situation or a person is hopeless, you are slamming the door in the face of God.
CHARLES L. ALLEN

It is hope which maintains most of mankind.
SOPHOCLES

Hope is a waking dream.
ARISTOTLE

The hopeful man sees success where others see failure, sunshine where others see shadows and storm.
ORISON SWETT MARDEN

I am prepared for the worst, but hope for the best.
BENJAMIN DISRAELI

A little more persistence, a little more effort, and what seemed hopeless failure may turn to glorious success.
ELBERT HUBBARD

Let your hopes, not your hurts, shape your future.
ROBERT SCHULLER

Everything that is done in the world is done by hope.
MARTIN LUTHER

We have always held to the hope, the belief, the conviction that there is a better life, a better world, beyond the horizon.
FRANKLIN D. ROOSEVELT

A whole stack of memories never equal one little hope.
CHARLES M. SCHULZ

We must free ourselves of the hope the sea will ever rest. We must learn to sail in high winds.
ARISTOTLE ONASSIS

Hope is important because it can make the present moment less difficult to bear. If we believe that tomorrow will be better, we can bear a hardship today.
THICH NHAT HANH

All human wisdom is summed up in two words, wait and hope.
ALEXANDER DUMAS

He that lives upon hope will die fasting.
BENJAMIN FRANKLIN

My hope still is to leave the world a bit better than when I got here.
JIM HENSON

The work goes on, the cause endures, the hope still lives, and the dreams shall never die.
EDWARD KENNEDY

Be prepared, work hard, and hope for a little luck. Recognize that the harder you work and the better prepared you are, the more luck you might have.
ED BRADLEY

The miserable have no other medicine but only hope.
WILLIAM SHAKESPEARE

I always entertain great hopes.
ROBERT FROST

Neither should a ship rely on one small anchor, nor should life rest on a single hope.
EPICTETUS

Once we start to act, hope is everywhere. So instead of looking for hope, look for action. Then, and only then, hope will come.
GRETA THUNBURG

A leader is a dealer in hope.
NAPOLEON BONAPARTE

Desire is the starting point of all achievement, not a hope, nor a wish, but a keen pulsating desire which transcends everything.
NAPOLEON HILL

If it were not for hopes, the heart would break.
THOMAS FULLER

Without hope men are only half alive. With hope they dream and think and work.
CHARLES SAWYER

Great hopes make great men.
THOMAS FULLER

Hope is one of those things in life you cannot do without.
LEROY DOUGLAS

The important thing is not that we can live on hope alone, but that life is not worth living without it.
HARVEY MILK

And thou shalt be secure because there is hope.
BIBLE

Hope! Of all the ills that men endure, the only cheap and universal cure.
ABRAHAM COWLEY

Our greatest good, and what we least can spare, is hope.
JOHN ARMSTRONG

Hope is the last thing that dies in man.
FRANCOIS DE LA ROCHEFOUCAULD

Strong hope is a much greater stimulant of life than any single realized joy could be.
FRIEDRICH NIETZSCHE

Hope arouses, as nothing else can arouse, a passion for the possible.
WILLIAM SLOAN COFFIN, JR.

Hope is the anchor of the soul, the stimulus to action, and the incentive to achievement.
ANONYMOUS

There are no hopeless situations; there are only men who have grown hopeless about them.
CLARE BOOTHE LUCE

Hope never abandons you, you abandon it.
GEORGE WEINBERG

Never despair.
HORACE

One should...be able to see things as hopeless and yet be determined to make them otherwise.
B. SCOTT FITZGERALD

While there's life, there's hope.
TERENCE

Hope is the poor man's bread.
GARY HERBERT

Hope is an adventure, a going forward, a confident search for a rewarding life.
KARL MENNONGER

Hope, like the gleaming taper's light, adorns and cheers our way; and still, as darker grows the night, emits a lighter ray.
OLIVER GOLDSMITH

Hope springs eternal in the human breast.
ALEXANDER POPE

Hope for a miracle. But don't depend on one.
TALMUD

Hope is itself a species of happiness, and, perhaps, the chief happiness which this world affords.
SAMUEL JOHNSON

He who has help has hope, and he who has hope has everything.
ARABIAN PROVERB

What one hopes for is always better than what has.
ETHIOPIAN PROVERB

Youth fades; love droops; the leaves of friendship fall; a mother's secret hope outlives them all.

OLIVWE WENDELL HOLMES

A religious hope does not only bear up the mind under her sufferings, but makes her rejoice in them.

JOSEPH ADDISON

Know the, whatever cheerful and serene supports the mind, supports the body too: hence, the most vital movement mortals feel is hope, the balm and lifeblood of the soul.

JOHN ARMSTRONG

Today well-lived...makes every tomorrow a vision of hope.

ANONYMOUS

Despite age, sickness, and sorrow, life is worth while if you still keep radiantly hopeful.

GRENVILLE KLEISER

Man is, properly speaking, based upon hope; he has no other possession but hope; this world of his emphatically the place of hope.

THOMAS CARLYLE

The man of hope can say with confidence, "Thou wilt keep him in perfect peace, whose mind is stayed on Thee; because he trusteth in Thee."

GRENVILLE KLEISER

What is hope? Hope is wishing for a thing to come true; faith is believing that it will come true. Hope is wanting something so eagerly that, in spite of all the evidence that you're not going to get it, you go right on wanting it. And the remarkable thing about it is that this very act of hoping produces a kind of strength of its own.

NORMAN VINCENT PEALE

Hope is the dream of a waking man.

DIOGENES

The greatest architect and the one most needed is hope.
HENRY WARD BEECHER

Hope ever urges us on, and tells us tomorrow will be better.
TIBULLUS

Without vision, there's no hope, and without hope, life is nothing more than a mere existence.
J. S. FELTS

Hope is necessary in every condition. The miseries of poverty, sickness, of captivity, would, without this comfort, be insupportable.
SAMUEL JOHNSON

A strong mind always hopes, and has always cause to hope.
POLYBUS

The hopeful man believes that the best is yet to be, and paints in roseate colors the good times in prospect. He is buoyant, enthusiastic, and confident when pessimism stalks ahead. He is an incorrigible optimist.
GRENVILLE KLEISER

HUMBLENESS

Self-praise is for losers. Be a winner. Stand for something. Always have class, and be humble.

JOHN MADDEN

Talent is God-given. Be humble. Fame is man-given. Be grateful. Conceit is self-given. Be careful.

HARVEY MACKAY

After crosses and losses men grow humbler and wiser.

BENJAMIN FRANKLIN

Humility, like darkness, reveals the heavenly lights.

HENRY DAVID THOREAU

It's hard to be humble, when you're as great as I am.

MUHAMMAND ALI

An able yet humble man is a jewel worth a kingdom.

WILLIAM PENN

The first test of a truly great man is his humility.

JOHN RUSKIN

Master your craft, be nice and stay humble.

ERICK MORILLO

I stand here before you not as a prophet, but as a humble servant of you, the people.
NELSON MANDELA

My religion consists of a humble admiration of the illimitable superior spirit who reveals himself in the slight details we are able to perceive with our frail and feeble mind.
ALBERT EINSTEIN

Don't be humble...you're not that great.
GOLDA MEIR

I'll never forget where I'm from. It's essential to remain humble and evolving.
FREIDA PINTO

It keeps me humble just to know exactly where I came from and all the hard work I had to put in to be here. It feels good to reminisce about the past.
HA HA CLINTON-DIX

I'm a simple man. Grew up in a small town. Came from humble beginnings. No silver spoon.
ROBIN SHARMA

I have learned that the biggest stars and the greatest players are the most humble ones, the ones who respect people the most.
KYLIAN MBAPPE

It is very difficult for the prosperous to be humble.
JANE AUSTEN

My aim is just to remain as humble and as godly as I can.
LETITIA WRIGHT

No amount of praise should go to your head. You should always remain humble.
MOHANLAL

I believe the first test of a truly great man is his humility.
JOHN RUSKIN

A mountain shames a molehill until they are both humbled by the stars.
ANONYMOUS

Pride is the cold mountain peak, sterile and bleak; humility is the quiet valley fertile and abounding in life, and peace lives there.
ANNE AUSTIN

We come nearest to the great when we are great in humility.
RABINDRANATH TAGORE

Humility is the first of virtues – for other people.
OLIVER WENDELL HOLMES

The reward for humility and fear of the Lord is riches and honour and life.
BIBLE

The proud man counts his newspaper clippings, the humble his blessings.
FULTON J. SHEEN

The greater you are, the more you must practice humility.
BEN SIRA

Whoever exalts himself will be humbled, and whoever humbles himself will be exalted.
BIBLE

Whoever humbles himself, God elevates him; whoever is proud, God brings him down. Whoever runs after honors, honors run away from him.
TALMUD

Life is a long lesson in humility.
JAMES M. BARRIE

God resisteth the proud, but giveth grace to the humble.
BIBLE

Do not consider yourself to have made any spiritual progress, unless you account yourself the least of all men. God walks with the humble; he reveals himself to the lowly; he gives understanding to the little ones; he discloses his meaning to pure minds, but hides his grace from the curious and the proud.
THOMAS A' KEMPIS

Humble we must be, if to heaven we go; high is the roof there; but the gate is low; when e're thou speak'st, look with a lowly eye; grace is increased by humility.
ROBERT HERRICK

Should you ask me: What is the first thing in religion? I should reply: The first, second, and third thing therein is humility.
SAINT AUGUSTINE

When he consults himself man knows that he is great. When he contemplates the universe around him he knows that he is little and his ultimate greatness consists in his knowledge of his littleness.
BLAISE PASCAL

Let another man praise thee, and not thine own mouth.
BIBLE

When pride comes, then comes disgrace, but with humility comes wisdom.
BIBLE

Before honour is humility.
BIBLE

It is always the secure who are humble.
GILBERT KEITH CHESTERTON

It is no great thing to be humble when you are brought low; but to be humble when you are praised is a great and rare attainment.
ST. BERNARD

The most thankful people are the humblest.
ARTHUR HELPS

Humility is the solid foundation for all the virtues.
CONFUCIUS

HUMOR

Everything is funny as long as it is happening to somebody else.
WILL ROGERS

Good humor is a tonic for mind and body. It is the best antidote for anxiety and depression. It is a business asset. It attracts and keeps friends. It lightens human burdens. It is the direct route to serenity and contentment.
GRENVILLE KLEISER

Laughter is the sun that drives winter from the human face.
VICTOR HUGO

Those who bring sunshine to the lives of others cannot keep it from themselves.
JAMES M. BARRIE

A good laugh is sunshine in a house.
WILLIAM MAKEPEACE THACKERAY

Laughter is the best medicine for a long and happy life. He who laughs – lasts.
WILFRED PETERSON

The sense of humor is the oil of life's engine. Without it, the machinery creaks and groans. No lot is so hard, no aspect of things is so grim, but it relaxes before a hearty laugh.
GEORGE S. MERRIAM

I could not tread these perilous paths in safety, if I did not keep a saving sense of humor.
LORD NELSON

Good humor is the best shield against the darts of satirical raillery.
CHARLES SIMMONS

Good humor is one of the best articles of dress one can wear in society.
WILLIAM MAKEPEACE THACKERAY

Good humor is the health of the soul; sadness is its poison.
STANISLAS

A good laugh does away with cares, worries, doubt, and relieves the great strain of modern life.
ORISON SWETT MARDEN

Humor is the harmony of the heart.
DOUGLAS WILLIAM JERROLD

Jokes are the cayenne pepper of conversation and the salt of life.
PAUL CHATFIELD

Mirth is like a flash of lighting, that breaks through a gloom of clouds, and glitters for a moment; cheerfulness keeps up a kind of daylight in the mind, and fills it with a steady and perpetual serenity.
JOSEPH ADDISON

Among those whom I like or admire, I can find no common denominator, but among those whom I love, I can: all of them make me laugh.
W. H. AUDEN

A difference of tastes in jokes is a great strain on the affections.
GEORGE ELIOT

The day most wholly lost is the one on which one does not laugh.
NICOLAS CHAMFORT

If we consider the frequent reliefs we receive from laughter, and how often it breaks the gloom which is apt to depress the mind, one would take care not to grow too wise for so great a pleasure of life.

JOSEPH ADDISON

'Tis easy enough to be pleasant, when life flows along like a song; but the man worth while is the one who will smile when everything goes dead wrong.

ELLA WHEELER WILCOX

The absolute truth is the thing that makes people laugh.

CARL REINER

Always laugh when you can. It is cheap medicine.

LORD BYRON

Man is distinguished from all other creatures by the faculty of laughter.

JOSEPH ADDISON

What sunshine is to flowers, smiles are to humanity. They are but trifles, to be sure, but, scattered along life's pathway, the good they do is inconceivable.

JOSEPH ADDISON

He deserves paradise who makes his companions laugh.

QUR'AN

A well-developed sense of humor is the pole that adds balance to your steps as you walk the tightrope of life.

WILLIAM ARTHUR WARD

For health and the constant enjoyment of life, give me a keen and ever present sense of humor; it is the next best thing to an abiding faith in providence.

GEORGE B. CHEEVER

A person without a sense of humor is like a wagon without springs. It's jolted by every pebble on the road.

HENRY WARD BEECHER

There is certainly no defense against adverse fortune which is, on the whole, so effectual as an habitual sense of humor.

THOMAS W. HIGGINSON

It is the ability to take a joke, not make one, that proves you have a sense of humor.

MAX EASTMAN

If you could choose one characteristic that would get you through life, choose a sense of humor.

JENNIFER JONES

Laugh as much as possible, always laugh. It's the sweetest thing one can do for oneself & one's fellow human beings.

MIGNON MCLAUGHLIN

The most thoroughly wasted of all days is that on which one has not laughed.

NICHOLAS CHAMFORT

A sense of humor can help you overlook the unattractive, tolerate the unpleasant, cope with the unexpected, and smile through the unbearable.

MOSHE WALDOKS

Humor can alter any situation and help us cope at the very instant we are laughing.

ALLEN KLEIN

Laughter is a tranquilizer with no side effects.

ARNOLD GLASGOW

If you don't learn to laugh at trouble, you won't have anything to laugh at when you grow old.

EDGAR WATSON HOWE

He who laughs, lasts.

MARY PETTIBONE POOLE

My way of joking is to tell the truth; it's the funniest joke in the world.
GEORGE BERNARD SHAW

One should take good care not to grow too wise for so great a pleasure of life as laughter.
JOSEPH ADDISON

A man isn't poor if he can still laugh.
RAYMOND HITCHCOCK

Time spent laughing is time spent with the gods.
JAPANESE PROVERB

A man without mirth is like a wagon without springs. He is jolted disagreeably by every pebble in the road.
HENRY WARD BEECHER

Laughter should dimple the cheek, and not furrow the brow with ruggedness.
OWEN FELTHAM

Life pays a bonus to those who learn that laughter is a vital part of living. It is one of God's richest gifts. The Lord loves a cheerful giver, but he also loves a cheerful – period. And so does everyone else.
EDWIN DAVIS

I'd rather laugh, a bright-haired boy, than reign, a gray-beard king.
OLIVER WENDELL HOLMES

Frame your mind to mirth and merriment which bar a thousand harms and lengthen life.
WILLIAM SHAKESPEARE

Laughter is a most healthful exertion; it is one of the greatest helps to digestion with which I am acquainted; and the custom prevalent among our forefathers, of exciting it at table by jesters and buffoons, was founded on true medical principles.
CHRISTOPH W. HUFELAND

A laugh is just like sunshine, it freshens all the day, it tips the peak of life with light, and drives the clouds away; the soul grows glad that hears it, and feels its courage strong; a laugh is just sunshine for cheering folks along.

ANONYMOUS

Man could direct his ways by plain reason, and support his life by tasteless food, but God has given us wit, and flavor, and brightness, and laughter to enliven the days of man's pilgrimage, and to charm his pained steps o'er the burning marle.

SYDNEY SMITH

I am persuaded that every time a man smiles, but much more when he laughs, it adds something to this fragment of life.

LAURENCE STERNE

Smiles are as catchin' as the measles and a whole lot more pleasant.

HARVEY HAMLYN

There is the laughter which is born out of the pure joy of living, the spontaneous expression of health and energy, the sweet laughter of the child. This is a gift of God. There is the warm laughter of the kindly soul which heartens the discouraged, gives health to the sick and comfort to the dying…There is, above all, the laughter that comes from the eternal joy of creation, the joy of expressing the inner riches of the soul, laughter that triumphs over pain and hardship in the passion for an enduring ideal, the joy of bringing the light of happiness, of truth and beauty into a dark world. This is divine laughter par excellence.

B. E. BOODIN

The laughter of girls is, and ever was, among the delightful sounds of earth.

THOMAS DE QUINCEY

Good-humor makes all things tolerable.

HENRY WARD BEECHER

INDEPENDENCE

True freedom is the capacity for acting according to one's true character, to be altogether one's self, to be self-determined and not subject to outside coercion.

CORLISS LAMONT

I cannot compromise or inhibit my independence.

WALTER ANNENBERG

Solitude is independence.

HERMANN HESSE

Nothing is more precious than independence and liberty.

HO CHI MINH

If money is your hope for independence, you will never have it. The only real security that a man will have in this world is reserve of knowledge, experience, and ability.

HENRY FORD

The American Dream is independence and being able to create that dream for yourself.

MARSHA BLACKBURN

The beauty of independence, departure, actions that rely on themselves.

WALT WHITMAN

Your life must be a progression towards ownership – first mentally of your independence, and then physically of your work, owning what you produce.

ROBERT GREENE

Independence is for the very few; it is a privilege of the strong.
FRIEDRICH NIETZSCHE

I don't have luxurious tastes or great needs, but my independence is worth a lot to me.
EMMANUEL MACRON

I don't want to be any more interesting than I am, I love the life that I get to live, which is one of real independence and privacy and autonomy.
ALLISON WILLIAMS

I work hard, I make my own living, and I love it. I like having financial independence.
SALMA HAYEK

I was born with a fierce need for independence.
MICHELLE WILLIAMS

Liberty, when it begins to take root, is a plant of rapid growth.
GEORGE WASHINGTON

Life without liberty is like a body without spirit.
KAHLIL GIBRAN

I am no bird; and no net ensnares me; I am a free human being with an independent will.
JANE EYRE

Guard with jealous attention the public liberty. Suspect everyone who approaches that jewel. Unfortunately, nothing will preserve it, but downright force. Whenever you give up that force, you are inevitably ruined.
PATRICK HENRY

I know, but one freedom, and that is the freedom of the mind.
ANTOINE DE SAINT-EXUPERY

The most courageous act is still to think for yourself. Aloud.
COCO CHANEL

To find yourself, think for yourself.
SOCRATES

Don't let the noise of other's opinions drown out your own inner voice.
STEVE JOBS

People have only as much liberty as they have the intelligence to want and the courage to take.
EMMA GOLDMAN

In the word of no master am I bound to believe.
HORACE

He that is good is free, though he be a slave; he that is evil is a slave, though he be a king.
SAINT AUGUSTINE

Depend upon it, that the lovers of freedom will be free.
EDMUND BURKE

Is life so dear, or peace so sweet, as to be purchased at the price of chains and slavery? Forbid it, Almighty God! I know not what course others may take; but as for me, give me liberty or give me death!
PATRICK HENRY

Liberty means responsibility. That is why most dread it.
GEORGE BERNARD SHAW

INTELLIGENCE

We pay a high price for being intelligent. Wisdom hurts.
EURIPIDES

It is not enough to have a good mind; the main thing is to use it well.
RENE DESCARTES

To the dull mind, all nature is leaden. To the illumined mind, the whole world burns and sparkles with light.
RALPH WALDO EMERSON

One good head is better than a hundred strong hands.
THOMAS FULLER

A good mind possesses a kingdom.
LUCIUS ANNAEUS SENECA

Many complain of their looks, but none of their brains.
YIDDISH PROVERB

A man is not necessarily intelligent because he has plenty of ideas any more than he is a good general because he has plenty of soldiers.
NICOLAS CHAMFORT

You cannot gauge the intelligence of an American by talking with him.
ERIC HOFFER

A moment's insight is sometimes worth a life's experience.
OLIVER WENDELL HOLMES

Intelligence – yes, but of what kind and aim? There is the intelligence of Socrates and the intelligence of a thief or a forger.
RALPH WALDO EMERSON

You can't beat brains.
JOHN F. KENNEDY

Intelligence alone, without wisdom and empathy for suffering, is hollow.
JOHN G. STOESSINGER

Unintelligent people always look for a scapegoat.
ERNEST BEVIN

Brains aren't everything, but they're important.
WILLIAM FEATHER

The best buy by way of management is brains – at any price.
MALCOLM FORBES

When you hire people who are smarter than you are, you prove you are smarter than they are.
R. H. GRANT

The most fertile soil does not necessarily produce the most abundant harvest. It is the use we make our faculties which render them valuable.
THOMAS W. HIGGINSON

I use not only all the brains I have but all I can borrow.
WOODROW WILSON

Intelligence consists in recognizing opportunity.
CHINESE PROVERB

The difference between intelligence and education is this – that intelligence will make you a good living.
CHARLES F. KETTERING

Do not always assume that the other fellow has intelligence equal to yours. He may have more.
TERRY-THOMAS

Education is no substitute for intelligence.
FRANK HERBERT

It is better to have a fair intellect that is well-used than a powerful one that is idle.
BRYANT H. MCGILL

If we encounter a man of rare intellect, we should ask him what books he reads.
RALPH WALDO EMERSON

Common sense is genius dressed in its working clothes.
RALPH WALDO EMERSON

A smart man makes a mistake, learns from it, and never makes that mistake again. But a wise man finds a smart man and learns from him how to avoid the mistake altogether.
ROY WILLIAMS

Talent hits a target no one else can hit; genius hits a target no one else can see.
ARTHUR SCHOPENHAUER

It is frequently a misfortune to have very brilliant men in charge of affairs. They expect too much of ordinary men.
THUCYDIDES

I think I only appear smart by staying quiet as often as possible.
SALLY ROONEY

Man is genius when he is dreaming.
AKIRA KUROSAWA

The true sign of intelligence is not knowledge but imagination.
ALBERT EINSTEIN

Common sense is not so common.
VOLTAIRE

Everyone is a genius at least once a year. The real geniuses simply have their bright ideas closer together.
GEORG C. LICHTENBERG

The higher the voice the smaller the intellect.
ERNEST NEWMAN

Intelligence is quickness in seeing things as they are.
GEORGE SANTAYANA

JUSTICE

To give every man his due, that is supreme justice.
MARCUS TULLIUS CICERO

Of all the things of a man's soul which he has within him, justice is the greatest good and injustice the greatest evil.
PLATO

Justice will not condemn even the Devil himself wrongfully.
THOMAS FULLER

The triumph of justice is the only peace.
ROBERT GREEN INGERSOLL

Justice delayed is democracy denied.
ROBERT F. KENNEDY

By the just, we mean that which is lawful and that which is fair and equitable.
ARISTOTLE

If we do not maintain justice, justice will not maintain us.
FRANCIS BACON

It is better to risk saving a guilty man than to condemn an innocent one.
VOLTAIRE

A man should not act as a judge either for someone he loves or for someone he hates. For no man can see the guilt of someone he loves or the good qualities in someone he hates.

TALMUD

Justice will not be served until those who are unaffected are as outraged as those who are.

BENJAMIN FRANKLIN

If you want peace, work for justice.

POPE JOHN PAUL VI

If we are to keep our democracy, there must be one commandment: Thou shalt not ration justice.

SOPHOCLES

Ethics and equity and the principles of justice do not change with the calendar.

B. H. LAWRENCE

Justice is the sum of all moral duty.

WILLIAM GODWIN

At his best, man is the noblest of all animals; separated from law and justice, he is the worst.

ARISTOTLE

Justice is truth in action.

BENJAMIN DISRAELI

Truth never damages a cause that is just.

MAHATMA GANDHI

Don't judge anybody before you hear both stories.

GREEK PROVERB

Justice consists not in being neutral between right and wrong, but finding out right and upholding it, wherever found, against the wrong.

THEODORE ROOSEVELT

There is a higher court than courts of justice and that is the court of conscience. It supersedes all other courts.

MAHATMA GANDHI

Until the great mass of the people shall be filled with the sense of responsibility for each other's welfare, social justice can never be attained.

HELEN KELLER

The probability that we may fail in the struggle ought not to deter us from the support of a cause we believe to be just.

ABRAHAM LINCOLN

He who spares the bad injures the good.

PUBLILIUS SYRUS

Justice is like the north star, which is fixed, and all the rest revolves about it.

CONFUCIUS

The judge weighs the arguments and puts a brave face on the matter, and, since there must be a decision, decides as he can, and hopes he has done justice and given satisfaction to the community.

RALPH WALDO EMERSON

He hears but half who hears one party only.

AESCHYLUS

Justice remains the greatest power on earth. To that tremendous power alone will we submit.

HARRY S. TRUMAN

KINDNESS

It takes courage to be kind.
MAYA ANGELOU

Practice kindness all day to everybody, and you will realize you're already in heaven.
JACK KEROUAC

The greatest thing a man can do for his heavenly Father is to be kind to some of his other children.
HENRY DRUMMOND

To speak kindly does not hurt the tongue.
FRENCH PROVERB

Be kind, for everyone you meet is fighting a battle you know nothing about.
WENDY MASS

Never lose a chance of saying a kind word.
WILLIAM MAKEPEACE THACKERAY

But remember, boy, that a kind act can sometimes be as powerful as a sword.
RICK RIORDAN

In a world where you can be anything, be kind.
CLARE POOLEY

Kind words promote peace in our thoughts and our lives.
ALLENE VANOIRCHOT

Kindness is its own type of magic, don't you think?
ALYSSA COLMAN

Though the world needs reproof and correction, it needs kindness more; though it needs the grasp of the strong hand, it needs, too, the open palm of love and tenderness.
HENRY WARD BEECHER

You cannot do kindness too soon, for you never know how soon it will be too late.
RALPH WALDO EMERSON

Be kind whenever possible. It is always possible.
DALAI LAMA

Always be a little kinder than necessary.
JAMES M. BARRIE

A kind word is like a spring day.
RUSSIAN PROVERB

Forget injuries; never forget kindness.
CONFUCIUS

Kindness is the golden chain by which society is bound together.
JAHANN WOLFGANG VON GOETHE

Kindness begins with the understanding that we all struggle.
CHARLES GLASSMAN

It is the characteristic of the magnanimous man to ask no favor but to be ready to do kindness to others.
ARISTOTLE

The words of kindness are more healing to a drooping heart than balm or honey.
SARAH FIELDING

Wherever there is a human being, there is an opportunity for a kindness.
LUCIUS ANNAEUS SENECA

You can accomplish by kindness what you cannot by force.
PUBLILIUS SYRUS

When words are both true and kind, they can change the world.
BUDDHA

No act of kindness, no matter how small, is ever wasted.
AESOP

To kindness and love, the things we need most.
THE GRINCH

How do we change the world? One random act of kindness at a time.
MORGAN FREEMAN

When I was young, I admired clever people. Now that I am old, I admire kind people.
ABRAHAM JOSHUA HESCHEL

Constant kindness can accomplish much. As the sun makes ice melts, kindness causes misunderstanding, mistrust, and hostility to evaporate.
ALBERT SCHWEITZER

The simplest acts of kindness are by far more powerful than a thousand heads bowing in prayer.
MAHATMA GANDHI

There's no use in doing a kindness if you do it a day too late.
CHARLES KINGSLEY

I expect to pass through life but once. If, therefore, there can be any kindness I can show, or any good thing I can do to any fellow human being, let me do it now.
WILLIAM PENN

Wise sayings often fall on barren ground, but a kind word is never thrown away.
ARTHUR HELPS

Life is mostly froth and bubbles; only two things stand like stone: kindness in another's troubles, courage in your own.
MARK TWAIN

If you want to lift yourself up, lift up someone else.
BOOKER T. WASHINGTON

A great man shows his greatness by the way he treats little men.
THOMAS CARLYLE

Kind words do not cost much. They never blister the tongue or lips. Mental trouble was never known to arise from such quarters. Though they do not cost much yet they accomplish much. They make other people good natured. They also produce their own image on men's souls, and a beautiful image it is.

BLAISE PASCAL

Have you had a kindness shown? Pass it on; 'twas not given for thee alone, pass it on; let it travel down the years, let it wipe another's tears, 'till in heaven the deed appears, pass it on.
HENRY BURTON

I shall pass through this world but once. Anything, therefore, that I can do, or any kindness that I can show to any human being, let me do it now. Let me not defer it or neglect it, for I shall not pass this way again!
WILLIAM PENN

Little dees of kindness, little words of love, help to make earth happy like the heaven above.
JULIA A. FLETCHER CARNEY

Whoever gives a small coin to a poor man has six blessings bestowed upon him, but he who speaks a kind word to him obtains eleven blessings.
TALMUD

Kind words produce their own image in men's souls; and a beautiful image it is. They soothe and quiet and comfort the hearer. They shame him out of his sour, morose, unkind feelings. We have not yet begun to use kind words in such abundance as they ought to be used.

BLAISE PASCAL

The happiness of life may be greatly increased by small courtesies in which there is no parade, whose voice is too still to tease, and which manifest themselves by tender and affectionate looks, and little kind acts of attention.

LAURENCE STERNE

So many gods, so many creeds, so many paths that wind and wind, while just the art of being kind is all the sad world needs.

ELLA WHEELER WILCOX

The whole worth of a kind deed lies in the love that inspires it.

TALMUD

How beautiful a day can be when kindness touches it!

ELLISTON

Acts of kindness shown to good men are never thrown away.

TITUS M. PLAUTUS

Be kind, for everyone is fighting a hard battle.

JOHN WATSON

Three things in human life are important. The first is to be kind. The second is to be kind. And the third is to be kind.

HENRY JAMES

What wisdom can you find that is greater than kindness?

JEAN-JACQUES ROUSSEAU

I wonder why it is that we are not all kinder to each other than we are. How much the world needs it! How easily it is done!

HENRY DRUMMOND

Guard within yourself that treasure kindness. Know how to give without hesitation, how to lose without regret, how to acquire without meanness.

GEORGE SAND

Human kindness has never weakened the stamina or softened the fiber of a free people. A nation does not have to be cruel in order to be tough.

FRANKLIN D. ROOSEVELT

KNOWLEDGE

The more one knows, the less one knows.
LARRY JOHN PHILLIPS

Knowledge is knowing. Wisdom is knowing, then doing. This is the unbeatable combination.
ALFRED ARMAND MONTAPERT

KNOWLEDGE is power. It is nothing of the sort! Knowledge is only potential power. It becomes power only when if it is organized into definite plans of actions, and directed to a definite end.
NAPOLEON HILL

Knowledge is of two kinds. We know a subject ourselves, or we know where we can find information upon it.
SAMUEL JOHNSON

One part of knowledge consists in being ignorant of such things as are not worthy to be known.
CRATES

It is not the quantity, but the quality of knowledge which determines the mind's dignity.
WILLIAM ELLERY CHANNING

Successful men, in all callings, never stop acquiring specialized knowledge related to their major purpose, business, or profession.
NAPOLEON HILL

The desire for knowledge, like the thirst of riches, increases ever with the acquisition of it.

LAURENCE STERNE

It is not a question how much a man knows, but what use he can make of what he knows.

JOSIAH GILBERT HOLLAND

As knowledge increases, wonder deepens.

CHARLES MORGAN

Knowledge is the food of the soul.

PLATO

You can never know too little of what is not worth knowing at all.

ANONYMOUS

Knowledge is a comfortable and necessary retreat and shelter for us in an advanced age; and if we do not plant it while young, it will give us no shade when we grow old.

EARL OF CHESTERFIELD

'Tis not knowing much, but what is useful, that makes a wise man.

THOMAS FULLER

A little knowledge that acts is worth infinitely more than much knowledge that is idle.

KAHLIL GIBRAN

...learned one thing - people who know the least anyways seem to know it the loudest.

ANDY CAPP

The saying that knowledge is power is not quite true. Used knowledge is power, and more than power. It is money, and service, and better living for our fellowmen, and a hundred other good things. But mere knowledge, let unused, has no power in it.

DR. EDWARD E. FREE

Without knowledge, action is useless, and knowledge without action is futile.
ABU BAKR

Risk comes from not knowing what you're doing.
WARREN BUFFETT

To acquire knowledge, one must study, but to acquire wisdom, one must observe.
MARILYN VOS SAVANT

Knowledge is better than riches.
AFRICAN PROVERB

Knowledge itself is power.
FRANCIS BACON

In expanding the field of knowledge we but increase the horizon of ignorance.
HENRY MILLER

Knowing others is wisdom. Know the self is enlightenment.
LAO TZU

He is wise who knows the sources of knowledge – who knows who has written and where it is to be found.
B. A. HODGE

Wisdom is the right use of knowledge. To know is not to be wise. Many men know a great deal, and are all the greater fools for it. There is no fool so great a fool as a knowing fool. But to know how to use knowledge is to have wisdom.
CHARLES SPURGEON

Seek knowledge from the cradle to the grave.
MUHAMMAD

Not to know is bad; not to wish to know is worse.
WOLOF

It is the peculiarity of knowledge that those who really thirst for it always get it.
JEFFERIES

If you have knowledge, let others light their candles at it.
MARGARET FULLER

Knowledge cannot be stolen from us. It cannot be bought or sold. We may be poor, and the sheriff may come and sell our furniture, or drive away our cow, or take our pet lamb, and leave us homeless and penniless; but he cannot lay the law's hand upon the jewelry of our minds.
BURRITT

Three-fourths of the mistakes a man makes are made because he does not really know the things he thinks he knows.
JAMES BRYCE

A little knowledge is a dangerous thing.
ALEXANDER POPE

He that increaseth knowledge increaseth sorrow.
BIBLE

It is better to know nothing than to know what ain't so.
JOSH BILLINGS

He who has knowledge spares his words.
BIBLE

To be conscious that you are ignorant is a great step to knowledge.
BENJAMIN DISRAELI

LEISURE

The end of labor is to gain leisure.
ARISTOTLE

What is this life if, full of care, we have no time to stand and stare?
W. H. DAVIES

It's not a man's working hours that is important, it is how he spends his leisure time.
MARILYNNE ROBINSON

Leisure is a time for doing something useful. This leisure, the diligent person will obtain the lazy one never.
BENJAMIN FRANKLIN

Employ thy time well, if thou meanest to gain leisure.
BENJAMIN FRANKLIN

Business is leisure when you find pleasure in it.
PETER ADEJIMI

If the use of leisure time is confined to looking at TV for a few extra hours every day, we will deteriorate as a people.
ELEANOR ROOSEVELT

I'd rather spend my leisure time doing what some people call my work, and I call my fun.
JARED DIAMOND

Sunday, the day for the language of leisure.
ELFRIEDE JELINEK

In our leisure, we reveal what kind of people we are.
OVID

What we do during our working hours determines what we have, what we do in our leisure hours determines what we are.
GEORGE EASTMAN

What the banker sighs for, the meanest clown may have, - leisure and a quiet mind.
HENRY DAVID THOREAU

Cultivated leisure is the aim of man.
OSCAR WILDE

Money and time are the heaviest burdens of life, and the unhappiest of all mortals are those who have more of either than they know how to use.
JOHNSON

Marry in haste and repent at leisure.
PROVERB

When you like your work, every day is a holiday.
TYGER

We are closer to the ants than the butterflies. Very few people can endure much leisure.
GERALD BRENAN

He has hard-working who has nothing to do.
PROVERB

Leisure is a beautiful garment, but it will not do for constant wear.
ANONYMOUS

The life of leisure and life of laziness are two things, there will be sleeping enough in the grave.
BENJAMIN FRANKLIN

Leisure, some degree of it, is necessary to the health of every man's spirit.
HARRIET MARTINEAU

He does not seem to me to be a free man who does not sometimes do nothing.
MARCUS TULLIUS CICERO

Only a person who can live with himself can enjoy the gift of leisure.
HENRY GREBER

It's the leisure hours, happily used, that have often opened up a new world to many a person.
GEORGE MATTHEW ADAMS

If you are losing your leisure, look out; you may be losing your soul.
LOGAN PEARSALL SMITH

The most difficult thing in the world to administer effectively is leisure.
MANLY HALL

They talk of the dignity of work. The dignity is in leisure.
HERMAN MELVILLE

Leisure activities such as contemplation, going for a stroll or a bike ride boost our overall health, well-being, and creativity,
JENS MARTIN SKIBSTED

To be able to fill leisure intelligently is the last product of civilization.
ARNOLD J. TOYNBEE

Leisure should be time that you can just goof off.
ANONYMOUS

Work is toil; what one does only to earn a living. If it gives pleasure, it is leisure.
MORTIMER ADLER

To describe my scarce leisure time in today's terms, I always default to reading.
JIMMY BUFFETT

If adults are not enjoying something they're doing in their leisure time, they should stop doing it.
NICK HORNBY

A life without festivities is a long road without inns.
DEMOCRITUS

The mind should be allowed some relaxation, that it may return to its work all the better for the rest.
LUCIUS ANNAEUS SENECA

We don't stop playing because we grow old; we grow old because we stop playing.
GEORGE BERNARD SHAW

I would not exchange my leisure hours for all the wealth in the world.
MIRABEAU

LIFE

A man can do nothing better than to eat and drink and find satisfaction in his work.
BIBLE

Live as if you were to die tomorrow. Learn as if you were to live forever.
MAHATMA GANDHI

It is not the years in your life but the life in your years that counts.
ADLAI STEVENSON

The journey, not the arrival, matters; the voyage, not the landing.
LOUIS THEROUX

You had better live your best, think your best and do your best today – for today will soon be tomorrow and tomorrow will soon be forever.
ADOLPH PHILIP GOUTHEY

The closing years of life are like the end of a masquerade party, when the masks are dropped.
ARTHUR SCHOPENHAUER

The quality of a life is determined by its activities.
ARISTOTLE

The unexamined life is not worth living.
SOCRATES

In three words I can sum up everything I've learned about life: it goes on.
ROBERT FROST

There are only two things to aim at in life; to get what you want; and, after that, to enjoy it. Only the wisest of mankind achieve the second.
LOGAN SMITH

The way I see it, if you want the rainbow, you gotta put up with the rain.
DOLLY PARTON

Life imposes things on you that you can't control, but you still have the choice of how you are going to live through this.
CELINE DION

It is not miserable to be blind; it is miserable to be incapable of enduring blindness.
JOHN MILTON

Life is really simple, but men insist on making it complicated.
CONFUCIUS

Life is a succession of lessons which must be lived to be understood.
HELEN KELLER

Don't settle for what life gives you; make life better and build something.
ASHTON KUTCHER

When God sorts out the weather and sends rain, why rain's my choice.
RILEY

Work spares us from three great evils: boredom, vice and need.
VOLTAIRE

The healthiest response to life is joy.
DEEPAK CHOPRA

Go confidently in the direction of your dreams! Live the life you've imagined! As you simplify your life, the laws of the universe will be simpler, solitude will not be solitude, poverty will not be poverty, nor weakness weakness.

HENRY DAVID THOREAU

The great majority of men exist but do not live. The power of the passions, the force of the will, the creative energy of the imagination, these make life, and reveal to us a world of which the millions are entirely ignorant.

BENJAMIN DISRAELI

Life is what we make it, always has been, always will be.

GRANDMA MOSES

When you cease to dream, you cease to live.

MALCOM FORBES

Don't cry because it's over, smile because it happened.

DR. SEUSS

The best way to predict your future is to create.

ABRAHAM LINCOLN

Life consists not in holding good cards but in playing those you hold well.

JOSH BILLINGS

The only disability in life is a bad attitude.

SCOTT HAMILTON

Such was the rule of life! I worked my best, subject to ultimate judgment, God's, not man's.

BROWNING

In the end, it's not the years in your life that count. It's the life in your years.

ABRAHAM LINCOLN

We carry with us the wonders we seek without us.
THOMAS BROWNE

Our entire life, with our fine moral code and our precious freedom, consists ultimately in accepting ourselves as we are.
JEAN ANOUILH

To be good company for ourselves we must store our minds well, fill them with happy and pure thoughts, with pleasant memories of the past, and reasonable hopes of the future.
JOHN LUBBOCK

Do not let making a living prevent you from making a life.
JOHN WOODEN

Not in the clamor of the crowded street, not in the shouts and plaudits of the throng, but in ourselves are triumph and defeat.
HENRY WADSWORTH LONGFELLOW

Life is either a daring adventure or nothing at all.
HELEN KELLER

I've learned that people will forget what you said, people will forget what you did, but people will never forget how you made them feel.
MAYA ANGELOU

To go slowly and to live a long time are two brothers.
DUTCH PROVERB

Life is 10% what happens to me and 90% of how I react to it.
CHARLES SWINDOLL

To be, or not to be, that is the question.
WILLIAM SHAKESPEARE

The battles that count aren't the ones for gold medals. The struggles within yourself – the invisible battles inside all of us – that's where it's at.

JESSE OWENS

Two roads diverged in a wood, and I – I took the one less traveled by, and that has made all the difference.

ROBERT FROST

Life is not measured by the number of breaths we take, but by the moments that take our breath away.

MAYA ANGELOU

Life will give you what you ask of her if only you ask long enough and plainly enough.

EDITH NESBIT

Not life, but a good life, is to be chiefly valued.

SOCRATES

Remember that not getting what you want is sometimes a wonderful stroke of luck.

DALAI LAMA

Don't count the days, make the days count.

MUHAMMAD ALI

You will face many defeats in life, but never let yourself be defeated.

MAYA ANGELOU

There is just one life for each of us: our own.

EURIPIDES

The business of life is to enjoy oneself, everything else is a mockery.

NORMAN DOUGLAS

Do not dwell in the past, do not dream of the future, concentrate the mind on the present moment.

BUDDHA

A man sooner or later discovers that he is the master-gardener of his soul, the director of his life.

JAMES ALLEN

Every man dies. Not every man really lives.

WILLIAM WALLACE

It is not length of life, but depth of life.

RALPH WALDO EMERSON

Most people have never learned that one of the main aims in life is to enjoy it.

SAMUEL BUTLER

The great use of life is to spend it for something that will outlast it.

WILLLIAM JAMES

Life well spent is long.

LEONARDO DA VINCI

No man is a failure who is enjoying life.

WILLIAM FEATHER

Life will always be to a large extent what we ourselves make it.

SAMUEL SMILES

The art of life is to know how to enjoy a little and to endure very much.

WILLIAM HAZLITT

He most lives who thinks most, feels the noblest, acts the best.

P. J. BAILEY

Life can't give me joy and peace – it's up to me to will it. Life just gives me time and space – it's up to me to fill it.

WILLIAM MAKEPEACE THACKERAY

Be not afraid of life. Believe that life is worth living, and your belief will help create the fact.

WILLIAM JAMEES

What we have done for ourselves alone dies with us. What we have done for others and the world remains and is immortal.

ALBERT PINE

Fear less, hope more; eat less, chew more; whine less, breathe more; talk less, say more; hate less, love more; and all good things are yours.

SWEDISH PROVERB

May you live all the days of your life.

JONATHAN SWIFT

What is a great life? It is the dream of youth realized in old age.

ALFRED DE VIGNY

How small a portion of our life it is that we really enjoy? In youth we are looking forward to things that are to come; in old age we are looking backward to things that are gone past; in manhood, although we appear indeed to be more occupied in things that are present, yet even that is too often absorbed in vague determinations to be vastly happy on some future day when we have time.

CHARLES CALEB COLTON

To live content with small means; to seek elegance rather than luxury; and refinement rather than fashion; to be worthy, not respectable; and wealthy, not rich; to study hard, think quietly, talk gently, act frankly; to listen to stars and birds, to babes and sages, with open heart; to bear all cheerfully, do all bravely, await occasion, hurry never; in a word, to let the spiritual, unbidden and unconscious grow up through the common. This is to be my symphony.

WILLIAM HENRY CHANNING

Life is too short to be little.

BENJAMIN DISRAELI

Life must be measured by thought and action, not by time.

JOHN LUBBOCK

Four things to learn: to think clearly without hurry or confusion; to love everybody sincerely; to act in everything with the highest motives; to trust God unhesitatingly.

HELEN KELLER

Let others lead small lives, but not you. Let others argue over small things, but not you. Let others cry over small hurts, but not you. Let others leave their future in someone else's hands, but not you.

JIM ROHN

Learn from yesterday, live for today, hope for tomorrow.

ALBERT EINSTEIN

Twenty years from now you will be more disappointed by the things that you didn't do than by the ones you did do. So throw off the bowlines. Sail away from the safe harbor. Catch the trade winds in your sails. Explore. Dream. Discover.

MARK TWAIN

The best day of your life is the one on which you decide your life is your own. No apologies or excuses. No one to lean on, rely on, or blame. The gift is yours – it is an amazing journey – and you alone are responsible for the quality of it. This is the day that your life rally begins.

BOB MOAWAB

The man who has accomplished all that he thinks worth while, has begun to die.

E. T. TRIGG

The art of living rightly is like all arts; it must be learned and practiced with incessant care.

JOHANN WOLFGANG VON GOETHE

Slow down and enjoy life. It's not only the scenery you miss by going too fast – you also miss the sense of where you're going and why.

EDDIE CANTOR

Every man should eat and drink and enjoy the good of all his labor, it is the gift of God.

BIBLE

LOVE

Absence is to love what wind is to fire; it extinguishes the small, it enkindles the great.

COMTE DE BUSSY-RABUTIN

All love is vanquished by a succeeding love.

OVID

And so we know and rely on the love God has for us. God is love. Whoever lives in love lives in God, and God in him.

BIBLE

Do not rebuke an older man harshly, but exhort him as if he were your father. Treat younger men as brothers, older women as mothers, and younger women as sisters, with absolute purity.

BIBLE

Friendship often ends in love; but love, in friendship – never.

CHARLES CALEB COLTON

The only victory over love is flight.

NAPOLEON BONAPARTE

Love makes your soul crawl out from its hiding place.

ZORA NEALE HURSTON

Time which strengthens friendship, weakens love.

JEAN DE LA BRUYERE

Who are wise in love, love most, say least.
ALFRED TENNYSON

Love yourself first, and everything falls into line.
LUCILLE BALL

The heart has its reasons of which reason know nothing.
BLAISE PASCAL

Love is friendship that has caught fire.
ANN LANDERS

A simple "I Love You" means more than money.
FRANK A. SINATRA

You don't marry someone you can live with - you marry someone you cannot live without.
ANONYMOUS

Tis better to have loved and lost, than never to have loved at all.
ALFRED TENNYSON

The smile is the beginning of love.
MOTHER TERESA

You had me at hello.
JERRY MAGUIRE

When you love someone, you love the person as they are, and not as you'd like them to be.
LEO TOLSTOY

Fortune and love favor the brave.
OVID

All you need is love. But a little chocolate now and then doesn't hurt.
CHARLES M. SCHULZ

The best and most beautiful things in the world cannot be seen, nor touched ...but are felt in the heart.
HELEN KELLER

All love that has not friendship for its base, is like a mansion built upon the sand.
ELLA WHEELER WILCOX

We are most alive when we're in love.
JOHN UPDIKE

The one you love and the one who loves you are never, ever the same person.
CHUCK PALAHNIUK

There is only one happiness in this life, to love and be loved.
GEORGE SAND

To love is nothing. To be loved is something. But to love and be loved, that's everything.
THEMIS TOLIS

Love and kindness are never wasted. They always make a difference. They bless the one who receives them, and they bless you, the giver.
BARBARA DE ANGELIS

Love, the itch, and a cough cannot be hid.
THOMAS FULLER

Love is more than a noun - it is a verb; it is more than a feeling - it is caring, sharing, helping, sacrificing.
WILLIAM ARTHUR WARD

If you do a good deed for other people, you will end up healing yourself too. Because a dose of love is the best spiritual cure.

ANONYMOUS

Love is shown in your deeds, not in your words.

FATHER JEROME CUMMINGS

Spread love everywhere you go. Let no one ever come to you without leaving happier.

MOTHER TERESA

Love is composed of a single soul inhabiting two bodies.

ARISTOTLE

A flower cannot blossom without sunshine, and man cannot live without love.

MAX MULLER

A kiss makes the heart young again and wipes out the years.

RUPERT BROOKE

Love is a force more formidable than any other. It is invisible – it cannot be seen or measured, yet it is powerful enough to transform you in a moment, and offer you more joy than any material possession could.

BARBARA DE ANGELIS

I like not only to be loved, but also to be told I am loved.

GEORGE ELIOT

Absence – that common cure of love.

LORD BYRON

The best thing to hold onto in life is each other.

AUDREY HEPBURN

Blessed is the influence of one true, loving human soul on another.

GEORGE ELIOT

Looking back, I have this to regret, that too often when I loved, I did not say so.
DAVID GRAYSON

One is loved because one is loved. No reason is needed for loving.
PAULO COELHO

The sweetness of all sounds is that of the voice of the woman we love.
JEAN DE LA BRUYERE

Tell me who admires and loves you, and I will tell you who you are.
ANTOINE DE SAINT-EXUPERY

Love is love's reward.
JOHN DRYDEN

Love is the great miracle cure. Loving ourselves works miracles in our lives.
LOUISE L. HAY

If you would be loved, love, and be loveable.
BENJAMIN FRANKLIN

There is more pleasure in loving than in being beloved.
THOMAS FULLER

To witness two lovers is a spectacle for the gods.
JOHANN WOLFGANG VON GOETHE

They who love are but one step from heaven.
JAMES RUSSELL LOWELL

If thou wishest to be loved, love.
LUCIUS ANNAEUS SENECA

The first duty of love is to listen.
PAUL TILLICH

Love conquers all.
VIRGIL

Love is the river of life in this world.
HENRY WARD BEECHER

Those who love deeply never grow old; they may die of old age, but they die young.
ARTHUR WING PINERO

Love is a great beautifier.
LOUISA ALCOTT

There is no fear in love; but perfect love casts out fear, because fear brings punishment. And he who fears is not perfected in love. Let us therefore love, because God first love us.
BIBLE

Love is the master key that opens the gates of happiness.
OLIVER WENDELL HOLMES

We are all born for love. It is the principle of existence, and its only end.
BENJAMIN DISRAELI

There is no power greater than true affection.
LUCIUS ANNAEUS SENECA

To love is to find pleasure in the happiness of the person loved.
LEIBNITZ

How far that little candle throws his beams! So shines a good deed in a naughty world.
WILLIAM SHAKESPEARE

We are most of us very lonely in this world; you who have any who love you, cling to them and thank God!
WILLIAM MAKEPEACE

Life has taught us that love does not consist in gazing at each other but in looking together in the same direction.
ANTOINE DE SAINT-EXUPERY

There is no disguise which can hide love for long where it exists, or simulate it where it does not.
FRANCOIS DE LA ROCHEFOUCAULD

Treasure each other in the recognition that we do not know how long we shall have each other.
JOSHUA LIEBMAN

Let no one who loves be called altogether unhappy. Even love unreturned has its rainbow.
JAMES M. BARRIE

If there is anything better than to be loved it is loving.
ANONYMOUS

Love is the word used to label the sexual excitement of the young, the habituation of the middle-aged, and the mutual dependence of the old.
JOHN CIARDI

Who, being loved, is poor?
OSCAR WILDE

Women fall in love through their ears and men through their eyes.
WOODROW WYATT

LOYALTY

Nothing is more noble, nothing more venerable, than loyalty.
MARCUS TULLIUS CICERO

There is one element that is worth its weight in gold and that is loyalty. It will cover a multitude of weaknesses.
PHILIP ARMOUR

You don't earn loyalty in a day. You earn loyalty day by day.
JEFFREY GITOMER

Loyalty is rare. It can only be proven under test.
ALFRED ARMAN MONTAPERT

Be loyal and trustworthy. Do not befriend anyone who is lower than yourself in this regard.
CONFUCIUS

You cannot buy loyalty. You cannot buy the devotion of hearts, minds, and souls. You have to earn these things.
CLARENCE FRANCIS

True loyalty is proven, not proclaimed.
GRAIG GROESCHEL

I'll take fifty percent efficiency to get one hundred percent loyalty.
SAMUEL GOLDWYN

Unless you can find some sort of loyalty, you cannot find unity and peace in your active living.
JOSIAH ROYCE

What I value most in my friends is loyalty.
DAVID MAMET

The scholar does not consider gold and jade to be precious treasures, but loyalty and good faith.
CONFUCIUS

Loyalty means giving me your honest opinion, whether you think I'll like it or not.
COLIN POWELL

Loyalty to the Nation all the time, loyalty to the Government when it deserves it.
MARK TWAIN

The test of good citizenship is loyalty to country.
BAINBRIDGE COLBY

I entirely appreciate loyalty to one's friends, but loyalty to the cause of justice and honor stands above it.
THEODORE ROOSEVELT

Never esteem anything as of advantage to you that will make you break your word or lose self-respect.
MARCUS AURELIUS

There is no friend as loyal as a book.
ERNEST HEMINGWAY

Loyalty is the greatest good in the human heart.
LATIN PROVERB

An ounce of loyalty is worth a pond of cleverness.
ANONYMOUS

Loyalty is one thing a leader cannot do without. It is as priceless as it is rare. It creates a quiet confidence in the heart of any leader and is the assurance of success in any enterprise.

ADOLPH PHILIP GOUTHEY

MATURITY

It is unjust to claim the privileges of age, and retain the playthings of childhood.
SAMUEL JOHNSON

The turning point in the process of growing up is when you discover the core of strength within you that survives all hurt.
MAX LERNER

It takes a certain level of maturity to get hit and get knocked down and get back up.
JAMAI CRAWFORD

When I can look life in the eyes, grown calm and very coldly wise, life will have given me the truth, and taken in exchange - my youth.
SARA TEASDALE

If you want to pull yourself into a glorious adulthood and personal fulfillment, do not permit yourself to live an uncharted life.
RHODA LACHAR

When I was a child, I spake as a child, I understood as a child, I thought as a child; but when I became a man, I put away childish things.
BIBLE

True maturity is only reached when a man realizes he has become a father figure to his girlfriends' boyfriends - and he accepts it.
LARRY MCMURTRY

Age is no guarantee of maturity.
LAWANA BLACKWELL

Maturity is achieved when a person postpones immediate pleasures for long-term values.
JOSHUA L. LIEBMAN

Most of us don't mind doing what we ought to do when it doesn't interfere with what we want to do, but it takes discipline and maturity to do what we ought to do whether we want to or not.
JOSEPH B. WIRTHLIN

A truly great book should be read in youth, again in maturity and once more in old age, as a fine building should be seen by morning light, at noon and by moonlight.
ROBERTSON DAVIES

As I grow older, I pay less attention to what men say, I just watch what they do.
ANDREW CARNEGIE

One of the signs of maturity is a man takes ownership of those things he does.
LARRY JOHN PHILLIPS

Maturity is when you live your life by your commitments, not by your feelings.
RICK WARREN

Maturity comes not with age but with the acceptance of responsibility. You are only young once, but immaturity can last a lifetime!.
EDWIN LOUIS COLE

It is not a sign of weakness, but a sign of high maturity, to rise to the level of self-criticism.
MARTIN LUTHER KING, JR.

Maturity is the ability to reap without apology and not complain when things don't go well.
JIM ROHN

I believe that the sign of maturity is accepting deferred gratification.
PEGGY CAHN

Maturity is when your world opens up and you realize that you are not the center of it.
M. J. CROAN

Young men are fitter to invent than to judge; fitter for execution than for counsel; and fitter for new projects than for settled business.
FRANCIS BACON

One sign of maturity is knowing when to ask for help.
DENNIS WHOLEY

MODERATION

I will not be a slave to myself, for it is a perpetual, a shameful, and the most heavy of all servitudes; and this end I may gain by moderate desires.
LUCIUS ANNAEUS SENECA

It is circumstance and proper measure that give an action its character, and make it either good or bad.
PLUTARCH

It is just as unpleasant to get more than you bargain for as to get less.
GEORGE BERNARD SHAW

You never know what is enough unless you know what is more than enough.
WILLIAM BLAKE

It may seem paradoxical, but it is certainly true, that in the long run, the moderate man will derive more enjoyment even from eating and drinking than the glutton or the drunkard will ever obtain.
JOHN LUBBOCK

Moderation is the inseparable companion to wisdom.
CHARLES CALEB COLTON

The best of things, beyond their measure, cloy.
HOMER

The choicest pleasures of life lie within the ring of moderation.
MARTIN FARQUHAR TUPPER

To go beyond is as wrong as to fall short.
CONFUCIUS

To learn moderation is the essence of sound sense and real wisdom.
JACQUES BENIGNE BOSSUET

Too much work and too much energy kill a man just as effectively as too much-assorted vice or too much drink.
RUDYARD KIPLING

Once one becomes a man, he can and must make his own decisions. But I do offer warning. Even a good thing can become destructive if taken to excess.
BRANDON SANDERSON

The ideas are louder when there are fewer of them.
DAVID DAY

Moderation and limitation represent the highest with regard to human strivings.
HELMUTH PLESSNER

Our world does not need tepid souls. It needs burning hearts, men who know the proper place of moderation.
ALBERT CAMUS

Every single thing has a balance, and the moment we overdo that balance, something has to give, and we are punished by fate in one way or another.
LLWARD ISA

Sometimes what we lack is the thrill of anticipation or the delay of gratification. We enjoy things far more when we've really desired them but had to wait for them. The real value is found in our self-control and patience, which allows to delay gratification and build anticipation. Letting desire build is an abstract way to achieve balance and moderation in your life...Moderation just may be the answer to boredom – go figure.
CRIS FRANK

This I consider to be a valuable principle in life, not to do anything in excess.
TERENCE

Be moderate in order to taste the joys of life in abundance.
EPICTETUS

Pleasures are enhanced that are sparingly enjoyed.
JUVENAL

Enough is enough, and too much spoils.
ITALIAN PROVERB

Fortify yourself with moderation; for this is an impregnable fortress.
EPICTETUS

Moderation should run through the whole of life. Moderation is strength, not weakness; it implies self-command and self-control.
JOHN LUBBOCK

Moderation is the key of lasting enjoyment.
HOSEA BALLOU

The motto is: Live every day to the fullest – in moderation.
LINDSAY LOHAN

Everything in moderation, and there's a perfect balance in this life if we can find it.
RYAN ROBBINS

Out of moderation, pure happiness springs.
JOHANN WOLFGANG VON GOETHE

Moderation is the secret of survival.
MANLY HALL

One action gives life its strength, as only moderation gives it its charm.
JEAN PAUL RICHTER

The heart is great which shows moderation in the midst of prosperity.
MARCUS ANNAEUS SENECA

MONEY

All that is really useful to us can be bought for little money; it is only the superfluous that is put up for sale at a high price.

AXEL MUNTHE

An inheritance quickly gained at the beginning will not be blessed at the end.

BIBLE

Regardless of one motives for amassing money, the results will not be what you hope for. Instead, the wise teachers of tradition tell us to go ahead and do the things we want and become good at them. In that lies our freedom.

MIKE PHILLIPS

He is not fit for riches who is afraid to use them.

THOMAS FULLER

Poor men seek meat for their stomach, rich men stomach for their meat.

ENGLISH PROVERB

He is rich who hath enough to be charitable.

THOMAS BROWNE

A man's treatment of money is the most decisive test of his character, how he makes it and how he spends it.

JAMES MOFFATT

Money is neither good or bad; it is the use of it which determines its value.

ALFRED ARMAND MONTAPERT

Always keep accounts, and keep them carefully. Keep them so that you know how the money goes and how much things cost you. No man who knows what his income is, and what he is spending, will run into extravagance.
JOHN LUBBOCK

As far as you can possibly, pay ready money for everything you buy, and avoid bills.
EARL OF CHESTERFIELD

Before buying anything, it is well to ask whether one could not do without it.
JOHN LUBBOCK

Do not wear yourself out to get rich; have the wisdom to show restraint.
BIBLE

Have a plan to earn money. Have a plan to carefully spend your money. Have a plan to save money. Have a plan to invest money.
ALFRED ARMAND MONTAPERT

I think any man diligently plying himself to labor seven or eight hours a day, may acquire as much as is necessary for his subsistence.
JAMES DONALDSON

It is neither wealth nor splendor, but tranquility and occupation, which give happiness.
THOMAS JEFFERSON

It is not large funds that are wanted, but a constant supply, like a small stream that never dies. To have a great capital is not so necessary as to know how to manage a small one and never be without a little.
WILLIAM COOPER

It is not what comes into a man's hands that enriches him, but what he saves from slipping through them. The saving habit grows rapidly, and your money grows, with it.
GRENVILLE KLEISER

It is good to have money and the things money can buy. But it's good too, to check up once in a while and make sure that you haven't lost the things that money can't buy.

GEORGE HORACE LORIMER

Money often costs too much, and power and pleasure are not cheap.

RALPH WALDO EMERSON

Most rich people are the poorest people I know.

ELSA MAXWELL

Most wealthy people are little more than janitors of their possessions.

FRANK LLOYD WRIGHT

Superfluous wealth can buy superfluities only. Money is not required to buy one necessity of the soul.

HENRY DAVID THOREAU

There is a certain Buddhistic calm that comes from having…money in the bank.

AYN RAND

There is nothing in money's nature to produce happiness. The more a man has, the more he wants. Instead of filling a vacuum, it makes one.

BENJAMIN FRANKLIN

A little with quiet.

GEORGE HERBERT

The first goal of a value minded spending plan should be accelerated repayment of debts. The second goal is to establish a capital reserve fund.

ALFRED ARMAND MONTAPERT

The secret to making money is saving it. It is not what a man earns, not the amount of his income, but the relation of his spending to his income that determines his poverty or wealth.

CHARLES CALEB COLTON

What is the proper limit for wealth? It is first, to have what is necessary; and, second, to have what is enough.

LUCIUS ANNAEUS SENECA

Whoever loves money never has enough; whoever loves wealth is never satisfied with his income. This too is meaningless.

BIBLE

Neither a borrower nor a lender be; for a loan oft loses both itself and friends; and borrowing dulls the edge of husbandry.

WILLIAM SHAKESPEARE

With money in your pocket, you are wise and you are handsome and you sing well too.

YIDDISH PROVERBS

Enough is as good as a feast.

JOHN HEYWOOD

A wise man will desire no more than what he may get justly, use soberly, distribute cheerfully, and leave contently.

BENJAMIN FRANKLIN

The cost of a thing is the amount of what I call life which is required to be exchanged for it, immediately or in the long run.

HENRY DAVID THOREAU

Buy when everyone else is selling and hold until everyone else is buying. That's not just a catchy slogan. It's the very essence in successful investing.

B. PAUL GETTY

Too many people spend money they earned ... to buy things they don't want ...to impress people that they don't like.

WILL ROGERS

It takes a great deal of boldness and a great deal of caution to make a great fortune; and when you have got it, it requires ten times as much wit to keep it.

RALPH WALDO EMERSON

Investment in knowledge pays the best interest.

BENJAMIN FRANKLIN

I will tell you the secret to getting rich on Wall Street. You try to be greedy when others are fearful. And you try to be fearful when others are greedy.

WARREN BUFFETT

It is not the man who has too little, but the man who craves more, that is poor.

LUCIUS ANNAEUS SENECA

The real measure of your wealth is how much you'd be worth if you lost all your money.

ANONYMOUS

Measure wealth not by the things you have, but by the things you have for which you would not take money.

ANONYMOUS

The buyer has need of a hundred eyes, the seller of but one.

ITALIAN PROVERB

After a certain point, money is meaningless. It ceases to be the goal. The game is what counts.

ARISTOTLE ONASSIS

A man is usually more careful of his money than of his principles.

OLIVER WNEDELL HOMES, JR.

It is not the creation of wealth that is wrong, but the love of money for its own sake.

MARGARET THATCHER

The only thing I can say about money, is that it's better to have it than not to have it.

LARRY JOHN PHILLIPS

Money may be the husk of many things, but not the kernel. It brings you food, but not appetite; medicine, but not health; acquaintances, but not friends; servants, but not faithfulness; days of joy, but not peace or happiness.

HENRIK IBSEN

If a rich man is proud of his wealth, he should not be praised until it is known how he employs it.

SOCRATES

No man can tell whether he is rich or poor by turning to his ledger. It is the heart that makes a man rich. He is rich according to what he is, not according to what he has.

HENRY WARD BEECHER

The use of money is all the advantage there is in having money.

BENJAMIN FRANKLIN

The surplus wealth we have gained to some extent at least belongs to our fellow beings; we are only the temporary custodians of our fortunes, and let us be careful that no just complaint can be made against our stewardship.

JACOB H. SCHIFF

If money is all that a man makes, then he will be poor – poor in happiness, poor in all that makes life worth living.

HERBERT N. CASSON

Save a part of your income and begin now, for the man with a surplus controls circumstances and the man without a surplus is controlled by circumstances.

HENRY H. BUCKLEY

It is where a man spends his money that shows where his heart lies.

B. EDWIN KEIGWIN

I have about concluded that wealth is a state of mind, and that anyone can acquire a wealthy state of mind by thinking rich thoughts.
YOUNG

Wealth is like seawater; the more we have, the thirstier we become, and the same is true for fame.
ARTHUR SCHOPENHAUER

Wealth is the product of man's capacity to think.
AYN RAND

Let us spare where we may, so that we may spend where we should.
THOMAS FULLER

Seek not proud riches, but rather such as thou mayest get justly, use soberly, distribute cheerfully, and leave contentedly.
FRANCIS BACON

That man is richest whose pleasures are the cheapest.
HENRY DAVID THOREAU

The richer your friends, the more they will cost you.
ELIZABETH MARBURY

If all the gold in the world were melted down into a solid cube it would be about the size of an eight-room house. If a man got possession of all that gold – billions of dollars worth, he could not buy a friend, character, peace of mind, clear conscience, or a sense of eternity.
CHARLES F. BANNING

Neither great poverty nor great riches will hear reason.
HENRY FIELDING

When money speaks the truth is silent.
RUSSIAN PROVERB

I never been in no situation where havin' money made it any worse.
CLINTON JONES

One reason why some men are always in debt is because they cannot do without the things they do not need.
ROY L. SMITH

Resolve not to be poor; whatever you have, spend less. Poverty is a great enemy to human happiness; it certainly destroys liberty, and it makes some virtues impracticable and others extremely difficult.
SAMUEL JOHNSON

Two of the hardest things to accomplish in this world are to acquire wealth by honest effort and, having gained it, to learn how to use it properly.
ELMER H. BOBST

Wealth is of all things the most esteemed by men and has the greatest power of all things in the world.
EURIPIDES

OPPORTUNITY

Opportunities should never be lost, because they can hardly be regained.
WILLIAM PENN

Small opportunities are often the beginning of great enterprises.
DEMOSTHENES

The wise man will make more opportunities than he finds.
FRANCIS BACON

No great man ever complains of want of opportunity.
RALPH WALDO EMERSON

Who seeks, and will not take when once 'tis offer'd, shall never find it more.
WILLIAM SHAKESPEARE

When one door closes, another opens. But we often look so long and so regretfully
upon the closed odor that we do not see the one which has opened for us.
ALEXANDER GRAHAM BELL

Thou strong seducer. Opportunity!
JOHN DRYDEN

It still holds true that man is most uniquely human when he turns obstacles into
opportunities.
ERIC HOFFER

The man who works need never be a problem to anyone. Opportunities multiply as they are seized; they die when neglected. Life is a long line of opportunities. Wealth is not in making money, but in making the man while he is making money. Production, not destruction, leads to success.

JOHN WICKER

Many do with opportunities as children do at the seashore; they fill their little hands with sand, and then let the grains fall through, one by one, till all are gone.

T. JONES

A pessimist is one who makes difficulties of his opportunities; an optimist is one who makes opportunities of his difficulties.

REGINALD B. MANSELL

There is no security on this earth; there is only opportunity.

DOUGLAS MACARTHUR

Whenever you see darkness, there is extraordinary opportunity for the light to burn brighter.

BONO

Problems can become opportunities when the right people come together.

ROBERT REDFORD

Entrepreneurs are simply those who understand that there is little difference between obstacle and opportunity and are able to turn both to their advantage.

VICTOR KIAM

I always tried to turn every disaster into an opportunity.

JOHN D. ROCKEFELLER

Every twist and turn in life is an opportunity to learn something new about yourself, your interests, your talents, and how to set and then achieve goals.

JAMEELA JAMIL

Victory comes from finding opportunities in problems.

SUN TZU

Innovation is the ability to see change as an opportunity, not a threat.
STEVE JOBS

Turn your obstacles into opportunities and your problems into possibilities.
ROY T. BENNETT

What is the difference between an obstacle and an opportunity? Our attitude toward it. Every opportunity has a difficulty, and every difficulty has an opportunity.
J. SIDLOW BAXTER

Opportunities are like sunrises. If you wait too long, you miss them.
WILLIAM ARTHUR WARD

Circumstances may cause interruptions and delays, but never lose sight of your goal. Prepare yourself in every way you can by increasing your knowledge and adding to your experience, so that you can make the most of opportunity when it occurs.
MARIO ANDRETTI

One secret of success in life is for a man to be ready for his opportunity when it comes.
BENJAMIN DISRAELI

At various points in your careers, you will be called to take a risk. And I think you will find, as I have found, those will be the times of your greatest opportunities.
RAYMOND V. GILMARTIN

If a window of opportunity appears, don't pull down the shade.
TOM PETERS

Our lives re defined by opportunities. Even the ones we miss.
F. SCOTT FITZGERALD

Life opens up opportunities to you, and you either take them or you stay afraid of taking them.
JIM CARREY

Nothing is more expensive than a missed opportunity.
H. JACKSON BROWN JR.

Jump at opportunities to take on responsibilities. People should try new things, that's how you grow.
KEVIN MURRAY

When a great moment knocks on the door of your life, it is often no louder than the beating of your heart, and it is very easy to miss it.
BORIS PASTERNAK

When opportunity presents itself, don't be afraid to go after it.
EDDIE KENNISON

The sad truth is that opportunity doesn't knock twice.
GLORIA ESTEFAN

He who refuses to embrace a unique opportunity loses the prize as surely as if he had tried and failed.
WILLIAM JAMES

Most people miss great opportunities because of their misperception of time. Don't wait! The time will never be just right.
STEPHEN C. HOGAN

Most do not understand the wonderful opportunities life gives until they look back at their life.
ERIC HANDLER

Opportunities? They are all around us…There is power lying latent everywhere waiting for the observant eye to discover it.
ORISON SWETT MARDEN

Your regrets aren't what you did, but what you didn't do. So I take every opportunity.
CANERON DIAZ

OPTIMISM

It is worth a thousand pounds a year to have the habit of looking on the bright side of things.

SAMUEL JOHNSON

The right mental attitude means a great deal. A mind filled with optimistic thoughts has no room for pessimism.

B. F. GIRARD

Perpetual optimism is annoying. It is a sign that you are not paying attention.

MAUREEN DOWD

Bein' optimistic after you've got every'thing you want don't count.

KIN HUBBARD

An optimist is a guy that never had much experience.

DON MARQUIS

The man who is a pessimist before the age of forty-eight knows too much; if he is an optimist after it, he knows too little.

MARK TWAIN

Optimism. The doctrine or belief that everything is beautiful, including what is ugly.

AMBROSE BIERCE

Optimism is essential to achievement, and it is also the foundation of courage and true progress.

NICHOLAS M. BUTLER

An optimist understands that life can be a bumpy road, but at least it is leading somewhere. They learn from mistakes and failures, and are not afraid to fail again.
HARVEY MACKAY

Choose to be an optimist. It feels better.
DALAI LAMA

It is the hopeful, buoyant, cheerful attitude of mind that wins. Optimism is a success builder; pessimism an achievement killer.
ORISON SWETT MARDEN

Write in your heart that every day is the best day in the year.
RALPH WALDO EMERSON

Optimism is the faith that leads to achievement. Nothing can be done without hope and confidence.
HELEN KELLER

I am an optimist...I choose to be. There is a lot of darkness in our world, there is a lot of pain, and you can choose to see that, or you can choose to see the joy. If you try to respond positively to the world, you will spend your time better.
TOM HIDDLESTON

While we may not be able to control all that happens to us, we can control what happens inside us.
BENJAMIN FRANKLIN

Optimism can be more powerful than a battery of artillery or squadron of tanks. It can be contagious and it's necessary to be a leader.
GENERAL RICK HILLIER

The optimist sees the rose and not its thorns. The pessimist stares at the thorns, oblivious to the rose.
KHALIL GIBRAN

Gray skies are just clouds passing over.
DUKE ELLINGTON

Optimism is a happiness magnet. If you stay positive, good things and good people will be drawn to you.

MARY LOU RETTON

Optimism inspires, energizes, and brings out our best. It points the mind toward possibilities and helps us think creatively past problems.

PRICE PRITCHETT

Few things in the world are more powerful than a positive push. A smile. A word of optimism and hope. A 'you can do it' when things are tough.

RICHARD M. DEVOS

Pessimism leads to weakness, optimism to power.

WILLIAM JAMES

The optimist makes his own heaven, and enjoys it as he goes through life. The pessimist makes his own hell and suffers it as he goes through life.

WILLIAM C. HUNTER

The pessimist sees the difficulty in ever opportunity; the optimist sees the opportunity in every difficulty.

L. P. JACKS

The habit of looking on the bright side of every event is worth more than a thousand pounds a year.

SAMUEL JOHNSON

I am glad I am an optimist. The pessimist is half-licked before he starts. The optimist has won half of the battle, the most important half that applies to himself, when he begins his approach to a subject with the proper mental attitude. The optimist may not understand, or if he understands he may not agree with, prevailing ideas; but he believes, yes, knows, that in the long run and in due course there will prevail whatever is right and best.

THOMAS A. BUCKNER

Be too large for worry, too noble for anger, too strong for fear, and too happy to permit the presence of trouble. Think well of yourself and proclaim this fact to the world – not in loud words, but in great deeds.

OPTIMISTS' CREED

ORGANIZATION

Organizing is what you do before you do something so that when you do it, it is not all mixed up.
E. A. MINE

A good system shortens the road to the goal.
ORISON SWETT MARDEN

Organizing has to be a 12-month endeavor.
TOM PEREZ

The obvious rule of efficiency is you don't want to spend more time organizing than it's worth.
DANIEL LEVITIN

For every minute spent in organizing, an hour is earned.
BENJAMIN FRANKLIN

Organize your life around your dreams, and watch them come true.
ANONYMOUS

With organization comes empowerment.
RICHARD WAGNER

Get clear on what matters by getting rid of everything that doesn't.
COURTNEY CARVER

Have nothing in your house that you do not know to be useful or believe to be beautiful.
WILLIAM MORRIS

A place for everything and everything in its place.
BENJAMIN FRANKLIN

Organization isn't about perfection; it's about efficiency, reducing stress and clutter, saving time and money, and improving overall quality of life.
CHRISTINA SCALISE

Outer order contributes to inner calm.
GRETCHEN RUBIN

Organization is not an option; it is a fundamental survival skill and distinct competitive advantage.
PAM N. WOODS

Imagine yourself living in a space that only contains that spark of joy.
MARIE KONDO

Nothing is particularly hard if you divide it into small jobs.
HENRY FORD

PAST

There is never any good reason to look back except to gain knowledge, or to recall the things we have seen or done which gave us pleasure. Worrying over a thing that is past never helps in the least. We should do something about it – or forget it.

WILLIAM ROSS

Four things come not back: the spoken word, the sped arrow, the past life, and the neglected opportunity.

OMAR IBN AL-HALIF

No one should be dominated by his past, but it is a privilege to build a better future upon such foundations as are available.

MANLY HALL

To be able to look back upon one's past life with satisfaction is to live twice.

MARTIAL

The past with its pleasure, its rewards, its foolishness, its punishments, is there for each of us forever, and it should be.

LILLIAN HELLMAN

Be not the slave of your own past.

RALPH WALDO EMERSON

The illusion that times that were are better than those that are, has probably pervaded all ages.

HORACE GREELEY

There is no time like the old time when you and I were young.
OLIVER WENDELL HOLMES

Hindsight is always twenty-twenty.
BILLY WILDER

One's past is what one is, it is the only way by which people should be judged.
OSCAR WILDE

Those who cannot remember the past are condemned to repeat it.
GEORGE SANTAYANA

When I want to understand what is happening today or try to decide what will happen tomorrow, I look back.
OLIVER WENDELL HOLMES

Not the power to remember, but its very opposite, the power to forget, is a necessary condition for our existence.
SHOLEM ASCH

May I forget what ought to be forgotten; and recall, unfailing, all that ought to be recalled, each kindly thing, forgetting what might sting.
MARY CAROLINE DAVIES

Anyone who limits her vision to memories of yesterday is already dead.
LILY LANGTRY

I like the dreams for the future better than the history of the past.
THOMAS JEFFERSON

Fear not the future, weep not for the past.
PERCY BYSSHE SHELLEY

Every saint has a past, and every sinner has a future.
OSCAR WILDE

When I am anxious it is because I am living in the future. When I am depressed it is because I am living in the past.

ANONYMOUS

This time, like all times, is a very good one if we but know what to do with it.

RALPH WALDO EMERSON

I look back on my life like a good day's work; it is done and I am satisfied.

GRANDMA MOSES

That sign of old age, extolling the past at the expense of the present.

SYDNEY SMITH

PATIENCE

Trust God to weave your thread into the great web, though the pattern shows it not yet.

GEORGE MACDONALD

Adopt the pace of nature; her secret is patience.

RALPH WALDO EMERSON

A man who is master of patience is master of everything else.

LORD HALIFAX

Patience is bitter, but its fruit is sweet.

JEAN-JACQUES ROUSSEAU

Genius is eternal patience.

MICHELANGELO BUONARROTI

It is not necessary for all men to be great in action. The greatest and sublimest power is often simple patience

HORACE BUSHNELL

No great thing is created suddenly, more than a bunch of grapes or a fig. If you tell me that you desire a fig, I answer you that there must be time. Let it first blossom, then bear fruit, then ripen.

EPICTETUS

Patience, and the mulberry leaf become a silk gown.

CHINESE PROVERB

Our real blessings often appear to us in the shape of pains, losses, and disappointments; but let us have patience, and we soon shall see them in their proper figures.

JOSEPH ADDISON

Patient waiting is often the highest way of doing God's will.

JOHN PAYNE COLLIER

Rush is the enemy of growth. Leaf by leaf, the great oak grows into a sturdy tree. Forty years alone in the desert produced a Moses. Three years alone in the Arabian desert perfected Paul's vision and thought, made him a world citizen.

ADOLPH PHILIP GOUTHEY

He that can have patience, can have what he will.

BENJAMIN FRANKLIN

Patience and fortitude conquer all things.

RALPH WALDO EMERSON

Our patience will achieve more than our force.

EDMOND BURKE

Everything comes gradually and at its appointed hour.

OVID

Patience accomplishes its object, while hurry speeds to its ruin.

SA'DI

Patience and perseverance have a magical effect, before which difficulties disappear, and obstacles vanish.

JOHN QUINCY ADAMS

With patience bear the lot to thee assigned, nor think it chance, nor murmur at the load; for know what man calls fortune, is from God.

NICHOLAS ROWE

Patience is the key to paradise.
TURKISH PROVERB

Trying to understand is like straining through muddy water. Be still and allow the mud to settle.
LAO TZU

To lose patience is to lose the battle.
MAHATMA GANDHI

Patience attracts happiness; it brings near that which is far.
SWAHILI PROVERB

Learning patience can be a difficult experience, but once conquered, you will find life is easier.
CATHERINE PULSIFER

The key to everything is patience. You get the chicken by hatching the egg, not smashing it.
ARNOLD H. GLASOW

Patience is not the ability to wait, but the ability to keep a good attitude while waiting.
ANONYMOUS

One minute of patience, ten years of peace.
GREEK PROVERB

With love and patience, nothing is impossible.
DAISAKU IKEDA

Patience is the best remedy for every trouble.
TITUS M. PLAUTUS

Trees that are slow to grow bear the best fruit.
MOLIERE

I have just three things to teach: simplicity, patience, compassion. These three are your greatest treasures.

LAO TZU

One moment of patience may ward off a great disaster. One moment of impatience may ruin a whole life.

CHINESE PROVERB

How poor are they who have not patience! What wound did ever heal but by degree.

WILLIAM SHAKESPEARE

The road to success is not to be run by seven-leagued boots. Step by step, little by little, bit by bit – that is the way to wealth, that is the way to wisdom, that is the way to glory.

SIR THOMAS FOXWELL BUXTON

Have patience with all the world, but first of all with yourself.

FRANCIS DE SALES

Two things define you: your patience when you have nothing and your attitude when you have everything.

GEORGE BERNARD SHAW

God has perfect timing; never early, never late. It takes a little patience, and it takes a lot of faith, but it's worth the wait.

ANONYMOUS

Have patience. All things are difficult before they become easy.

MOSLIH EDDIN SAADI

Patience is a conquering virtue.

GEOFFREY CHAUCER

Patience and passage of time do more than strength and fury.

JEAN DE LA FONTAINE

There is nothing so bitter, that a patient mind cannot find some solace for it.
LUCIUS ANNAEUS SENECA

And many strokes, though with a little axe, hew down and fell the hardest-timbered oak.
WILLIAM SHAKESPEARE

Beware the fury of a patient man.
JOHN DRYDEN

All men commend patience, although few be willing to practice it.
THOMAS A' KEMPIS

Be still before the Lord and wait patiently for him; do not fret when men succeed in their ways, when they carry out their wicked schemes.
BIBLE

Be patience, good things take time.
ANONYMOUS

The strongest of all warriors are those two – time and patience.
LEO TOLSTOY

There's no advantage to hurrying through life.
SHIKAMARU NARA

Patience ensures victory.
ANONYMOUS

Don't cross the bridge until you come to it.
HENRY WADSWORTH LONGFELLOW

There is something good in all seeming failures. You are not to see that now. Time will reveal it. Be patient.
SWAMI SIVANANDA

At the gate of patience, there is no crowding.
MOROCCAN SAYING

Be not afraid growing slowly, be afraid only of standing still.
CHINESE PROVERB

Serene I fold my hands and wait.
JOHN BURROUGHS

I'm extraordinarily patient provided I get my own way in the end.
MARGARET THATCHER

A noble, courageous man is recognizable by the patience he shows in adversity.
PACHACUTEC INCA YUPANQUI

Strength comes from waiting.
JOSE MARTI

I had no special sagacity, only the power of patient thought. I kept the subject constantly before me and waited until the first dawnings opened little by little into the full light.
ISAAC NEWTON

At least bear patiently, if thou canst not joyfully.
THOMAS A' KEMPIS

Patience is the companion of wisdom.
SAINT AUGUSTINE

It's easy finding reasons why other folks should be patient.
GEORGE ELIOT

To know how to wait is the great success of success.
JOSEPH M. DE MAISTRE

They also serve who only stand and wait.
JOHN MILTON

Heaven is not reached at a single bound, we build the ladder by which we rise from the lowly earth to the vaulted skies, and we mount to its summit round by round.
JOSIAH GILBERT HOLLAND

He that has patience may compass anything.
RABELAIS

As you grow ready for it, somewhere or other you will find what is needful for you, in a book, or a friend, or best of all, in your own thoughts, the eternal thought speaking in your thought.
GEORGE MACDONALD

Let us not become weary in doing good, for at the proper time we will reap a harvest if we do not give up.
BIBLE

They that wait upon the Lord shall renew their strength; they shall mount up with wings as eagles; they shall run, and not be weary, and they shall walk, and not faint.
BIBLE

My brethren, count it all joy when ye fall into divers temptations; knowing this, that the trying of your faith worketh patience. But let patience have her perfect work, that ye may be perfect and entire, wanting nothing. If any of you lack wisdom, let him ask of God, that giveth to all men liberally, and upbraideth not; and it shall be given him.
BIBLE

A handful of patience is worth more than a bushel of brains.
DUTCH PROVERB

Patience is a necessary ingredient of genius.
BENJAMIN DISRAELI

Patience denotes self-composure, self-confidence and self-assurance. It is the capacity to realize that all conditions and situations are only temporary; if you exercise forbearance and remain cool, calm, and collected, the most trying situations will right themselves. Patience teaches us to grin and bear it. Trials, tribulations, obstacles, delays, disappointments and failures are only stalking shadows that instantly disappear in the light of patience. They will all soon disappear. "In your patience possess ye your souls."

EARL PREVETTE

One of the greatest drawbacks to success is the common American trait of impatience. Each of us would like to accomplish great things right-away-quick.

A. B. ZU TAVERN

PEACE OF MIND

You should feel beautiful and you should feel safe. What you surround yourself with should bring you peace of mind and peace of spirit.

STACY LONDON

Resign every forbidden joy; restrain every wish that is not referred to God's will; banish all eager desires, all anxiety; desire only the will of God; seek him alone and supremely, and you will find peace.

FRANCOIS FENELON

From the cradle to his grave a man never does a single thing which has any first and foremost object save one, to secure peace of mind, spiritual comfort, for himself.

MARK TWAIN

Where there is peace, God is.

GEORGE HERBERT

Nothing can disturb your peace of mind unless you allow.

ROY T. BENNETT

Nothing is more conductive to peace of mind than not having any opinions at all.

GEORG CHRISTOPH LICHTENBERG

Stay away from conflictive, negative people that pull you down, because they contaminate your energy and impede your progress. Search for people who look at the world with optimism, that inspire you, make you happy and provide peace of mind.

PABLO

Happiness is a choice. Peace is a state of mind. Both are free.
AMY LEIGH MERCREE

Anger is the ultimate destroyer of peace of mind.
DALAI LAMA

Never ignore your conscience, yet always be conscious of reason. Make your heart and mind friends and you will have peace of mind throughout life's seasons.
SUZY KASSEM

Set peace of mind as your highest goal and organize your life around it.
ANONYMOUS

You'll never find peace of mind until you listen to your heart.
GEORGE MICHAEL

Do not let the behavior of others destroy your inner peace.
DALAI LAMA

Nobody can bring you peace but yourself.
RALPH WALDO EMERSON

If you cannot find peace within yourself, you will never find it anywhere else.
MARVIN GAYE

When things change inside you, things change around you.
ANONYMOUS

Whoever values peace of mind and the health of the soul will live the best of possible lives.
MARCUS AURELIUS

If you want to find inner peace find it in solitude, not speed, and if you would find yourself, look to the land from which you came and to which you go.
STEWART L. UDALL

To find peace of mind, you have to be willing to lose your connection with people, places and things that create all the noise.

ANONYMOUS

Peace of mind is found when you stop judging yourself and stop judging others. Aspire to what you were born into and don't let the limitations of your family background reduce the height of your potential.

KEMMY NOLA

Peace of mind comes from not wanting to change others.

AMPOLSKY

Peace for five minutes, that's what I crave.

ALANIS MORISSETTE

For peace of mind, we need to resign as general manager of the universe.

LARRY EISENBERG

You will find peace not by trying to escape problems, but by confronting them courageously. You will find peace not in denial, but in victory.

B. DONALD WALTERS

When you make peace with yourself, you make peace with the world.

MAHA GHOSANANDA

When you've seen beyond yourself, then you may find, peace of mind is waiting there.

GEORGE HARRISON

The measure of success is happiness and peace of mind.

BOBBY DAVRO

Never seize to constantly remind yourself that your positive thoughts and beliefs are the pillars of your peace of mind.

EDMOND MBIAKA

Success is peace of mind which is a direct result of self-satisfaction in knowing you did your best to become the best you are capable of becoming.

JOHN WOODEN

When you do the right thing, you get the feeling of peace and serenity associated with it. Do it again and again.

ROY T. BENNETT

There is no greater prize than a quiet, peaceful mind.

RASHEED OGUNLARU

If you are depressed you are living in the past if you are anxious you are living in the future, if you are at peace, you are living in the present.

LAO TZU

No person, no place, and nothing has any power over us, for "we" are the only thinkers in our mind. When we create peace and harmony and balance in our minds, we will find it in our lives.

LOUISE HAY

This is the gift that God reserves for his special proteges, talent and beauty he gives to many. Wealth is commonplace, fame not rare. But peace of mind – that is his final guerdon of approval, the fondest sign of his love. He bestows it. Most men are never blessed with it, others wait all their lives – yes, far into advanced age – for this gift to descend upon them.

JOSHUA LIEBMAN

Nothing can bring you peace but yourself. Nothing can bring you peace but the triumph of principles.

RALPH WALDO EMERSON

Lovely, lasting peace of mind, sweet delight of human kind.

THOMAS PARNELL

I take it that what all men are really after is some form of, perhaps only some formula, of peace.

JAMES CONRAD

The mind is never right but when it is at peace within itself.
LUCIUS ANNAEUS SENECA

I am searching for that which every man seeks – peace and rest.
DANTE ALIGHIERI

In back of tranquility lies always conquered unhappiness.
DAVID GRAYSON

If you wish to strive for peace of soul and pleasure, then believe.
HEINRICH HEINE

If you do not find peace in yourself you will never find it anywhere else.
PAULA A. BENDRY

The opportunities for enjoyment in your life are limitless. If you feel you are not experiencing enough joy, you have only yourself to blame.
DAVID E. BRESLER

For peace of mind, resign as general manager of the universe.
ANONYMOUS

Do not lose your inward peace for anything whatsoever, even if your whole world seems upset.
FRANCIS DE SALES

People are afraid to think, or they don't know how. They fail to realize that, while emotions can't be suppressed, the mind can be strengthened. All over the world people are seeking peace of mind, but there can be no peace of mind without strength of mind.
ERIC B. GUTKIND

Thou will keep him in perfect peace, whose mind is stayed on thee: because he trusteth in thee.
BIBLE

Five great enemies to peace inhabit with us: viz., avarice, ambition, envy, anger and pride. If these enemies were to be banished, we would infallibly enjoy perpetual peace.

PETRARCH

It is still true that God is the best cure for a troubled mind. "Thou wilt keep him in perfect peace, whose mind is stayed on Thee."

JOHN MILLER

PERCEPTION

What we perceive and understand depends upon what we are.
ALDOUS HUXLEY

The outer sense alone perceives visible things, and the eyes of the heart alone sees the invisible.
RICHARD OF SAINT-VICTOR

A fool sees not the same tree that a wise man sees.
WILLIAM BLAKE

People only see what they are prepared to see.
RALPH WALDO EMERSON

Perceptions about people can be powerful. They can also be powerfully wrong.
CRAIG DRESANG

Every man takes the limits of his own field of vision for the limits of the world.
ARTHUR SCHOPENHAUER

Truth is universal. Perception of truth is not.
ANONYMOUS

That is certainly one way to look at the matter. There are others.
PATRICIA C. WREDE

One has not only an ability to perceive the world but an ability to alter one's perception of it; more simply, one can change things by the manner in which one looks at them.

TOM ROBBINS

Perception is reality. If you are perceived to be something, you might as well be it because that's the truth in people's minds.

STEVE YOUNG

In the kingdom of the blind, the one-eyed man is king.

DESIDERIUS ERASMUS

We see with our brains, not with our eyes.

NORMAN DOIDGE

Life is about perception. The quicker I learned that the happier I was.

ANONYMOUS

What is behind your eyes holds more power than what is in front of them.

GARY ZUKAV

It's not what you look at that matters, it's what you see.

HENRY DAVID THOREAU

Your perception creates your reality. You can look at life and see scarcity or abundance. It depends on your mindset.

JOE VITALE

The moment you change your perception is the moment you rewrite the chemistry of your body.

DR. BRUCE LIPTON

Your perception of the world is not necessarily the same as what is actually occurring.

PETER RALSTON

Life is all about perception. Positive versus negative. Whichever you choose will affect, and more than likely reflect your outcomes
SONYA TECLAI

One's perception of themselves has a much bigger role than has been acknowledged to determine who succeeds and who does not.
SAL KHAN

The world is full of magic things, patiently waiting for our senses to grow sharper.
WILLIAM BUTLER YEATS

Humans see what they want to see.
RICK RIORDAN

PERSEVERANCE

Great works are performed not by strength but by perseverance.
SAMUEL JOHNSON

Success in life is a matter not so much of talent or opportunity as of concentration and perseverance.
WENDTE

The will to persevere is often the difference between failure and success.
DAVID SARNOFF

Should various misfortunes assail thee, persevere in patience of body, speech, and mind.
BUDDHIST SCRIPTURE

God is with those who patiently persevere.
QUR'AN

Perseverance is a great element of success. If you only knock long enough and loud enough at the gate, you are sure to wake up somebody.
HENRY WADSWORTH LONGFELLOW

"Tis Perseverance that prevails.
THOMAS FULLER

Perseverance is the hard work you do after you get tired of doing the hard work you already did.
NEWT GINGRICH

Perseverance is failing 19 times and succeeding on the 20th.
B. ANDREWS

However small in proportion the benefit which follows individual attempts to do good, a great deal may be accomplished by perseverance, even in the midst of discouragement and disappointments.
GEORGE CRABBE

In the realm of ideas, everything depends on enthusiasm; in the real world, all rests on perseverance.
JOHANN WOLFGANG VON GOETHE

Whoever perseveres will be crowned.
JOHANN GOTTFRIED VON HERDER

Genius is perseverance in disguise.
MIKE NEWLIN

All the performances of human art, at which we look with praise or wonder, are instances of the resistless force of perseverance.
SAMUEL JOHNSON

By perseverance, the snail reached the Ark.
CHARLES SPURGEON

To persevere in one's duty and be silent, is the best answer to calumny.
GEORGE WASHINGTON

Without perseverance, talent is a barren bed.
WELSH PROVERB

To persevere, trusting in what hopes he has, is courage in a man.
The coward despairs.
EURIPIDES

With ordinary talent and extraordinary perseverance, all things are attainable.
SIR THOMAS FOXWELL BUXTON

Victory belongs to the most persevering.
NAPOLEON BONAPARTE

If you wish to succeed in life, make perseverance your bosom friend.
JOSEPH ADDISON

No one succeeds without effort...Those who succeed owe their success to their perseverance.
RAMANA MAHARSHI

Sure I am of this, that you have only to endure to conquer. You have only to persevere to save yourselves.
WINSTON CHURCHILL

We conquer by continuing.
GEORGE MATHESON

Don't be discouraged. It's often the last key in the bunch that opens the lock.
ANONYMOUS

Be of good cheer. Do not think of today's failures, but of the success that may come tomorrow. You have set yourselves a difficult task, but you will succeed if you persevere; and you will find a joy in overcoming obstacles. Remember, no effort that we make to attain something beautiful is ever lost.
HELEN KELLER

If thou believest a thing impossible, thy despondency shall make it so; but he that persevereth, shall overcome all difficulties.
EARL OF CHESTERFIELD

Clear your mind of can't'.
SAMUEL JOHNSON

Perseverance is more prevailing than violence; and many things which cannot be overcome when they are together, yield themselves up when taken little by little.

QUINTUS SERTORIUS

If you should put even a little on a little, and should you do this often, soon this too would become big.

HESIOD

We can do anything we want to do if we stick to it long enough.

HELEN KELLER

Men fail much oftener from want of perseverance than from want of talent.

WILLIAM COBBETT

Most successes are built on failures. That is more than a paradox; it is an actual fact. Most successes have been built on failures, not on one failure alone but on several. A majority of the great historic accomplishments of the past have been the final result of persistent struggle against discouragement and failure. A man is never beaten until he thinks he is. Without perseverance, the chances of his succeeding are small indeed.

CHARLES GOW

There is no magic in the world except the occasional magic of human personality and the human mind. It takes time and perseverance to do big things. It will not do to be faint-hearted. One meets with failure occasionally, but one has yet to go on. Success does not come suddenly or without setbacks.

JAWAHARIAL NEHRU

PERSISTENCE

Fall seven times, stand up eight.
JAPANESE PROVERB

He conquers who endures.
PERSIUS

The drops of rain make a hole in the stone not by violence but by oft falling.
LUCRETIUS

Keep on going, and the chances are that you will stumble on something, perhaps when you are least expecting it. I never heard of anyone ever stumbling on something sitting down.
CHARLES F. KETTERING

Our glory is not in never failing, but in rising up every time we fail.
RALPH WALDO EMERSON

Difficult things take a long time, impossible things a little longer.
ANONYMOUS

Success seems to be largely a matter of hanging in after others have let go.
WILLIAM FEATHER

Don't let the fear of the time it will take to accomplish something stand in the way of your doing it. The time will pass anyway; we might just as well put that passing time to the best possible use.
EARL NIGHTINGALE

Look at the stone cutter hammering away at his rock, perhaps a hundred times without as much as a crack showing in it. Yet at the hundred-and-first blow it will split in two, and I know it was not the last blow that did it, but all that had gone before.

JACOB A. RIIS

There is no use whatever trying to help people who do not help themselves. You cannot push anyone up a ladder unless he be willing to climb himself.

ANDREW CARNEGIE

If we are facing in the right direction, all we have to do is keep on walking.

BUDDHIST SAYING

There aren't any great men. There are just great challenges that ordinary men like you and me are forced by circumstances to meet.

WILLIAM F. HALSEY

There is no failure except in no longer trying. There is no defeat except from within, no really insurmountable barrier save our own inherent weakness of purpose.

KIN HUBBARD

The greatest test of courage on earth is to bear defeat without losing heart.

ROBERT GREEN INGERSOLL

Getting ahead in a difficult profession requires avid faith in yourself. That is why some people with mediocre talent, but with great inner drive, go much further than people with vastly superior talent.

SOPHIA LOREN

What is defeat? Nothing but education, nothing but the first step to something better.

WENDELL PHILLIPS

I have learned that success is to be measured not by the position that one has reached in life as by the obstacles which he has overcome while trying to succeed.

BOOKER T. WASHINGTON

Big shots are only little shots who keep trying.
CHRISTOPHER MORLEY

Little by little does the trick.
AESOP

Nothing in this world can take the place of persistence. Talent will not; nothing is more common than unsuccessful people with talent. Genius will not; unrewarded genius is almost a proverb. Education will not; the world is full of educated derelicts. Persistence and determination alone are omnipotent. The slogan "press on" has solved and always will solve the problems of the human race.
CALVIN COOLIDGE

Most of the important things in the world have been accomplished by people who have kept on trying when there seemed to be no help at all.
ANDREW CARNEGIE

Talent is nothing without persistence.
DEAN CRAWFORD

Success is not final, failure is not fatal: it is the courage to continue that counts.
WINSTON CHURCHILL

Success seems to be connected with action. Successful men keep moving. They make mistakes, but they don't quit.
CONRAD HILTON

Never give up. Never, never give up! We shall go on to the end.
WINSTON CHURCHILL

It is not that I'm so smart, it's just that I stay with the problems longer.
ALBERT EINSTEIN

Energy and persistence conquer all things.
BENJAMIN FRANKLIN

As long as there's breath in you persist.
BERNARD KELVIN CLIVE

Champions keep playing until they get it right.
BILLY JEAN KING

Persistence and determination are always rewarded.
CHRISTINE RICE

A little persistence, a little more effort, and what seemed hopeless failure may turn to glorious success.
WINSTON CHURCHILL

Let me tell you the secret that has led to my goal. My strength lies solely in my tenacity.
LOUIS PASTEUR

Permanence, perseverance and persistence in spite of all obstacles, discouragement and impossibilities: It is this, that in all things distinguishes the strong soul from the weak.
THOMAS CARLYLE

I am not the smartest or most talented person in the world, but I succeed because I keep going, and going, and going.
SYLVESTER STALLONE

They who are the most persistent, and work in the true spirit, will invariably be the most successful.
SAMUEL SMILES

If at first you don't succeed, try, try, try again.
W. E. HICKSON

The winner never quits, and a quitter never wins.
ANONYMOUS

Continuous efforts - not strength or intelligence - is the key to unlocking our potential.

WINSTON CHURCHILL

Business is full of brilliant men who started out with a spurt and lacked the stamina to finish. Their places were taken by patient and unshowy plodders who never knew when to quit.

B. R. TODD

Never give up, for that is just the place and time that the tide will turn.

HARRIET BEECHER STOWE

Slow and steady wins the race.

AESOP

Many strokes overthrow the tallest oak.

JOHN LYLY

Rome was not built in one day.

JOHN HEYWOOD

Most of the things worth doing in the world were said to be impossible before they were done.

LOUIS BRANDEIS

The successful man has persistence: There isn't a problem anywhere that won't yield to the secret, for it's the last punch that counts; it's the last volt of power that puts things across. There's a key to every door. That key is persistence.

A. B. ZU TAVERN

Persistent people begin their success where others end in failure.

EDWARD EGGLESTON

PLEASURE

Your greatest pleasure is that which rebounds from hearts that you have made glad.
HENRY WARD BEECHER

I know what pleasure is, for I have done good work.
ROBERT LOUIS STEVENSON

The test of an enjoyment is the remembrance which it leaves behind.
JEAN PAUL RICHTER

Pleasure has three facets: anticipation, realization, remembrance.
DAVID DUNN

The master of pleasure is not the he who abstains from it, but he who uses it without being carried away by it.
ARISTIPPUS

The love of pleasure is one of the great elementary instincts of human nature.
ARISTOTLE

Variety is the soul of pleasure.
APHRA BEHN

The honest Man takes Pains, and then enjoys Pleasures; the Knave takes Pleasure, and then suffers Pains.
BENJAMIN FRANKLIN

No pleasure is evil in itself; but the means by which certain pleasures are gained bring pains many times greater than the pleasures.

EPICURUS

Pleasure is the object, the duty, and the goal of all rational creatures.

VOLTAIRE

A pleasure deferred is a pleasure intensified.

ADAIR LARA

Most men that do thrive in the world do forget to take pleasure during the time that they are getting their estate, but reserve that till they have got one and then it is too late for them to enjoy it.

SAMUEL PEPYS

Business before pleasure.

ENGLISH SAYING

Enjoy pleasures, but let them be your own, and then you will taste them.

EARL OF CHESTERFIELD

Pleasure is none, if not diversified.

JOHN DONNE

A life merely of pleasure, or chiefly of pleasure, is always a poor and worthless life.

THEODORE W. PARKER

I can think of nothing less pleasurable than a life devoted to pleasure.

JOHN D. ROCKEFELLER, JR.

Anticipation of pleasure is, in itself, a very considerable pleasure.

DAVID HUME

Enjoy present pleasures in such a way as not to injure future ones.

KAROLINA KURKOVA

One of the many pleasures of old age is giving things up.
MALCOLM MUGGERIDGE

Throw moderation to the winds, and the greatest pleasures bring the greatest pains.
DEMOCRITUS

The greatest pleasure of life is love.
EURIPIDES

Those who enjoy the large pleasures of advanced age are those who have sacrificed the small pleasures of youth.
CHARLES E. CARPENTER

Old age has its pleasures, which, though different, are not less than the pleasures of youth.
WILLIAM SOMERSET MAUGHHAM

He that loveth pleasure shall be a poor man.
BIBLE

We should rank a good talk very high among the pleasures of existence. It is an admirable tonic, food for both mind and body.
JOHN LUBBOCK

POSSESSION

The most precious possession that ever comes to a man in this world is a woman's heart.
JOSIAH GILBERT HOLLAND

Life itself is the most valuable thing any person possesses.
E. B. ZU TAVERN

Give thy mind more to what thou has to what thou hast not.
MARCUS AURELIUS

Things may come to those who wait, but only the things left by those who hustle.
ABRAHAM LINCOLN

You give but little when you give of your possessions. It is when you give of yourself that you truly give.
KHALIL GIBRAN

All my possessions for a moment of time.
ELIZABETH I

Material possessions, winning scores, and great reputations are meaningless in the eyes of the Lord, because He knows what we really are and that is all that matters.
JOHN WOODEN

Your peers will respect you for your integrity and character, not your possessions.
DAVID ROBINSON

My riches consist not in the extent of my possessions but in the fewness of my wants.
JOSEPH BROTHERTON

It is best to be moderate in all things including material possessions.
LARRY JOHN PHILLIPS

When you lose your desire for things that do not matter you will be free.
MORIHEI UESHIBA

We are not rich by what we possess but by what we can do without.
IMMANUEL KANT

He possesses most must be most afraid of loss.
LEONARDO DA VINCI

The more we simplify our material needs the more we are free to think of other things.
ELEANOR ROOSEVELT

We can never get enough of what you don't need to make you happy.
ERIC HOFFER

Many wealthy people are little more than the janitors of their possessions.
FRANK LLOYD WRIGHT

Of prosperity, mortals can never have enough.
AESCHYLUS

It is the preoccupation with possessions, more than anything else, that prevents us from living freely and nobly.
BERTRAND RUSSELL

Once you need less, you'll have more.
ANONYMOUS

You will be happy with stuff only if you can be happy without stuff.
THIBAUT

Own less, love more.
JOSHUA BECKER

People who live below their expectations, enjoy a freedom people who are busy upgrading their lifestyles can't afford.
NAVAL RAVIKANT

All the good things of the world are no further good to us than as they are of use; and of all we may heap up we enjoy only as much as we can use, and no more.
DANIEL DEFOE

If we did but know how little some enjoy of the great things that they possess, there would not be much envy in the world.
EDWARD YOUNG

If you have a garden and a library, you have everything you need.
MARCUS TULLIUS CICERO

The acquest of needless things tends to the ruin of the soul and body. And, when all's done, the enjoyment of them gives neither satisfaction to the one nor health to the other, but makes our wants the greater.
THOMAS TRYON

Riches consists not in the extent of possessions but in the fewness of wants.
ANONYMOUS

Riches do not consist in the possession of treasures, but in the use made of them.
NAPOLEON

Things are only worth what one makes them worth.
MOLIERE

Whatever one possesses, becomes of double value, when we have the opportunity of sharing it with others.
BOUILLY

The desires of man increase with his acquisitions.
SAMUEL JOHNSON

PURPOSE

The secret of success is constancy of purpose.
BENJAMIN DISRAELI

Definiteness of purpose is the starting point of all achievement.
W. CLEMENT STONE

The man without purpose is like a ship without a rudder; a waif, a nothing, a no-man. Have a purpose in life and having it, throw such strength of mind and muscle into your work as God has given you.
THOMAS CARLYLE

Many persons have a wrong idea of what constitutes true happiness. It is not attained through self-gratification but through fidelity to a worthy purpose.
HELEN KELLER

Happy are those whose purpose has found them.
ANONYMOUS

Purpose is what gives life a meaning.
CHARLES HENRY PARKHURST

The great and glorious masterpiece of man is to know how to live to purpose.
MICHEL DE MONTAIGNE

The only failure a man ought to fear is failure in cleaving to the purpose he sees to be best.
GEORGE ELIOT

We all have a purpose in life, and when you find yours you will recognize it.
CATHERINE PULSIFER

Live for something, have a purpose, and keep that purpose in view.
ROBERT WHITAKER

More men fail through lack of purpose than lack of talent.
BILLY SUNDAY

Nothing will divert me from my purpose.
ABRAHAM LINCOLN

Each of us is born for a purpose, and we want our lives to matter. I don't think it's unique to only some of us; it's longing of every human being.
GARRETT GRAVESEN

The purpose of life is to contribute in some way to make things better.
ROBERT F. KENNEDY

There is one quality which one must possess to win, and that is definiteness of purpose, the knowledge of what one wants, and a burning desire to possess it.
NAPOLEON HILL

If you want to know what your purpose is, it is to make the most of your talents and skills for the greater good, and that means starting with yourself.
TONY CLARK

Not everybody can identify a purpose in life. But when you do, and when you pursue it, you will be living the kind of life you feel you were meant to live. And what's more, you will be happy.
STEVE GOODIER

God planned for you to be here - right now - with a purpose.
PAULA WHITE

Life is never made unbearable by circumstances, but only by lack of meaning and purpose.
VIKTOR FRANKL

The two most important days in life are the day you born and the day you discover the reason why.
MARK TWAIN

Where there is no vision, the people perish.
BIBLE

The purpose of life is a life of purpose.
ROBERT BYRNE

Your purpose in life is to find your purpose and give your whole heart and soul to it.
BUDDAH

Efforts and courage are not enough without purpose and direction.
JOHN F. KENNEDY

Know what you want to do, hold the thought firmly, and do every day what should be done, and every sunset will see you that much nearer the goal.
ELBERT HUBBARD

To be what we are, and to become what we are capable of becoming, is the only end of life.
ROBERT LOUIS STEVENSON

You have to have a dream so you can get up in the morning.
BILLY WILDER

The poor man is not he who is without a cent, but he who is without a dream.
HARRY KEMP

Great minds have purposes, others have wishes.
WASHINGTON IRVING

Unless you give yourself to some great cause, you haven't even begun to live.
WILLIAM P. MERRILL

Without a purpose, nothing should be done.
MARCUS AURELIUS

No pleasure philosophy, no sensuality, no place nor power, no material success can for a moment give such inner satisfaction as the sense of living for good purpose.
MINO SIMONS

Lack of something to feel important about is almost the greatest tragedy a man may have.
CHARLES C. NOBEL

To grow and know what one is growing towards – that is the source of all strength and confidence in life.
JAMES BAILLIE

The world stands aside to let anyone pass who knows where he is going.
DAVID STARR JORDAN

Not only must we be good, but we must also be good for something.
HENRY DAVID THOREAU

The soul that has no established aim loses itself.
MICHEL DE MONTAIGNE

Laboring toward distant aims sets the mind in a higher key, and puts us at our best.
CHARLES HENRY PARKHURST

Strong lives are motivated by dynamic purposes.
KENNETH HILDEBRAND

One of the sources of pride in being a human being is the ability to bear present frustrations in the interests of longer purposes.
HELEN MERRELL LYND

If you don't know where you are going, how can you expect to get there?
BASIL S. WALSH

Fortunate is the person who has developed the self-control to steer a straight course toward his objective in life, without being swayed from his purpose by either commendation or condemnation.
NAPOLEON HILL

We can do whatever we wish to do provided our wish is strong enough...What do you want most to do? That's what I have to keep asking myself, in the face of difficulties.
KATHERINE MANSFIELD

A determinate purpose of life, and steady adhesion to it through all disadvantages, are indispensable conditions of success.
WILLIAM M. PUNSHON

I think the purpose of life is to be useful, to be responsible, to be honorable, to be compassionate. It is, after all, to matter: to count, to stand for something, to have made some difference that you lived at all.
LEO C. ROSTEN

It concerns us to know the purposes we seek in life, for then, like archers aiming at a definite mark, we shall be more likely to attain what we want.
ARISTOTLE

We succeed only as we identify in life, or in war, or in anything else, a single overriding objective, and make all other considerations bend to that one objective.
DWIGHT D. EISENHOWER

I have brought myself by long meditation to the conviction that a human being with a settled purpose must accomplish it, and that nothing can resist a will which will stake even existence upon its fulfillment.
BENJAMIN DISRAELI

You can do what you want to do, accomplish what you want to accomplish, attain any reasonable objective you may have in mind...Not all of a sudden, perhaps, not in on one swift and sweeping act of achievement... But you can do it gradually – day by day and play by play – if you want to do it, if you will to do it, if you work to do it, over a sufficiently long period of time.

WILLIAM E. HOLLER

What our deepest self craves is not mere enjoyment, but some supreme purpose that will enlist all our powers and will give unity and direction to our life. We can never know the profoundest joy without a conviction that our life is significant – not a meaningless episode. The loftiest aim of human life is the ethical perfecting of mankind – the transfiguration of humanity.

HENRY J. GOLDING

Having a purpose in life, throw into your work such strength of mind and muscle as God has given you.

THOMAS CARLYLE

The true worth of a man is to be measured by the objects he pursues.

MARCUS AURELIUS

Our plans miscarry because they have no aim. When a man does not know what harbour he is making for, no wind is the right wind.

LUCIUS ANNAEUS SENECA

In the long run men hit only what they aim at.

HENRY DAVID THOREAU

What makes life dreary is want of motive.

GEORGE ELIOT

If we have our own 'why' of life we shall get along with almost any 'how'.

FRIEDRICH NIETZSCHE

Firmness of purpose is one of the most necessary sinews of character, and one of the best instruments of success. Without it, genius wastes its efforts in a maze of inconsistencies.

EZRA SAMPSON

The minute you choose to do what you really want to do, it's a different kind of life.
BUCKMINSTER FULLER

Set goals that make you feel powerful, motivated, and driven when you focus on them.
STEVE PAVLINA

The worst thing that can happen to you is not striving for what you want.
JAKE STEINFELD

The world has the habit of making room for the man whose words and actions show that he knows where he is going.
NAPOLEON HILL

Without goals, and plans to reach them, you are like a ship that has set sail with no destination.
FITZHUGH DODSON

Concentrated effort along a single line of endeavor is boring, but it makes people rich.
LEE WINKLER

One principal reason why men are so often useless is, that they divide and shift their attention among a multiplicity of objects and pursuits.
EMMONS

A man travels the world over in search of what he needs and returns home to find it.
GEORGE MOORE

Man's aim in life is not to add from day to day to his material prospects and to his material possessions, but his predominant calling is from day to day to come nearer his Maker.
MAHATMA GANDHI

REPUTATION

You can't build a reputation on what you are going to do.
HENRY FORD

A reputation for good judgement, for fair dealing, for truth, and for rectitude, is itself a fortune.
HENRY WARD BEECHER

Some men seem remarkable to the world in whom neither their wives nor their valets saw anything extraordinary. Few men have been admired by their servants.
MICHEL DE MONTAIGNE

If your name is to live at all, it is so much more to have it live in people's hearts than only in their brains.
OLIVER WENDELL HOLMES

Reputation is the road to power.
JEREMY BENTHAM

What is said behind your back is the community's estimate of you.
EDGAR WATSON HOWE

I would rather make my name than inherit it.
WILLIAM MAKEPEACE THACKERAY

Have regard for your name, since it will remain for you longer than a great store of gold.
APOCRYPHA

It is generally much more shameful to lose a good reputation than never to have acquired it.
PLINY THE YOUNGER

It is easier to lose a good reputation than get one.
LARRY JOHN PHILLIPS

Associate yourself with men of good quality if you esteem your own reputation; for 'tis better to be alone than in bad company.
GEORGE WASHINGTON

Character is like a tree and reputation like its shadow. The shadow is what we think of it; the tree is the real thing.
ABRAHAM LINCOLN

Your reputation is in the hands of others. That's what reputation is. You can't control that. The only thing you can control is your character.
WAYNE W. DYER

Reputation is like fine china: Once broken it's very hard to repair.
ABRAHAM LINCOLN

Regard your good name as the richest jewel you can possibly be possessed of.
SOCRATES

It takes 20 years to build a reputation and five minutes to ruin it. If you think about that, you'll do things differently.
WARREN BUFFETT

He who worries about reputation, has a reputation to worry about.
EDWIN LEIBFREED

The way to gain a good reputation is to endeavor to be what you desire to appear.
SOCRATES

A good reputation is something that must be earned, yet can never be bought.
STEPHEN KING

If I take care of my character, my reputation will take care of me.
DWIGHT L. MOODY

You are what you do, not what you say you'll do.
CARL JUNG

We judge ourselves by what we feel capable of doing, others judge us by what we have already done.
HENRY WADSWORTH LONGFELLOW

A good name is seldom regained. When character is gone, all is gone, and one of the richest jewels of life is lost forever.
B. HEWES

It matters not what you are thought to be, but what you are.
PUBLILIUS SYRUS

If I can only keep my good name, I shall be ric**h enough.**
TITUS M. PLAUTUS

A good name, like good will, is got by many actions and lost by one.
LORD JEFFERY

RESPECT

Life is too short to waste your time on people who don't respect, appreciate, and value you.
ROY T. BENNETT

Respect yourself, and others will respect you.
CONFUCIUS

Men are respectable only as they respect.
RALPH WALDO EMERSON

Nothing is more despicable than respect based on fear.
ALBERT CAMUS

I firmly believe that respect is a lot more important, and a lot greater, than popularity.
JULIUS ERVING

One of the most sincere forms of respect is actually listening to what another has to say.
BRYANT H. MCGILL

I'm not concerned with your liking or disliking me...All I ask is that you respect me as a human being.
JACKIE ROBINSON

Respecting someone indicates the quality of your personality.
MOHAMMAD SAKHI

There is no respect for others without humility in one's self.
HENRI FREDERICK AMIEL

I cannot conceive of a greater loss than the loss of one's self-respect.
MAHATMA GANDHI

We should all consider each other as human beings, and we should respect each other.
MALALA YOUSAFZAI

Most good relationships are built on mutual trust and respect.
MONA SUTPHEN

Respect is what we owe; love, what we give.
PHILIP JAMES BAILEY

The final test of a gentleman is his respect for those who can be of no possible service to him.
WILLIAM LYON PHELPS

That you may retain your self-respect, it is better to displease the people by doing what you know is right, than to temporarily please them by doing what you know is wrong.
WILLIAM J. H. BOETCKER

And the greatest lesson that mom ever taught me though was this one. She told me there would be times in your life when you have to choose between being loved and being respected. Now she said to always pick being respected.
CHRIS CHRISTIE

Respect yourself above all.
PYTHAGORAS

In a civilized society, external advantages make us more respected. A man with a good coat upon his back meets with a better reception than he who has a bad one.
SAMUEL JOHNSON

Show regard for no one at the expense of your soul, and respect no one, to your own downfall.

BEN SIRA

Man does not live by bread alone, many prefer self-respect to food.

MAHATMA GANDHI

He that respects himself is safe from others; he wears a coat of mail that none can pierce.

HENRY WADSWORTH LONGFELLOW

A great man shows his greatness by the way he treats little men.

JOHN TIMOTHY STONE

When you are content to be simply yourself and don't compare or compete, everybody will respect you.

LAO TZU

Everybody, my friend, everybody lives for something better to come. That's why we want to be considerate of every man – who knows what's in him, why he was born and what he can do?

MAXIM GORKY

RESPONSIBILITY

The price of greatness is responsibility.
WINSTON CHURCHILL

Few things can help an individual more than to place responsibility on him, and to let him know that you trust him.
BOOKER T. WASHINGTON

Accept responsibility for your life. Know it is you who will get you where you want to go, no one else.
LES BROWN

In dreams begins responsibility.
WILLIAM BUTLER YEATS

The ability to accept responsibility is the measure of a man.
ROY L. SMITH

Man is fully responsible for his nature and his choices.
JEAN-PAUL SARTRE

Life is the responsibilities or their evasion; it is a business of meeting obligations or avoiding them. To every man, the choice is continually being offered, and by the manner of his choosing, you may fairly well measure him.
BEN AMES WILLIAMS

Everyone is the son of his own works.
FROM THE SPANISH

It is easy to dodge our responsibilities, but we cannot dodge the consequences of dodging our responsibilities.
JOSIAH STAMP

You cannot escape the responsibility of tomorrow by evading it today.
ABRAHAM LINCOLN

Responsibility, n. A detachable burden easily shifted to the shoulders of God, Fate, Fortune, Luck or one's neighbor. In the days of astrology, it was customary to unload it upon a star.
AMBROSE BIERCE

To be a man, is precisely, to be responsible.
ANTOINE DE SAINT-EXUPERY

The fault, dear Brutus, is not in our stars, but in ourselves, that we are underlings.
WILLIAM SHAKESPEARE

Responsibility alone drives a man to toil and brings out his gifts.
N. D. HILLIS

Unto whomsoever much is given, of him shall much be required.
BIBLE

Life always gets harder toward the summit – the cold increases, responsibility increases.
FREDERICH NIETZSCHE

Responsible persons are mature people who have taken charge of themselves and their conduct, who own their actions and own up to them – who answer for them.
WILLIAM JOHN BENNETT

Responsibility is the price of freedom.
ELBERT HUBBARD

We are responsible for actions performed in response to circumstances for which we are not responsible.

ALLAN MASSIE

Responsibility is the thing people dread most of all. Yet it is the one thing in the world that develops us, gives us manhood or womanhood fibre.

FRANK CRANE

You must create your own world. I am responsible for my world.

LOUISE NEVELSON

Every one is responsible for his own acts.

MIGUEL DE CERVANTES

The highest praise for a person is to give them responsibility.

SAYING

Responsibilities gravitate to the person who can shoulder them.

ELBERT HUBBARD

RETIREMENT

Given three requisites – means of existence, reasonable health, and an absorbing interest – those years beyond sixty can be the happiest and most satisfying of a lifetime.
ERNEST CALKINS

Cessation of work is not accompanied by cessation of expenses.
MARCUS PORCIUS CATO

Few men of action have been able to make a graceful exit at the appropriate time.
MALCOLM MUGGERIDGE

Lord Tyrawley and I have been dead these two years, but we don't choose to have it know.
EARL OF CHESTERFIELD

I advise you to go on living solely to enrage those who are paying your annuities. It is the only pleasure I have left.
VOLTAIRE

Retire from your job, but never retire your mind.
ANONYMOUS

I see retirement as just another of these reinventions, another chance to do new things and be a new version of myself.
WALT MOSSBERG

Retirement is the last opportunity for individuals to reinvent themselves, let go of the past, and find peace and happiness within.

ERNIE J. ZELINSKI

The first years of man must make provision for the last.

SAMUEL JOHNSON

Retirement, a time to enjoy all the things you never had time to do when you worked.

CATHERINE PULSIFER

Don't simply retire from something; have something to retire to.

HARRY EMERSON FOSDICK

A lot of our friends complain about their retirement. We tell'em to get a life.

LARRY LASER

Retirement kills more people than hard work ever did.

MALOCM FORBES

The harder you work, the harder it is to surrender.

VINCE LOMBARDI

Dare to live the life you have dreamed for yourself. Go forward and make your dreams come true.

RALPH WALDO EMERSON

You can retire, but you can't retire from being great!

ANONYMOUS

Retirement means doing whatever I want to do. It means choice.

DIANNE NAHIRNY

Retirement ... a time to experience a fulfilling life derived from many enjoyable and rewarding activities,

ERNIE J. ZELINSKI

If you believe that achievement ends with retirement, you will slowly fade away. First of all, keeping the mind active is one way to prolong your life and to enjoy life to its fullest for as long as possible.

BYRON PULSIFER

Retire from work, not from life.

SUKANT RATNAKAR

Retirement is a blank sheet of paper. It is a chance to redesign your life into something new and different.

PATRICK FOLEY

Retirement only means that it is time for a new adventure.

ANONYMOUS

Retirement is when you stop living at work and start working at living.

ANONYMOUS

Having purpose and vision during retirement is one of the most important determinants of mental, social, spiritual, and physical well-being in later life.

HAROLD G. KOENIG

Retirement is not the end of the road...it is simply a fork in the road, sending you off in a new direction.

HILARY HENDERSON

Retirement is the prison and punishment of the fool, the paradise of the wise and good.

RICHARD LUCAS

Retirement can and will be a glorious time in your life. You'll love the freedom and ability to try new things. It's a new phase of life; a chance to be a beginner again.

RICHARD CARLSON

SILENCE

A man of knowledge uses words with restraint, and a man of understanding is even-tempered.

BIBLE

Be silent, or speak something worth hearing.

THOMAS FULLER

A man who lives right, and is right, has more power in his silence than another has by his words.

PHILLIPS BROOKS

Blessed is the man who, having nothing to say, abstains from giving in words evidence of the fact.

GEORGE ELIOT

A word aptly spoken is like apples of gold in settings of silver.

BIBLE

Silence is the unbearable repartee.

GILBERT KEITH CHESTERTON

Better say nothing than nothing to the purpose.

ENGLISH PROVERB

I have often regretted my speech, never my silence.

SYRUS

Many a time, the thing left silent makes for happiness.
PINDAR

Saying nothing sometimes says the most.
EMILY DICKINSON

We need a reason to speak, but never to keep silent.
PIERRE NICOLE

Listen to silence. It has so much to say.
RUMI

All men's miseries derive from not being able to sit in a quiet room alone.
BLAISE PASCAL

A fool is known by his speech; and a wise man by his silence.
PYTHAGORAS

The quieter you become the more you are able to hear.
RUMI

It is better in prayer to have a heart without words than words without a heart.
MAHATMA GANDHI

When you have nothing to say, say nothing.
CHARLES CALEB COLTON

In the silence behind what can be heard lies the answers we have been searching for
for so long.
ANDREAS FRANNSON

Noise creates illusions. Silence brings truth.
MAXINE LAGACE

Speech is silver, silence is golden.
THOMAS CARLYLE

The good and the wise lead quiet lives.
EURIPIDES

Silence is the source of great strength.
LAO TZU

Silence is sorrow's best food.
LAO TZU

Inner silence is the mother of all talents.
SRI SRI RAVI SHANKAR

The closer you are to the truth, the more silent you become inside.
NAVAL RAVIKANT

I think 99 times and find nothing, swim in silence, and the truth comes to me.
ALBERT EINSTEIN

Three silences there are: the first of speech, the second of desire, the third of thought.
HENRY WADSWORTH LONGFELLOW

I've begun to realize that you can listen to silence and learn from it. It has a quality and a dimension all its own.
CHAIM POTOK

Silence is true wisdom's best reply.
EURIPIDES

Time and silence are the most luxurious things today.
TOM FORD

Silence is sometimes the best answer.
DALAI LAMA

Silence speaks when words can't.
ANONYMOUS

Keep silence for the most part, and speak only when you must, and then briefly.
EPICTETUS

Silence is a true friend who never betrays.
CONFUCIUS

Nothing strengthens authority so much as silence.
LEONARDO DA VINCI

Speak only if it improves upon the silence.
MAHATMA GANDHI

The right word may be effective, but no word was ever as effective as a rightly times pause.
MARK TWAIN

Silence is the ultimate weapon of power.
CHARLES DE GUALLE

Experience tells us that silence terrifies people the most.
BOB DYLAN

Let us be silent, that we may hear the whispers of the gods.
RALPH WALDO EMERSON

Silence is the element in which great things fashion themselves together.
THOMAS CARLYLE

The best cure for the body is a quiet mind.
NAPOLEON BONAPARTE

Real action is in silent moments.
RALPH WALDO EMERSON

The quiet mind is richer than a crown.
ROBERT GREENE

Under all speech that is good for anything, there lies a silence that is better.
THOMAS CARLYLE

Do not the most moving moments of our lives find us all without words?
MARCEL MARCEAU

Let a fool hold his tongue and he will pass for a sage.
PUBLILIUS SYRUS

A sage thing is timely silence, and better than any speech.
PLUTARCH

Speaking comes by nature, silence by understanding.
GERMAN PROVERB

The sin by silence when they should protest makes cowards of men.
ABRAHAM LINCOLN

No one has a finer command of language than the person who keeps his mouth shut.
SAM RAYBURN

He refuses to turn off our computers, turn off our phones, log off Facebook, and just sit in silence, because, in those moments, we might actually have to face up to who we really are.
JEFFERSON BETHKE

Well-timed silence hath more eloquence than speech.
MARTIN FARQUHAR TUPPER

When you have spoken the word, it reigns over you. When it is unspoken you reign over it.
ARABIAN PROVERB

The great gift of conversation lies less in displaying it ourselves than in drawing it out of others. He who leaves your company pleased with himself and his own cleverness is perfectly well pleased with you.
JEAN DE LA BRUYERE

A judicious silence is always better than truth spoken without charity.
FRANCIS DE SALES

Don't speak unless you can improve on the silence.
SPANISH PROVERB

Silence is a fence around wisdom.
HEBREW PROVERB

Silence is a great peacemaker.
HENRY WADSWORTH LONGFELLOW

Silence is deep as eternity, speech is shallow as time.
THOMAS CARLYLE

I think the first virtue is to restrain the tongue; he approaches nearest to the gods who knows how to be silent, even though he is in the right.
MARCUS PORCIUS CATO

Silence is one great art of conversation.
WILLIAM HAZLITT

Our lives begin to end the day we become silent about the things that matter.
ANONYMOUS

Silence is the most perfect expression of scorn.
GEORGE BERNARD SHAW

Silence is one of the hardest arguments to refute.
JOSH BILLINGS

Never rise to speak till you have something to say; and when you have said it, cease.
WITHERSPOON

Silence is also speech.
YIDDISH PROVERB

He that keepeth his mouth keepeth his life: but he that openeth wide his lips shall have destruction.
BIBLE

The sole cause of man's unhappiness is that he does not know how to stay quietly in his room.
BLAISE PASCAL

For a few minutes every day practice quietness. Choose a place where you can relax completely. Quietness and silence are a healing balm for a tired body and brain, frayed nerves, and needless foreboding.
GRENVILLE KLEISER

Silence at the proper season is wisdom, and better than any speech.
PLUTARCH

Be silent or let thy words be worth more than silence.
PYTHAGORAS

Whoso keepeth his mouth and his tongue keepeth his soul from troubles.
KING SOLOMON

SIMPLICITY

Beauty of style and harmony and grace and good rhythm depend on simplicity.
PLATO

Ask how little, not how much, can I get along with. To say-is it necessary? – when I am tempted to add one more accumulation to my life, when I am pulled toward one more centrifugal activity.
ANNE MORROW LINDBERGH

Less is more.
ROBERT BROWNING

Simplicity, simplicity, simplicity! I say, let your affairs be as two or three, and not a hundred or a thousand; instead of a million count half a dozen, and keep your accounts on your thumb-nail.
HENRY DAVID THOREAU

Teach us delight in simple things, and mirth that has no bitter springs.
RUDYARD KIPLING

And all the loveliest things there be come simply so, it seems to me.
EDNA ST. VINCENT MILLAY

It is proof of high culture to say the greatest matters in the simplest way.
RALPH WALDO EMERSON

The greatest truths are the simplest: and so are the greatest men.
JULIUS CHARLES HARE

To be simple is to be great.

RALPH WALDO EMERSON

To be simple is the best thing in the world; to be modest is the next best thing; I am not sure about being quiet.

GILBERT KEITH CHESTERTON

Reduce the complexity of life by eliminating the needless wants of life, and the labors of life reduce themselves.

EDWIN WAY TEALE

I must find a way to live more simply.

RUTH ST. DENIS

It is not a daily increase, but a daily decrease. Hack away at the inessentials.

BRUCE LEE

The ability to simplify means to eliminate the unnecessary so that the necessary may speak.

HANS HOFMANN

The essence of civilization consists not in the multiplication of wants but in their deliberate and voluntary renunciation.

MAHATMA GANDHI

Your life is what you make it. Your life can be simple if you will set it up with simplicity as a goal! It will take courage to cut away from the thousand and one hindrances that make life complex, but it can be done.

RHODA LACHAR

Great leaders are almost always great simplifiers who can cut through argument, debate, and doubt to offer a solution everybody can understand.

COLIN POWELL

Besides the noble art of getting things done, there is the noble art of leaving things undone. The wisdom of life consists in the elimination of neo-essentials.

LIN YUTANG

Simplicity is ultimately a manner of focus.
ANN VOSKAMP

Be the curator of your life. Slowly cut things out until you're left only with what you love, with what is necessary, with what makes you happy.
LEO BABAUTA

The greatest ideas are the simplest.
WILLIAM GOLDING

Simplicity is the ultimate sophistication.
LEONARDO DA VINCI

The art of art, the glory of expression, and the sunshine of the light of letters, is simplicity.
WALT WHITMAN

Don't make the process harder than it is.
JACK WELCH

Tis the gift to be simple. Tis the gift to be free...
JOSEPH BRACKETT

The core of beauty is simplicity.
PAULO COELHO

It is the essence of genius to make use of the simplest ideas.
CHARLES PEGUY

There is no greatness where there is not simplicity, goodness, and truth.
LEO TOLSTOY

Like all magnificent things, it's very simple.
NATALIE BABBITT

One day I will find the right words, and they will be simple.
JACK KEROUAC

The greatest artist and thinker are the simplifiers.
HENRI FREDERICK AMIEL

If your mind isn't clouded by unnecessary things, this is the best season of your life.
WU-MEN

Simplicity is not a simple thing.
CHAPLIN

Living simply makes loving simple.
ANONYMOUS

Possessions, outward success, publicity, luxury – to me these have always been contemptible. I believe that a simple and unassuming manner of life is best for everyone, best for both the body and mind.
ALBERT EINSTEIN

Truth is ever to be found in the simplicity, and not in the multiplicity and confusion of things.
ISAAC NEWTON

Simplicity is about subtracting the obvious and adding the meaningful,
JOHN MAEDA

Make it simple, but significant.
DON DRAPER

The less I needed the better I felt.
CHARLES BUKOWSKI

A simple life is its own reward.
GEORGE SANTAYANA

Simplicity is an exact medium between too little and too much.
SIR JOSHUA REYNOLDS

The wisdom of life consists in the elimination of nonessentials.
LIN YUTANG

Genius is the ability to reduce the complicated to the simple.
B. W. CERAM

The greatest men are the simplest.
ANONYMOUS

Nothing is more simple than greatness; indeed, to be simple is to be great.
RALPH WALDO EMERSON

There is a majesty in simplicity.
ALEXANDER POPE

The most valuable of all talents, that of never using two words where one will do.
THOMAS JEFFERSON

It is simplicity that makes the uneducated more effective than the educated when addressing popular audiences.
ARISTOTLE

A sentence should contain no unnecessary words, a paragraph no unnecessary sentences, for the same reason that a drawing should have no unnecessary lines and a machine no unnecessary parts.
WILLIAM STRUNK, JR.

The more you say, the less people remember. The fewer the words, the greater the profit.
FRANCIS DE SALES

Simplicity is making the journey of this life with just baggage enough.
CHARLES WARNER

SINCERITY

No one means all he says, and yet very few say all they mean.
HENRY ADAMS

Sincerity is the highest compliment you can pay.
RALPH WALDO EMERSON

Be as you would seem to be.
THOMAS FULLER

What is uttered from the heart alone will win the hearts of others to your own.
JOHANN WOLFGANG VON GOETHE

Sincerity is an opening of the heart; we find it in very few persons; and that which we see ordinarily is only a cunning deceit to attract the confidence of others.
FRANCOIS DE LA ROCHEFOUCAULD

Weak people cannot be sincere.
FRANCOIS DE LA ROCHEFOUCAULD

It's never what you say, but how you make it sound sincere.
MARYA MANNES

Never has there been one possessed of complete sincerity who did not move others. Never has there been one who had not sincerity who was able to move others.
MENCIUS

Sincerity may not help us make friends, but it will help us keep them.
JOHN WOODEN

The primary condition for being sincere is the same as for being humble: not to boast of it, and probably not even to be aware of it.
HENRI PEYRE

Perfect sincerity offers no guarantee.
CHUANG-TZU

When pure sincerity forms within, it is outwardly realized in other people's hearts.
LAO TZU

Sincerity makes the very least person to be of more value than the most talented hypocrite.
CHARLES SPURGEON

Live a sincere life, be natural, and be honest with yourself.
MEHER BABA

In life, sincerity is always the best strategy to win people's hearts.
MEHMET MURAT ILDAN

Sincere deeds invite new friends.
TOBA BETA

Be sincere with your compliments. Most people can tell the difference between sugar and saccharine.
E. C. MCKENZIE

Sincerity is to speak as we think, to do as we pretend and profess, to perform and make good what we promise, and really to be what we would seem and appear to be.
JOHN TILLOTSON

If knowledge and foresight are too penetrating and deep, unify them with ease and sincerity.

XUNZI

Sincerity of conviction and purity of motive will surely gain the day; and even a small minority, armed with these, is surely destined to prevail against all odds.

SWAMI VIVEKANANDA

I should say sincerity, a deep, great, genuine sincerity, is the first characteristic of all men in any way heroic.

THOMAS CARLYLE

Sincerity is the way of heaven.

CONFUCIUS

The tongue of the sincere is rooted in his heart; hypocrisy and deceit have no place in his words.

ROBERT DODSLEY

Where there is the greatest sincerity, there is the greatest humility; and where the least truth, there is the greatest pride.

ASEN NICHOLSON

He who as sincere hath the easiest task in the world, for truth being always consistent with itself, he is put to no trouble about his words and actions.

J. BEAUMONT

SOLITUDE

I live in that solitude which is painful in youth, but delicious in the years of maturity.
ALBERT EINSTEIN

In solitude the mind gains strength and learns to lean upon itself.
LAURENCE STERNE

Conversation enriches the understanding, but solitude is the school of genius.
EDWARD GIBBON

The monotony and solitude of a quiet life stimulates the creative mind.
ALBERT EINSTEIN

Loneliness is the poverty of self; solitude is the richness of self.
MAY SARTON

Seclusion is the price of greatness.
PARAMAHANSA YOGANANDA

The more powerful and original a mind, the more it will incline towards the religion of solitude.
ALDOUS HUXLEY

One can be instructed in society, one is inspired only in solitude.
JOHANN WOLFGANG VON GOETHE

Be able to be alone. Lose not the advantage of solitude, and the society of thyself.
THOMAS BROWNE

I like peace and solitude and silence.
CARLA BRUNI

Solitude is important to man. It is necessary to his achievement of peace and contentment. It is a well into which he dips for refreshment for his soul. It is his laboratory in which he distills the pure essence of worth from the raw materials of his experiences. It is his refuge when the very foundations of his life are being shaken by disastrous events.
MARGARET E. MULAC

Great men are like eagles, and build their nest on some lofty solitude.
ARTHUR SCHOPENHAUER

A creation of importance can only be produced when its author isolates himself, it is a child of solitude.
JOHANN WOLFGANG VON GOETHE

It is only in solitude that I ever find my own core.
ANNE MORROW LINDBERGH

Converse with men makes sharp the glittering wit, but God to man doth speak in solitude.
JOHN STUART BLACKIE

Extraordinary things happen in solitude.
MICHAEL FINKEL

Sit in solitude every day. Be quiet and be still. Calm your thoughts and get to know your inner voice.
JOHN SOFORIC

Without great solitude no serious work is possible.
PABLO PICASSO

When you have shut your doors and darkened your room, remember, never to say that you are alone; for you are not alone, but God is within, and your genius is within.
EPICTETUS

Better be alone than in bad company.
THOMAS FULLER

Solitary trees, if they grow at all, grow strong.
WINSTON CHURCHILL

I love to be alone. I never found a companion that was so companionable as solitude.
HENRY DAVID THOREAU

The happiest of all lives is a busy solitude.
VOLTAIRE

Nowhere can man find a quieter or more untroubled retreat than in his own soul.
MARCUS AURELIUS

Solitude is as needful to the imagination as society is wholesome for the character.
JAMES RUSSELL LOWELL

Solitude is the great teacher, and to learn its lessons you must pay attention to it.
DEEPAK CHOPRA

Solitude is not the absence of company, but the moment when our soul is free to speak to us and help us decide what to do with our lives.
PAULO COELHO

Solitude is creativity's best friend, and solitude is refreshment for our souls.
NAOMI JUDD

Solitude is where one discovers one is not alone.
GRETCHEN RUBIN

Solitude sharpens awareness of small pleasures otherwise lost.
KEVIN PATTERSON

You talk when you cease to be at peace with your thoughts.
KAHLIL GIBRAN

How can you hear your soul if everyone is talking?
MARY DORIA RUSSELL

Solitude is good for great minds but bad for small ones.
VICTOR HUGO

I don't see how you can respect yourself if you must look in the hearts and minds of others for your happiness.
HUNTER S. THOMPSON

It is difficult to find happiness within oneself, but it is impossible to find it anywhere else.
ARTHUR SCHOPENHAUER

Those who fly solo have the strongest wings.
ANONYMOUS

Get away from the crowd when you can. Keep yourself to yourself, if for a few hours daily.
ARTHUR BRISBANE

Sometimes solitude is one of the most beautiful things on earth.
CHARLES BUKOWSKI

In nature, in solitude, the soft voice of wisdom can be heard.
ANONYMOUS

Never be afraid to spend time in your own company getting to know yourself better. That's where true happiness is found.
ANONYMOUS

Ordinary men hate solitude. But the Master makes use of it, embracing his aloneness, realizing he is one with the whole universe.

LAO TZU

Make the time to be alone. Your best ideas live within solitude.

ROBIN SHARMA

Respect the child. Be not too much his parent. Trespass not on his solitude.

RALPH WALDO EMERSON

The secret of a good old age is simply an honorable pact with solitude.

GABRIEL GARCIA MARQUEZ

Blessed are those who do not fear solitude, who are not afraid of their own company, who are not always desperately looking for something to do, something to amuse themselves with, something to judge.

PAULO COELHO

It would do the world good if every man in it would compel himself occasionally to be absolutely alone. Most of the world's progress has come out of such loneliness.

BRUCE BARTON

To most people loneliness is a doom. Yet loneliness is the very thing which God has chosen to be one of the schools of training for his very own. It is the fire that sheds the dross and reveals the gold.

BERNARD M. MARTIN

A perfect life is like that of a ship of war which has its own place in the fleet and can share in its strength and discipline, but can also go forth alone in the solitude of the infinite sea. We ought to belong to society, to have our place in it, and yet be capable of a complete individual existence outside of it.

HAMERTON

The right to be alone – the most comprehensive of rights, and the right most valued by civilized man.

LOUIS BRANDEIS

Solitude: a good place to visit, but a poor place to stay.
JOSH BILLINGS

It is when a man is alone, away from the influence of other men and their acts, that he can work on himself. It is in solitude that he must correct his thoughts, driving out the bad and stimulating the good.
LEO TOLSTOY

The best thinking has been done in solitude. The worst has been done in turmoil
THOMAS ALVA EDISON

SORROW

The deeper that sorrow carves into your being, the more joy you can contain.
KAHLIL GIBRAN

He that conceals his grief finds no remedy for it.
TURKISH PROVERB

No emotion falls into dislike so readily as sorrow.
LUCIUS ANNAEUS SENECA

Grief even in a child hates the light and shrinks from human eyes.
THOMAS DE QUINCEY

Grief can't be shared. Everyone carries it alone, his own burden, his own way.
ANNE MORROW LINDBERGH

To weep is to make less the depth of grief.
WILLIAM SHAKESPEARE

A man's sorrow runs uphill; true it is difficult for him to bear, but it is also difficult
for him to keep.
DJUNA BARNES

Grief drives men into habits of serious reflection, sharpens the understanding and
softens the heart.
JOHN QUINCY ADAMS

Heavy hearts, like heavy clouds in the sky, are best relieved by the letting of a little water.
CHRISTOPHER MORLEY

Crying is cleansing. There's a reason for tears, happiness or sadness.
DIONNE WARWICK

Even in laughter the heart is sad, and the end of joy is grief.
BIBLE

Sorrow is better than laughter; for, by the sadness of the countenance, the heart is made better.
KING SOLOMON

Whenever sorrow comes, be kind to it. For God has placed a pearl in sorrow's hand.
RUMI

Bear and endure: this sorrow will one day prove to be for your good.
OVID

Truly, it is in darkness that one finds the light, so when we are in sorrow, then this light is nearest to all of us.
MEISTER ECKHART

Sorrow looks back, worry looks around, faith looks up.
RALPH WALDO EMERSON

Sorrow and silence are strong, and patient endurance is godlike.
HENRY WADSWORTH LONGFELLOW

It is better to drink of deep griefs than to taste shallow pleasures.
WILLIAM HAZLITT

It's the great mystery of human life that old grief passes gradually into quiet tender joy.
FYODOR DOSTOEVSKY

Grief is itself a medicine.
WILLIAM COWPER

Weeping may endure for a night, but joy cometh in the morning.
BIBLE

There is a sacredness in tears. They are not the mark of weakness, but of power. They speak more eloquently than ten thousand tongues. They are messengers of overwhelming grief, of deep contrition, or unspeakable love.
SAMUEL JOHNSON

Grief is like a physical pain which must be allowed to subside somewhat on its own.
PLUTARCH

Being in the debts of sadness is just as important an experience as being exuberantly happy.
MARLENE DIETRICH

Every man has his secret sorrows which the world knows not; and oftentimes we call a man cold, when he is only sad.
HENRY WADSWORTH LONGFELLOW

One must not let oneself be overwhelmed by sadness.
JACQUELINE KENNEDY-ONASSIS

The word 'happy' would lose its meaning if it were not balanced by sadness.
TRUMAN CAPOTE

Tears are words that need to be written.
PAULO COELHO

Behind every sweet smile, there is a bitter sadness that no one can ever see and feel.
TUPAC

The good life is not one immune to sadness but one in which suffering contributes to our development.
ALAIN DE BOTTON

Sadness gives depth. Happiness gives height. Sadness gives roots. Happiness gives branches. Happiness is like a tree going into the sky, and sadness is like the roots going down into the womb of the earth. Both are needed, and the higher a tree goes, the deeper it goes, simultaneously. The bigger the tree, the bigger will be its roots. In fact, it is always in proportion. That's its balance.

OSHO RAJNEESH

The mind profits by the wrecks of every passion, and we measure our road to wisdom by the sorrows we have undergone.

EDWARD BULWER-LYTTON

Some days are just bad days, that's all. You have to experience sadness to know happiness, and I remind myself that not every day is going to be a good day, that's just the way it is.

DITA VON TEESE

Every man must go through the fire. This means that during your lifetime you will experience great suffering or great sorrow, and you will need the help of God to win over your problems.

ALFRED ARMAND MONTAPERT

Tears come from the heart and not from the brain.

LEONARDO DA VINCI

Those who don't know how to weep with their whole heart, don't know how to laugh either.

GOLDA MEIR

Every human walks around with a certain kind of sadness. They may not wear it on their sleeves, but it's there if you look deep.

TARAJI P. HENSON

It doesn't hurt to feel sad from time to time.

WILLIE NELSON

Sadness flies away on the wings of time.

JEAN DE LA FONTAINE

What soap is for the body, tears are for the soul.
JEWISH PROVERB

Learn weeping, and thou shalt gain laughing.
GEORGE HERBERT

He truly sorrows who sorrows unseen.
MARTIAL

It is our human lot, it is heaven's will, that sorrow follow joy.
TITUS M. PLAUTUS

Sorrows remembered sweeten present joy.
ROBERT POLLOK

Happiness is good for the body but sorrow strengthens the spirit.
MARCEL PROUST

There is no greater sorrow than remembering happy times in the midst of misery.
DANTE

A day of sorrow is longer than a month of joy.
CHINESE PROVERB

Patience is a remedy for every sorrow.
PUBLIUS SYRUS

Sorrow comes unsent for.
JOHN RAY

'Tis held that sorrow makes us wise.
ALFRED TENNYSON

Sorrow is a fruit. God does not allow it to grow on a branch that is too weak to bear it.
VICTOR HUGO

Sorrow's best antidote is employment.
EDWARD YOUNG

The rose and thorn, and sorrow and gladness are linked together.
SA'DI

Be brave, and rise superior to your sorrows, and maintain a spirit that cannot be broken.
OVID

While grief is fresh, every attempt to divert only irritates.
SAMUEL JOHNSON

When you are sorrowful, look again in your heart, and you shall see that in truth you are weeping for that which has been your delight.
KHALIL GIBRAN

He that lacks time to mourn lacks time to mend.
HENRY TAYLOR

Sorrow makes men sincere.
HENRY WARD BEECHER

There can be no rainbow without a cloud and a storm.
J. H. VINCENT

Weeping makes the heart grow lighter.
YIDDISH PROVERB

SUCCESS

Success is the result of perfection, hard work, learning from failure, loyalty, and persistence.
COLIN POWELL

Self-belief and hard work will always earn your success.
VIRAT KOHLI

He who would climb the ladder must begin at the bottom.
ENGLISH PROVERB

There is no success without hardship.
SOPHOCLES

The ability to convert ideas to things is the secret of outward success.
HENRY WARD BEECHER

Success is a journey, not a destination.
BEN SWEETLAND

The heights by men reached and kept were not attained by sudden flight, but they, while their companions slept, were toiling upward in the night.
HENRY WADSWORTH LONGFELLOW

Success begins with a fellow's will. It's all in the state of mind.
WALTER D. WINTLE

The great thing in this world is not so much where we stand as in what direction we are moving.
OLIVER WENDELL HOLMES

One of the chief reasons for success in life is the ability to maintain a daily interest in one's work, to have a chronic enthusiasm, to regard each day as important.
WILLIAM LYONS PHELPS

Success consists of going from failure to failure without loss of enthusiasm.
WINSTON CHURCHILL

If a man does not keep pace with his companions, perhaps it is because he hears a different drummer. Let him step to the music which he hears, however measured or far away.
HENRY DAVID THOREAU

The secret of your success is determined by your daily agenda.
JOHN MAXWELL

Successful people do what unsuccessful people are not willing to do. Don't wish it were easier; wish you were better.
JIM ROHN

There is only one success – to be able to spend your life in your own way.
CHRISTOPHER MORLEY

It is no use to wait for your ship to come in unless you have sent one out.
BELGIAN PROVERB

All progress takes place outside the comfort zone.
MICHAEL JOHN BOBAK

Don't let the fear of losing be greater than the excitement of winning.
ROBERT T. KIYOSAKI

The successful warrior is the average man, with laser-like focus.

BRUCE LEE

If you really want to do something, you'll find a way. If you don't, you'll find an excuse.

JIM ROHN

It is better to fail in originality than to succeed in imitation.

HERMAN MELVILLE

One ship drives east an another west, with the self-same winds blow; 'tis the set of the sails and not the gales that determines where they go. Like the winds of the sea are the ways of fate, as we voyage along through life; 'tis the set of the soul that decides it goal – and not the calm or strife.

ELLA WHEELER WILCOX

From success you get a lot of things, but not that great inside thing that love brings you.

SAMUEL GOLDWYN

Success is not the key to happiness. Happiness is the key to success. If you love what you are doing, you will be successful.

ALBERT SCHWEITZER

To be yourself in a world that is constantly trying to make you something else is the greatest accomplishment.

RALPH WALDO EMERSON

If you can dream it, you can do it.

WALT DISNEY

The secret of success is to do the common thing uncommonly well.

JOHN D. ROCKEFELLER, JR.

I failed my way to success.

THOMAS ALVA EDISON

The secret to success is to know something nobody else knows.
ARISTOTLE ONASSIS

The only place where success comes before work is in the dictionary.
VIDAL SASSOON

It's not whether you get knocked down, it's whether you get up.
VINCE LOMBARDI

I'd rather attempt something great .... And fail, then attempt nothing ... and succeed.
ANONYMOUS

If one advances confidently in the direction of his dreams, and endeavors to live the life which he has imagined, he will meet with success unexpected in common hours.
HENRY DAVID THOREAU

You are never too old to set another goal or to dream a new dream.
B. S. LEWIS

Develop success from failures. Discouragement and failure are two of the surest stepping stones to success.
DALE CARNEGIE

Patience, persistence and perspiration make an unbeatable combination for success.
NAPOLEON HILL

You don't have to be great to start, but you have to start to be great.
ZIG ZIGLAR

Out of the will of God there is no such thing as success; in the will of God there cannot be any failure.
GRENVILLE KLEISER

For success, attitude is as important as ability.
HARRY F. BANKS

There's no elevator to success. You have to take the stairs.
ZIG ZIGLAR

Positive action combined with positive thinking results in success.
SHIV KHERA

The greater the difficulty, the more the glory in surmounting it.
EPICTETUS

It is a rough road that leads to the heights of greatness.
LUCIUS ANNAEUS SENECA

What is the use of running when we are not on the right road.
GERMAN PROVERB

People begin and become successful the minute they decide to be.
HARVEY MACKAY

It does not matter how slowly you go as long as you do not stop.
CONFUCIUS

Satisfaction lies in the effort, not in the attainment, full effort is full victory.
MAHATMA GANDHI

They succeed because they think they can.
VIRGIL

Success is to be measured not so much by the position that one has reached in life as by the obstacles which he has overcome while trying to succeed.
BOOKER T. WASHINGTON

Success is getting what you want. Happiness is wanting what you get.
DALE CARNEGIE

What's money? A man is a success if he gets up in the morning and goes to bed at night and in between does what he wants to do.

BOB DYLAN

There are no secrets to success. It is the result of preparation, hard work and learning from failure.

COLIN POWELL

In every failure the wise man will find the seed of success.

W. CLEMENT STONE

Whatever the mind of man can conceive and believe, it can achieve.

NAPOLEON HILL

Do not go where the path may lead, go instead where there is no path and leave a trail.

RALPH WALDO EMERSON

If you can dream it, you can achieve it.

ZIG ZIGLAR

They can because they think they can.

VIRGIL

The journey of a thousand miles begins with one step.

LAO TZU

Many of life's failures are people who did not realize how close they were to success when they gave up.

THOMAS ALVA EDISON

Success is walking from failure to failure with no loss of enthusiasm.

WINSTON CHURCHILL

Believe you can, and you're halfway there.

THEODORE ROOSEVELT

Always bear in mind that your own resolution to success is more important than any other one thing.
ABRAHAM LINCOLN

The successful person is the individual who forms the habit of doing what the failing person doesn't like to do.
DOANLD RIGGS

Success follows doing what you want to do. There is no other way to be successful.
MALCOLM FORBES

He did it with all his heart, and prospered.
BIBLE

Every man is the architect of his own fortune.
SALLUST

No man will succeed unless he is ready to face and overcome difficulties and prepared to assume responsibilities.
WILLIAM J. H. BOETCKER

To get profit without risk, experience without danger and reward without work is as impossible as it is to live without being born.
ADOLPH PHILIP GOUTHEY

Courage to start and willingness to keep everlasting at it are the requisites for success.
ALONZO NEWTON BENN

Success is dependent on effort.
SOPHOCLES

Striving for success without hard work is like trying to harvest where you haven't planted.
DAVID BLY

If you can't accept losing, you can't win.
VIINCE LOMBARDI

I know the price of success: dedication, hard work and an unremitting devotion to the things you want to see happen.
FRANK LLOYD WRIGHT

It takes time to succeed because success is merely the natural reward for taking time to do anything well.
JOSEPH ROSS

Success has always been easy to measure. It is the distance between one's origins and one's final achievement.
MICHAEL KORDA

The man who has done his level best, and who is conscious that he has done his best, is a success, even though the world may write him down a failure.
B. C. FORBES

If you've had a good time playing the game, you're a winner even if you lose.
MALCOLM FORBES

The reward of a thing well done is to have done it.
RALPH WALDO EMERSON

Starting out to make money is the greatest mistake in life. Do what you have a flair for doing, and if you are good enough at it, the money will come.
GREER GARSON

We should not judge people by their peak of excellence; but by the distance they have traveled from the point where they started.
HENRY WARD BEECHER

When it is obvious that the goals cannot be reached, don't adjust the goals, adjust the action steps.
CONFUCIUS

If you want to succeed you should strike out on new paths rather than travel the worn paths of accepted success.

JOHN D. ROCKEFELLER

No legitimate business man ever got started on the road to permanent success by any other means than that of hard, intelligent work, coupled with an earned credit, plus character.

F. D. VAN AMBURGH

Take the course opposite to custom and you will almost always do well.

JEAN-JACQUES ROUSSEAU

Men who have attained things worth having in this world have worked while others idled, have persevered when others gave up in despair, have practiced early in life the valuable habits of self-denial, industry, and singleness of purpose. As a result, they enjoy in later life the success so often erroneously attributed to good luck.

GRENVILLE KLEISER

It is not the ship so much as the skillful sailing that assures the prosperous voyage.

GEORGE WILLIAM CURTIS

Success often comes to those who dare and act; it seldom goes to the timid who are ever afraid of the consequences.

JAWAHARIAL NEHRU

He has achieved success who has lived well, laughed often, and loved much.

MRS. A. J. STANLEY

The common idea that success spoils people by making them vain, egotistic, and self-complacent is erroneous; on the contrary it makes them, for the most part, humble, tolerant, and kind. Failure makes people bitter and cruel.

WILLIAM SOMERSET MAUGHAM

This is the foundation of success nine times out of ten – having confidence in yourself and applying yourself with all your might to your work.

THOMAS E. WILSON

Chiefly, the mould of a man's fortune is in his own hands.

FRANCIS BACON

A strong will, a settled purpose, an invincible determination, can accomplish almost anything; and in this lies the distinction between great men and little men.

THOMAS FULLER

No man was ever great by imitation.

SAMUEL JOHNSON

The very first step towards success in any occupation is to become interested in it.

SIR WILLIAM OSLER

No man is truly great who is great only in his lifetime. The test of greatness is the page of history.

WILLIAM HAZLITT

Success doesn't come from what you occasionally do, but what you consistently do.

SAYING

You will recognize your own path when you come upon it because you will suddenly have all the energy and imagination you will ever need.

SARA TEASDALE

You've achieved success in your field when you don't know whether what you're doing is work or play.

WARREN BEATTY

Success has ruined many a man.

BENJAMIN FRANKLIN

Life's greatest achievement is the continual re-making of yourself so that at last you know how to live.

WINFRED RHODES

If you have something to do that is worthwhile doing, don't talk about it, but do it. After you have done it, your friends and enemies will talk about it.

GEORGE W. BLOUNT

The three great essentials to achieve anything worthwhile are first, hard work; second, stick-to-itiveness; third, common sense.

THOMAS ALVA EDISON

My definition of success is this: The power with which to acquire whatever one demands of life without violating the rights of others.

ANDREW CARNEGIE

SUFFERING

We should feel sorrow, but not sink under its oppression.
CONFUCIUS

Great souls suffer in silence.
FRIEDRICH SCHILLER

There is no sorrow which length of time will not diminish and soothe.
MARCUS TULLIUS CICERO

If you are distressed by anything external, the pain is not due to the thing itself but to your own estimate of it; and this you have the power to revoke at any moment.
MARCUS AURELIUS

Although the world is full of suffering, it is full also of the overcoming of it.
HELLEN KELLER

Most people get a fair of amount of fun out of their lives, but on balance life is suffering, and only the very young or the very foolish imagine otherwise.
GEORGE ORWELL

Pain makes man think. Thought makes man wise. Wisdom makes life endurable.
JOHN HENRY PATRICK

Suffering is above, not below. And everyone thinks that suffering is below. And everyone wants to rise.
ANTONIO PORCHIA

No gain without pain.
ANONYMOUS

To a great extent, suffering is a sort of need felt by the organism to make itself familiar with a new state, which makes it uneasy, to adapt its sensibility to that state.
MARCEL PROUST

Sorrow makes us all children again.
RALPH WALDO EMERSON

Some of my best moments of enlightenment come soon after mental and emotional struggling.
LARRY JPHN PHILLIPS

Take this sorrow to thy heart, and make it a part of thee, and it shall nourish thee till thou are strong again.
HENRY WADSWORTH LONGFELLOW

We are healed of suffering only by experiencing it to the full.
MARCEL PROUST

Peace does not dwell in outward things, but within the soul; we may preserve it in the midst of the bitterness pain, if our will remains firm and submissive. Peace in this life springs from acquiescence to, not in an exemption from, suffering.
FRANCOIS FENELON

It is the lot of man to suffer.
BENJAMIN DISRAELI

There is nothing the body suffers that the soul may not profit by.
GEORGE MEREDITH

We learn from the things we suffer.
AESOP

Without the bitterest suffering, we cannot rise above others.
CHINESE PROVERB

Afflictions refine some, they consume others.
THOMAS FULLER

Blessed art Thou Lord, who giveth suffering as a divine remedy for our impurities.
CHARLES BAUDELAIRE

We rejoice in our sufferings, knowing that suffering produces endurance, and endurance produces character, and character produces hope.
BIBLE

The person who risks nothing, does nothing, has nothing, is nothing. He may avoid suffering and sorrow, but he cannot learn, feel change, grow or live...
WILLIAM ARTHUR WARD

A deep distress hath humanized my soul.
WLLIAM WORDSWORTH

Sorrow is better than laughter, because a sad face is good for the heart.
BIBLE

The most beautiful people we have known are those who have known defeat, known suffering, know struggle, know loss, and have found their way out of those depths.
ELIZABETH KUBLER-ROSS

Storms make oaks take deeper root.
ELBERT HUBBARD

Men cannot remake himself without suffering for he is both marble and the sculptor.
ALEXIS CARREL

Be still, sad heart! And cease repining; behind the clouds is the sun still shining; thy fate is the common fate of all, into each life some days must be dark and dreary.
WILLIAM WADSWORTH

The reward of suffering is experience.
HARRY S. TRUMAN

Suffering becomes beautiful when anyone bears great calamities with cheerfulness, not through insensibility but through greatness of mind.
ARISTOTLE

Oh, fear not in a world like this, and thou shall know erelong, know how sublime a thing it is to suffer and be strong.
HENRY WADSWORTH LONGFELLOW

In heaven above and earth below, they best can serve true gladness who meet most feelingly the calls of sadness.
WILLIAM WORDSWORTH

Without pain, there would be no suffering, without suffering we would never learn from our mistakes. To make it right, pain and suffering is the key to all windows, without it, there is no way of life.
ANGELINA JOLIE

Suffering is part of our training program for becoming wise.
RAM DASS

Pain and suffering are always inevitable for a large intelligence and a deep heart. The really great men must, I think, have great sadness on earth.
FYODOR DOSTOEVSKY

Until you have suffered much in your heart, you cannot learn humility.
ELDER THADDEUS OF VITOVNICA

Human misery must somewhere have a stop; there is no wind that always blows a storm.
EURIPIDES

You will suffer and you will hurt. You will have joy and you will have peace.
ALISON CHEEK

Pain is hard to bear...but with patience, day by day, even this shall pass away.
THEODORE TILTON

We shall draw from the heart of suffering itself the means of inspiration and survival.
WINSTON CHURCHILL

Out of suffering have emerged the strongest souls; the most massive characters are seared with scars.
EDWIN HUBBEL CHAPIN

If you suffer, thank God! It is a sure sign that you are alive.
ELBERT HUBBARD

Character cannot be developed in ease and quiet. Only through experience of trial and suffering can the soul be strengthened, vision cleared, ambition inspired, and success achieved.
HELEN KELLER

Only the willingness to suffer can conquer suffering.
DAVID J. BOSCH

Pain is pain and sorrow is sorrow. It hurts. It limits. It impoverishes. It isolates. It restrains. It works devastation deep within the personality. It circumscribes in a thousand different ways. There is nothing good about it. But the gifts God can give with it are the richest the human spirit can know.
MARGARET CLARKSON

If God is in charge and loves us, then whatever is given is subject to his control and is meant ultimately for our joy.
ELISABETH ELLIOT

God prepares great men for great tasks by great trials.
J. K. GRESSETT

It is suffering and then glory. Not to have the suffering means not to have the glory.
ROBERT C. MCQUILKIN

It is by those who have suffered that the world has been advanced.
LEO TOLSTOY

Great men suffer hours of depression through introspection and self-doubt. That is why they are great. That is why you will find modesty and humility the characteristics of such men.
BRUCE BARTON

There is no man in the world fee from trouble or anguish, though he were King or Pope.
THOMAS A' KEMPIS

By suffering comes wisdom.
AESCHYLUS

TALENT

The man who is born with a talent which he meant to use, finds his greatest happiness in using it.

JOHANN WOLFGANG VON GOETHE

Hide not your talents, they for use were made. What's a sun dial in the shade?

BENJAMIN FRANKLIN

Each man has his own vocation; his talent is his call. There is one direction in which all space is open to him.

RALPH WALDO EMERSON

More will be accomplished, and better, and with more ease, if every man does what he is best fitted to do, and nothing else.

PLATO

Whatever you are by nature, keep to it; never desert your line of talent. Be what nature intended you for, and you will succeed.

SYDNEY SMITH

Nothing is so frequent as to mistake an ordinary human gift for a special and extraordinary endowment.

OLIVER WENDELL HOLMES

It is very rare thing for a man of talent to succeed by his talent.

JOSEPH ROUX

God has given each normal person a capacity to achieve some end. True, some are endowed with more talent than others, but God has left none of us talentless.
MARTIN LUTHER KING, JR.

A true talent delights the possessor first.
RALPH WALDO EMERSON

There is no substitute for talent. Industry and all the virtues are of no avail.
ALDOUS HUXLEY

To do easily what is difficult for others is the mark of talent.
HENRI FREDERIC AMIEL

No one respects a talent that is concealed.
DESIDERIUS ERASMUS

If the power to do hard work is not talent, it is the best possible substitute for it.
JAMES A. GARFIELD

There must always be some advantage on one side or the other, and it is better that advantage should be had by talents than by chance.
SAMUEL JOHNSON

Each man has to seek out his own special aptitude for a higher life in the midst of the humble and inevitable reality of daily existence. Than this, there can be no nobler aim in life.
MAURICE MAETERLINCK

Hidden talent counts for nothing.
NERO

Nature has concealed at the bottom of our minds talents and abilities of which we are not aware.
FRANCOIS DE LA ROCHEFOUCAULD

Life's greatest gift is natural talent.
P. K. THOMAJAN

There is no so wretched and coarse soul wherein some particular faculty is not seen to shine.
MICHEL DE MONTAIGNE

Talent without working hard is nothing.
ANONYMOUS

If a man can write a better book, preach a better sermon, or make a better mouse-trap, than his neighbor, though he builds his house in the woods, the world will make a beaten path to his door.
RALPH WALDO EMERSON

Winning takes talent, to repeat takes character.
JOHN WOODEN

Your talent is God's gift to you. What you do with it is your gift back to God.
LEO BUSCAGLIA

The real tragedy of life is not being limited to one talent, but in failing to use that one talent.
EDGAR WATSON HOWE

Too many people overvalue what they are not and undervalue what they are.
MALCOLM FORBES

If a man has a talent and cannot use it, he has failed. If he has a talent and uses only half of it, he has partly failed. If he has a talent and learns somehow to use the whole of it, he has gloriously succeeded, and won a satisfaction and a triumph few men ever know.
THOMAS WOLFE

The aim of life is self-development, to realize one's nature perfectly.
OSCAR WILDE

Never desert your own line of talent. Be what nature intended you for, and you will succeed.
SYDNEY SMITH

They are happy men whose natures sort with their vocations.
FRANCIS BACON

Hard work without talent is a shame, but talent without hard work is a tragedy.
ROBERT HALF

The weakest among us has a gift, however seemingly trivial, which is peculiar to him and which worthily used will be a gift also to his race.
JOHN RUSKIN

Doing easily what others find difficult is talent; doing what is impossible for talent is genius.
HENRI FREDERICK AMIEL

The same man cannot well be skilled in everything; each has his special excellence.
EURIPIDES

Skills vary with the man. We must tread a straight path and strive by that which is born in us.
PINDAR

You were born an original. Don't die a copy.
JOHN MASON

Buried seeds may grow but buried talents never.
ROGER BABSON

THOUGHT

With the new day comes new strength and new thoughts.
ELEANOR ROOSEVELT

The happiness of your life depends upon the quality of your thoughts, therefore, guard accordingly, and take care that you entertain no notions unsuitable to virtue and reasonable nature.
MARCUS AURELIUS

We are what our thoughts have made us, so take care about what you think. Words are secondary. Thoughts live, they travel far.
SWAMI VIVEKANANDA

All that we are is the result of what we have thought.
BUDDHA

Concentrate all your thoughts upon the work at hand. The sun's rays do not burn until brought to a focus.
ALEXANDER GRAHAM BELL

A man is but the product of his thoughts what he thinks, he becomes.
MAHATMA GANDHI

The more man meditates upon good thoughts, the better will be his world and the world at large.
CONFUCIUS

Thinking good thoughts, positive and cheerful thoughts, will improve the way you feel. What affects your mind also affects your body.
W. CLEMENT STONE

All truly wise thoughts have been thought already thousands of times; but to make then truly ours, we must think them over again honestly, till they take root in our personal experience.
JOHANN WOLFGANG VON GOETHE

They are never alone who are accompanied with noble thoughts.
PHILIP SIDNEY

In your thoughts today you are building the blueprint of what you will become tomorrow.
THOMAS BLANDI

You will never be any better or higher than your best thoughts.
ALFRED ARMAND MONTAPERT

Our life is what our thoughts make it.
MARCUS AURELIUS

Change your thoughts and you change the world.
NORMAN VINCENT PEALE

Our life always expresses the result of our dominant thoughts.
SOREN KIERKEGAARD

Nurture your minds with great thoughts. To believe in the heroic makes heroes.
BENJAMIN DISRAELI

You are today where your thoughts have brought you, you will be tomorrow where your thoughts take you.
JAMES ALLEN

If you realized how powerful your thoughts are, you would never think a negative thought.

PEACE PILGRIM

What consumes your mind, controls your life.

ANONYMOUS

If you have good thoughts, they will shine out of your face like sunbeams and you will always look lovely.

ANONYMOUS

The highest possible stage in moral culture is when we recognize that we ought to control our thoughts.

CHARLES DARWIN

What is the hardest task in the world? To think.

RALPH WALDO EMERSON

Those that think must govern those that toil.

OLIVER GOLDSMITH

Sow a thought, and you reap an act; sow an act and you reap a habit; sow a habit, and you reap a character, sow a character, and you reap a destiny.

ANONYMOUS

Great thoughts come from the heart.

VAUVENARGUES

My thoughts are my company; I can bring them together, select them, detain them, dismiss them.

WALTER SAVAGE LANDOR

The thoughts that come often unsought, and, as it were, drop into the mind, are commonly the most valuable of any we have.

JOHN LOCKE

Over thinking is the biggest cause of unhappiness.
ANONYMOUS

Thinking is, or ought to be, a coolness and a calmness; and our poor hearts throb, and our poor brains beat too much for that.
HERMAN MELVILLE

I have no riches but my thoughts, yet these are wealth enough for me.
SARA TEASDALE

Man's greatness lies in his power of thought.
BLAISE PASCAL

If a man speaks or acts with an evil thought, pain follows him, as the wheel follows the foot of the ox that draws the carriage.
BUDDHA

Associate reverently and as much as you can, with your loftiest thoughts.
HENRY DAVID THOREAU

The body always ends by being a bore. Nothing remains beautiful and interesting except thought, because the thought is life.
GEORGE BERNARD SHAW

Thought is essentially practical in the sense that but for thought no motion would be an action, no change a progress.
GEORGE SANTAYANA

What we think, we become.
BUDDHA

All that a man does outwardly is but the expression and completion of his inward thought. To work effectively, he must think clearly; to act nobly, he must think nobly.
WILLIAM ELLERY CHANNING

The life each of us lives is the life within the limits of our own thinking. To have life more abundant, we must think in limitless terms of abundance.

THOMAS DREIER

Our destiny changes with our thoughts; we shall become what we wish to become, do what we wish to do, when our habitual thoughts correspond with our desires.

ORISON SWETT MARDEN

Our best friends and our worst enemies are our thoughts. A thought can do us more good than a doctor or a banker or a faithful friend. It can also so as more harm than a brick.

FRANK CRANE

A man's life is what his thoughts make it.

MARCUS AURELIUS

Every man is free to rise as far as he's able or willing, but the degree to which he thinks determines the degree to which he'll rise.

AYN RAND

The wisdom of all ages and cultures emphasizes the tremendous power our thoughts have over our character and circumstances.

LIANE CORDES

The relationship of a man's soul to God is best evidenced by those things that occupy his thoughts.

KENNETH L. DODGE

A wise man will be master of his mind, a fool will be its slave.

PUBLILIUS SYRUS

Nothing pains some people more than having to think.

MARTIN LUTHER KING, JR.

Thought is free.

WILLIAM SHAKESPEARE

We cannot employ the mind to advantage when we are filled with excessive food and drink.

MARCUS TULLIUS CICERO

Ideas are the mightiest influence on earth. One great thought breathed into a man may regenerate him.

WILLIAM ELLERY CHANNING

Keep your thoughts right - for as you think, so you are. Thoughts are things, therefore, think only the things that will make the world better and you unashamed.

HENRY H. BUCKLEY

A man would do well to carry a pencil in his pocket, and write down the thoughts of the moment. Those that come unsought for are commonly the most valuable, and should be secured, because they seldom return.

FRANCIS BACON

Thinking, for many, is life's most painful activity. For the fortunate others, there's not much in life that approaches it.

CARTH CATE

Great men are they who see that spiritual is stronger than any material force; that thoughts rule the world.

RALPH WALDO EMERSON

Our thought is the key which unlocks the doors of the world.

SAMUEL MCCHORD CROTHERS

You all have powers you never dreamed of. You can do things you never thought you could do. There are no limitations in what you can do except the imitations in your own mind as to what you cannot do. Don't think you cannot. Think you can.

DARWIN P. KINGSLEY

Do not think that what your thoughts dwell upon is of no matter. Your thoughts are making you.

BISHOP STEERE

Some thoughts always find us young and keep us so. Such a thought is the love of the universal and eternal beauty.
RALPH WALDO EMERSON

Speech is the gift which reveals moral purpose, but thought of few.
CATO

All things that we see standing accomplished in the world are properly the outer material result, the practical realization and embodiment of thoughts that dwell in the great men sent into the world.
THOMAS CARLYLE

The pleasantest things in the world are pleasant thoughts; and the great art of life is to have as many of them as possible.
MICHEL DE MONTAIGNE

Thoughts are pleasant companions if we choose them as well as we should other company.
CHANNING POLLOCK

As he thinketh in his heart, so is he.
BIBLE

A man who does not think for himself does not think at all.
OSCAR WILDE

Finally, brothers, whatever is true, whatever is noble, whatever is right, whatever is pure, whatever is lovely, whatever is admirable if anything is excellent or praiseworthy think about such things.
BIBLE

A simple man believes anything, but a prudent man gives thought to his steps.
BIBLE

Great thought reduced to practice become great acts.
WILLIAM HAZLITT

If we are not responsible for the thoughts that pass our doors, we are at least responsible for those we admit and entertain.

CHARLES B. NEWCOMB

All that a man achieves and all that he fails to achieve is the direct result of his own thoughts.

JAMES ALLEN

A man is what he thinks about all day long.

RALPH WALDO EMERSON

The way we think determines how we live.

JOHN MILLER

All the great thinkers of the past have done their best thinking in solitude.

ROY L. SMITH

First we think, then we act. To consciously think that we "can" impels the subconscious faculties into action.

WALTER MATTHEWS

What we think most about is constantly weaving itself into the fabric of our career, becoming a part of ourselves, increasing the power of our mental magnet to attract those things which we most ardently desire.

ORISON SWETT MARDEN

Every good thought you think is contributing its share to the ultimate result of your life.

GRENVILLE KLEISER

Let a man strive to purify his thoughts. What a man thinketh, that is he; this is the eternal mystery. Dwelling within himself with thoughts serene, he will obtain imperishable happiness. Man becomes what of which he thinks.

UPANISHADS

The optimistic thinker fills his mind with cheerful thoughts. To him the day opens auspiciously. He dwells on the sunny side of life. He plans for the best. His uniformly bright thoughts cause him to be confident, buoyant, and enthusiastic.

GRENVILLE KLEISER

Give your mind positive thoughts to chew on but keep them realistic. You can control your thoughts, and your thoughts control your life.

DORA ALBERT

To get the most out of your life, plant in your mind seeds of constructive power that will yield fruitful results. Acquire the habit of substituting positive ideas for negative ones, and gradually your life will become more and more successful.

GRENVILLE KLEISER

TIME

Time, indeed, is a sacred gift, and each day is a little life.

JOHN LUBBOCK

You wake up in the morning, and lo! Your purse is magically filled with twenty-four hours of the unmanufactured tissue of the universe of your life. It is yours. It is the most precious of possessions. No one can take it from you. It is unstealable. And no one receives more or less than you receive.

ARNOLD BENNETT

All this shall pass away. Then why not enjoy the few days we have on our earthly home. All we have is just loaned to us. When a man has accumulated enough of the material goods to live comfortably why does he keep loading himself up with more and more? Instead of enjoying what he has. Enjoy your little, while the fool is in search for more.

ALFRED ARMAND MONTAPERT

The value of time. What are friends, books or health, the interest of travel, or the delights of home, if we have not time for their employment.

JOHN LUBBOCK

We always have time enough, if we will but use it right.

JOHANN WOLFGANG VON GOETHE

Hours and days, month and years, pass away, and time once past never returns.

MARCUS TULLIUS CICERO

Time is the most valuable thing a man can spend.

THEOPHRASTUS

Know the true value of time; snatch, seize, and enjoy every moment of it.
EARL OF CHESTERFIELD

To everything there is a season and a time to every purpose under the heaven. A time to be born, and a time to die; a time to plant and a time to pluck up that which is planted.
BIBLE

Happy the man and happy he alone, he who can call today his own; he who, secure within, can say, tomorrow, do thy worst, for I have lived today.
JOHN DRYDEN

No person will have occasion to complain of the want of time who never loses any. It is wonderful how much may be done if we are always doing.
THOMAS JEFFERSON

The years pass more quickly as we become older.
ARHTUR SCHOPENHAUER

Time you enjoy wasting is not wasted time.
MARTHE TROLY-CURTIN

The thief to be most wary of is the one who steals your time.
ANONYMOUS

At times it is folly to hasten; at other times, to delay. The wise do everything in its proper time.
OVID

Dost thou love life, then do not squander time, for that's the stuff life is made of.
BENJAMIN FRANKLIN

When one day is like all others, then they are all like one; complete uniformity would make the longest life seem short, and as though it had stolen away from us unawares.
THOMAS MANN

Time, which changes people, does not alter the image we have retained of them.
MARCEL PROUST

Half of our life is spent trying to find something to do with the time we have rushed through life trying to save.
WILL ROGERS

Time heals what reason cannot.
LUCIUS ANNAEUS SENECA

The butterfly counts not months but moments, and has time enough.
RABINDRANATH TAGORE

One realizes the full importance of time only when there is little of it left. Every man's greatest capital asset is his unexpired years of productive life.
P. W. LITCHFIELD

The bad news is time flies. The good news is you're the pilot.
MICHAEL ALTSHULER

Life, if well lived, is long enough.
LUCIUS ANNAEUS SENECA

Seize the hour.
SOPHOCLES

Possessions dwindle: I mourn their loss. But I mourn the loss of time much more, for anyone can save his purse, but none can win back lost time.
LATIN PROVERB

Minutes are worth more than money. Spend them wisely.
THOMAS P. MURPHY

Dollars cannot buy yesterday.
ADMIRAL HAROLD R. STARK

Lost time is never found again.
BENJAMIN FRANKLIN

If a person gives you his time, he can give you no more precious gift.
TYGER

Time isn't a commodity, something you pass around like cake. Time is the substance of life. When anyone asks you to give your time, they're really asking for a chunk of your life.
ANTOINETTE BOSCO

The ability to concentrate and to use time well is everything.
LEE IACOCCA

No matter how much time you've wasted in the past, you still have an entire tomorrow. Success depends upon using it wisely – by planning and setting priorities.
DENIS WAITELY

Make use of time, let not advantage slip.
WILLIAM SHKESPEARE

The highest value in life is found in the stewardship of time.
ROBERT M. FINE

I wish I could stand on a busy corner, hat in hand, and beg people to throw me all their wasted hours.
BERNARD BERENSON

Wasted time means wasted lives.
R. SHANNON

All that time is lost which might be bettered employed.
JEAN-JACQUES ROUSSEAU

What we love to do we find time to do.
JOHN LANCASTER SPALDING

An earnest purpose finds time, or makes it. It seizes on spare moments, and turns fragments to golden account.
WILLIAM ELLERY CHANNING

Each day should be passed as though it were our last.
PUBLILIUS SYRUS

Time is nothing absolute; its duration depends on the rate of thought and feeling.
JOHN DRAPER

An hour of pain is as long as a day of pleasure.
ANONYMOUS

If you don't have time to do it right, when will you have time to do it over.
JOHN WOODEN

Time is money.
BENJAMIN FRANKLIN

Guard well your spare moments. They are like uncut diamonds. Discard them and their value will never be known. Improve them and they will become the brightest gems in a useful life.
RALPH WALDO EMERSON

Look not mournfully into the past, it comes not back again. Wisely improve the present, it is thine. Go forth to meet the shadowy future without fear and with a manly heart.
HENRY WADSWORTH LONGFELLOW

As every thread of gold is valuable, so is every moment of time.
JOHN MASON

What I do today is important because I'm exchanging a day of my life for it.
JOHN WESLEY

The ultimate of being successful is the luxury of giving yourself the time to do what you want to do.

LEONTYNE PRICE

Time is the one thing that can never be retrieved. One may lose and regain a friend; one may lose and regain money; opportunity once spurned may come again; but the hours that are lost in idleness can never be brought back to be used in gainful pursuits. Most careers are made or marred in the hours after supper.

C. R. LAWTON

Don't be fooled by the calendar. There are only as many days in the year as you make use of. One man gets only a week's value out of a year while another man gets a full year's value out of a week.

CHARLES RIICHARDS

A man who dares to waste one hour of life has not discovered the value of life.

CHARLES DARWIN

Time wasted is existence; used is life.

EDWARD YOUNG

Nothing is more highly to be prized than the value of each day.

JOHANN WOLFGANG VON GOETHE

Ordinary people think merely how they shall spend their time; a man of intellect tries to use it.

ARTHUR SCHOPENHAUER

Every man's life lies within the present; for the past is spent and done with, and the future is uncertain.

MARCUS AURELIUS

Time is all you have. And you may find one day that you have less than you think.

RANDY PAUSCH

If you love life, don't waste time, for time is what life is made up of.

BRUCE LEE

Time is more valuable than money. You can get more money, but you cannot get more time.

JIM ROHN

The days are long, but the years are short.

ANONYMOUS

Time gives good advice.

MALTESE PROVERB

One today is worth two tomorrows.

BENJAMIN FRANKLIN

Time is the wisest of all counselors.

PLUTARCH

Tomorrow, tomorrow, not today, hear the lazy people say.

GERMAN PROVERB

Short as life is, we make it still shorter by the careless waste of time.

VICTOR HUGO

It is well to be up before daybreak for such habits contribute to health, wealth, and wisdom.

ARISTOTLE

The early morning hours have gold in their mouth.

DUTCH PROVERB

He that riseth late must trot all day, and shall scarce overtake his business at night.

BENJAMIN FRANKLIN

How careful we are about how we handle our money. Are we as careful about investing our time? Time is our most valuable asset, it is worth far more to us than money which we safeguard so carefully.

DR. PAUL PARKER

TOLERANCE

Tolerance is the positive and cordial effort to understand another's beliefs, practices, and habits without necessarily sharing or accepting them.

JOSHUA LIEBMAN

Tolerance is no excuse for the toleration of evil.

ROGER BABSON

It is easy to be tolerant when you do not care.

CLEMENT F. ROGERS

In the practice of tolerance, one's enemy is the best teacher.

DALAI LAMA

The peak of tolerance is most readily achieved by those who are not burdened with convictions.

ALEXANDER CHASE

True greatness is not without that germ of greatness that can bear with patience the mistakes of the ignorant.

CHARLES CALEB COLTON

Laws alone cannot secure freedom of expression; in order that every man present his views without penalty there must be a spirit of tolerance in the entire population.

ALBERT EINSTEIN

Tolerance implies no lack of commitment to one's own beliefs. Rather it condemns the oppression or persecution of others.

JOHN F. KENNEDY

It is a good thing to demand liberty for ourselves and for those who agree with us, but it is better and a rarer thing to give liberty to others who do not agree with us.

FRANKLIN D. ROOSEVELT

In order to have faith in his own path, he does not need to prove that someone else's path is wrong.

PAULO COELHO

Tolerance isn't about not having beliefs. It's about how your beliefs lead you to treat people who disagree with you.

TIMOTHY KELLER

I do not like what you say but I will defend to the death your right to say it.

VOLTAIRE

Tolerance becomes a crime when applied to evil.

THOMAS MANN

Tolerance is accepting differences in other people. It is thinking 'It is OK that you are different from me.

CYNTHIA AMOROSO

Tolerance is the ability to forgive those who tend to speak before thinking.

CATHERINE PULSIFER

Tolerance is being wise enough to have no difference with those who differ from us.

PAUL CHATFIELD

Discord is the great ill of mankind; and tolerance is the only remedy for it.

VOLTAIRE

Tolerance is the ability to smile when someone else's child behaves as badly as your own.

EVAN ESAR

If people but knew their own religion, how tolerant they would become, and how free from any grudge against the religion of others.

HAZRAT INAYAT KHAN

Since others have to tolerate my weaknesses, it is only fair that I should tolerate theirs.

WILLIAM ALLEN WHITE

Tolerant people are the happiest, so why not get rid of prejudices that hold you back.

WILLIAM MOULTON MARSTON

TRUST

Trust men and they will be true to you; treat them greatly and they will show themselves great.
RALPH WALDO EMERSON

Trust thyself only, and another shall not betray thee.
THOMAS FULLER

Love all, trust a few.
WILLIAM SHAKESPEARE

It's a vice to trust all, and equally a vice to trust none.
SENECA

Put your trust in God and keep your powder dry.
OLIVER CROMWELL

Never be afraid to trust an unknown future to a known God.
CORRIE TEN BOOM

To be trusted is a greater compliment than being loved.
GEORGE MACDONALD

All I have seen teaches me to trust the creator for all I have not seen.
RALPH WALDO EMERSON

A man who doesn't trust himself can never really trust anyone else.
CARDINAL DE RETZ

He who does not trust enough, will not be trusted.
LAO TZU

The most important lesson that I learned is to trust God in every circumstance. Lots of times we go through difficult trials and following God's plan seems like it doesn't make any sense at all. God is always in control and he will never leave us.
ALLYSON FELIX

Trusting our intuition often saves us from disaster.
ANNE WILSON SCHAEF

Men trust their ears less than their eyes.
HERODOTUS

When I get logical, and I don't trust my instincts – that is when I get in trouble.
ANGELINA JOLIE

Trust everyone, but cut the cards.
FINLEY PETER DUNNE

Trust in the Lord with all thine heart; and lean not unto thine own understanding. In all ways acknowledge him, and he shall direct thy paths.
BIBLE

Quit questioning God and start trusting Him!
JOEL OSTEEN

A body of men holding themselves accountable to nobody ought not to be trusted by anybody.
THOMAS PAINE

Don't trust people who tell you other people's secrets.
DAN HOWELL

Peace and trust take years to build and seconds to shatter.
MAHOGANY SILVERRAIN

Let your life reflect the faith you have in God. Fear nothing and pray about everything. Be strong, trust God's word, and trust the process.
GERMANY KENT

A man who trusts nobody is apt to be the kind of man nobody trusts.
HAROLD MACMILLAN

The more you trust your intuition, the more empowered you become, the stronger you become, and the happier you become.
GISELE BUNDCHEN

Trust your hunches. They're usually based on facts filed away just below the conscious level.
DR. JOYCE BROTHERS

It's a delight to trust somebody so completely.
JEFF GOLDBLUM

Trust yourself, you know more than you think you do.
BENJAMIN SPOCK

Put your trust in the Lord and go ahead. Worry gets you no place.
ROY ACUFF

And having thus chosen our course without guile and with pure purpose, let us renew our trust in God and go forward without fear and with manly hearts.
ABRAHAM LINCOLN

It is better to trust in the Lord than to put confidence in man.
BIBLE

Whoever is careless with the truth in small matters cannot be trusted in important affairs.
ALBERT EINSTEIN

The way to learn whether a person is trustworthy is to trust him.
ERNEST HEMINGWAY

TRUTH

It would be wrong to put friendship before the truth.
ARISTOTLE

Truth sits upon the lips of dying men.
MATTHEW ARNOLD

The truth shall make you free.
BIBLE

Look on this beautiful world, and read the truth in her fair page.
WILLIAM CULLEN BRYANT

How often have I said to you that when you have eliminated the impossible, whatever remains, however improbable, must be the truth?
SIR ARTHUR CONAN DOYLE

It is morally as bad not to care whether a thing is true or not, so long as it makes you feel good, as it is not to care how you got your money so long as you have got it.
EDWIN WAY TEALE

Truth and oil always come to the surface.
SPANISH PROVERB

The truth is always the strongest argument.
SOPHOCLES

We know the truth, not only by the reason, but also by the heart.
PASCAL

The truth is cruel, but it can be loved, and it makes free those who have loved it.
GEORGE SANTAYANA

The love of truth has its reward in heaven and even on earth.
FRIEDRICH NIETZSCHE

Truth fears no trial.
THOMAS FULLER

Time trieth truth.
ENGLISH PROVERB

Great is truth and strongest of all.
APOCRYPHA

Dear friends, we must buy truth even if the price is ever so dear. Every parcel of truth is precious, as the filings of gold. We must either live it, or die for it.
THOMAS BROOKS

Great truths can only be forgotten and can never be falsified.
GILBERT KEITH CHESTERTON

A lie gets halfway around the world before the truth has a chance to get its pants on.
WINSTON CHURCHILL

Peace if possible, truth at all costs.
MARTIN LUTHER

Truth matters supremely because in the end, without truth there is no freedom. Truth, in fact, is not only essential to freedom; it is freedom, and the only way to a free life lies in becoming a person of truth and learning to live in truth. Living in truth is the secret of living free.
OS GUINNESS

The further a society drifts from the truth, the more it will hate those that speak it.
GEORGE ORWELL

I have no greater joy than to hear that my children are walking in the truth.
BIBLE

If you look for truth, you may find comfort in the end; if you look for comfort you will not get either comfort or truth only soap and wishful thinking to begin, and in the end, despair.
C. S. LEWIS

We cannot help it if the truth offends people, but we must always make sure that it is the truth that is offending them and not us.
MARTYN LLOYD-JONES

I would rather be divided by truth than united with error.
MARTIN LUTHER

Error does not become Truth because it is widely accepted; Truth does not become error, even when it stands alone.
JOHN MACARTHUR

The truth does not change according to our ability to stomach it.
FLANNERY O'CONNOR

The truth will set you free. But first it will make you miserable.
JOHN ORTBERG

During times of universal deceit, telling the truth becomes a revolutionary act.
GEORGE ORWELL

Truth carries with it confrontation. Truth demands confrontation; loving confrontation, but confrontation nevertheless.
FRANCIS SCHAEFFER

You can resolve to live your life with integrity. Let your credo be this: Let the lie come into the world, let it even triumph. But not through me.
ALEXANDER SOLZHENITSYN

Of course it's the same old story. Truth usually is the same old story.
MARGARET THATCHER

There are two ways to be fooled. One is to believe what isn't true; the other is to refuse to believe what is true.
SOREN KIERKEGAARD

Truth will always be truth, regardless of lack of understanding, disbelief or ignorance.
W. CLEMENT STONE

Three things cannot be hidden: the sun, the moon, and the truth.
CONFUCIUS

I never did give anybody hell. I just told the truth and they thought it was hell.
HARRY S. TRUMAN

WISDOM

The heart of a fool is in his mouth, but the mouth of a wise man is in his heart.
BENJAMIN FRANKLIN

Wise men are not wise all the time.
RALPH WALDO EMERSON

He is not a wise man that cannot play the fool on occasion.
THOMAS FULLER

Wisdom is the principal thing; therefore get wisdom; and with all thy getting get understanding.
BIBLE

Wisdom comes alone through suffering.
AESCHYLUS

Happy is the man that findeth wisdom, and the man that getteth understanding....her ways are ways of pleasantness, and all her paths are peace.... wisdom is the principal thing; therefore get wisdom; and with all thy getting get understanding.
BIBLE

Common-sense in an uncommon degree is what the world calls wisdom.
SAMUEL TAYLOR COLERIDGE

The art of being wise is the art of knowing to overlook.
WILLIAM JAMES

He is happy in his wisdom who learned at another's expense.
TITUS M. PLAUTUS

The price of wisdom is above rubies.
BIBLE

The beginning of wisdom is to call things by their right names.
CHINESE PROVERB

The fear of the Lord is the beginning of wisdom.
BIBLE

It is the province of knowledge to speak, and it is the privilege of wisdom to listen.
OLIVER WENDELL HOLMES

Nine-tenths of wisdom consists in being wise in time.
THEODORE ROOSEVELT

It is wisdom to believe the heart.
GEORGE SANTAYANA

Wisdom is the power to put our time and our knowledge to proper use.
THOMAS J. WATSON

The wise Man, even when he holds his Tongue, says more than the Fool when he speaks.
THOMAS FULLER

The wise does at once what the fool does at last.
BALTASAR GRACIAN

Little is needed to make a wise man happy, but nothing can content a fool.
FRANCOIS DE LA ROCHEFOUCAULD

Wise men talk because they have something to say: fools because they have to say something.

PLATO

A hundred fools together will not make one wise man.

ARTHUR SCHOPENHAUER

The wise seek wisdom; the fool has found it.

SAYING

The wise learn from their mistakes of others; the foolish, not even from their own.

SAYING

Keep the gold and keep the silver, but give us wisdom.

ARABIAN PROVERB

As a solid rock is not shaken by a strong gale, so wise persons remain unaffected by praise or censure.

BUDDHA

Wise men learn more from fools than fools from the wise.

CATO

Be wiser than other people if you can; but do not tell them so.

EARL OF CHESTERFIELD

A single conversation across the table with a wise man is worth a month's study of books.

CHINESE PROVERB

By three methods we may learn wisdom: First, by reflection, which is noblest; Second, by imitation, which is easiest; and third by experience, which is the bitterest.

CONFUCIUS

A good head and a good heart are always a formidable combination.

NELSON MANDELA

The only true wisdom is in knowing you know nothing.
SOCRATES

Cleverness is not wisdom.
EURPIDES

There is a wisdom of the head, and a wisdom of the heart.
CHARLES DICKENS

Wisdom is the reward you get for a lifetime of listening when you'd have preferred to talk.
DOUG LARSON

Wisdom is the supreme part of happiness.
SOPHOCLES

A short saying oft contains much wisdom.
SOPHOCLES

A fool doth think he is wise, but the wise man knows himself a fool.
WILLIAM SHAKESPEARE

It is a characteristic of wisdom not to do desperate things.
HENRY DAVID THOREAU

Wisdom is not wisdom when it is derived from books alone.
HORACE

Good people are good because they've come to wisdom through failure. We get very little wisdom from success, you know.
WILLIAM SARAYAN

Great men are the commissioned guides of mankind, who rule their fellows because they are wiser.
THOMAS CARLYLE

The wisest have the most authority.
PLATO

The price of wisdom is eternal thought.
FRANK BIRCH

Wisdom is the power that enables us to use knowledge for the benefit of ourselves and others.
THOMAS J. WATSON

Wisdom is knowing when to speak your mind and when to mind your speech.
EVANGEL

The wisest mind has something yet to learn.
GEORGE SANTAYANA

In seeking wisdom, thou art wise; in imagining that thou hast attained it, thou art a fool.
BEN SIRA

Wisdom makes her sons exalted, and lays hold of those who seek her. Whoever loves her, loves life. And those who seek her early will be filled with joy.
BEN SIRA

If one extends knowledge to the utmost, one will have wisdom. Having wisdom, one can then make choices.
CHENG YI

Great is wisdom; infinite is the value of wisdom. It cannot be exaggerated; it is the highest achievement of man.
THOMAS CARLYLE

Wisdom is to the mind what health is to the body.
FRANCOIS DE LA ROCHEFOUCAULD

The mintage of wisdom is to know that rest is rust, and that real life is in love, laughter, and work.
ELBERT HUBBARD

To finish the moment, to find the journey's end in every stop of the road, to live the greatest number of good hours, is wisdom.
RALPH WALDO EMERSON

Wisdom is knowing what to do next; virtue is doing it.
DAVID STARR JORDAN

The invariable mark of wisdom is to see the miraculous in the common.
RALPH WALDO EMERSON

The clouds may drop down titles and estates; wealth may seek us; but wisdom must be sought.
EDWARD YOUNG

The growth of wisdom may be gauged accurately by the decline of ill-temper.
FRIEDRICH NIETZSCHE

Wisdom denotes the pursuing of the best ends by the best means.
FRANCES HUTCHESON

It takes a wise man to discover a wise man.
DIOGENES

Time ripens all things. No man is born wise.
MIGUEL DE CERVANTES

He bids fair to grow wise who has discovered that he is not so.
PUBLILIUS SYRUS

The wisest man could ask no more of fate than to be simple, modest, manly, true, safe from the many, honored by the few; nothing to court in church, or world, or state, but inwardly in secret to be great.
JAMES RUSSELL LOWELL

I don't think much of a man who is not wiser today than he was yesterday.
ABRAHAM LINCOLN

The wise man corrects his own errors by observing those of others.
PUBLILIUS SYRUS

A wise man reflects before he speaks; a fool speaks, and then reflects on what he has uttered.
FRENCH PROVERB

The fool wonders, the wise man asks.
BENJAMIN DISRAELI

Wisdom is more precious than rubies, and all the things thou canst desire are not to be compared unto her.
BIBLE

Man who know little say much. Man who know much say little.
SAYING

WORK

Work smarter, not harder.
AMERICAN SAYING

Discover as soon as possible the time of the day at which you work best.
A. B. ZU TAVERN

Let every man be occupied, and occupied in the highest employment of which his nature is capable, and die with the consciousness that he has done his best.
SYDNEY SMITH

The most important thing in life is the choice of a profession.
BLAISE PASCAL

Work expands so as to fill the time available for its completion.
C. NORTHCOTE PARKINSON

Work keeps from three great evils: boredom, vice, and want.
VOLTAIRE

It is not real work unless you would rather be doing something else.
JAMES M. BARRIE

When work is a pleasure, life is a joy. When work is a duty, life is slavery.
MAXIM GORKY

As a remedy against all ills – poverty, sickness, and melancholy – only one thing is absolutely necessary: a liking for work.
CHARLES BAUDELAIRE

Work is the means of living, but it is not living.
JOSIAH GILBERT HOLLAND

Love labor: for if thou dost not want it for food, thou mayest for physic. It is wholesome for thy body and good for thy mind.
WILLIAM PENN

A man is not idle because he is absorbed in thought. There is a visible labour and there is an invisible labour.
VICTOR HUGO

Thou, O God, dost sell us all good things at the price of labor.
LEONARDO DA VINCI

It is a poor art that maintains not the artisan.
ITALIAN PROVERB

Do your work with your whole heart and you will succeed – there is so little competition!
ELBERT HUBBARD

It is necessary to work, if not from inclination, at least from despair. Everything considered, work is less boring than amusing oneself.
CHARLES BAUDELAIRE

His brow is wet with honest sweat, he earns whate'er he can, and looks the whole world in the face, for he owes not any man.
HENRY WADSWORTH LONGFELLOW

In any given group, the most will do the least and the least the most.
MERLE P. MARTIN

It's not work, if you love what you're doing.
STEVE SEARS

Work is the price you pay for money.
ANONYMOUS

Your time is limited, so don't waste it living someone else's life. Don't be trapped by dogma – which is living with the results of other people's thinking.
STEVE JOBS

Most people spend most of their days doing what they do not want to in order to earn the right, at times, to do what they may desire.
JOHN MASON BROWN

There is only one thing for a man to do who is married to a woman who enjoys spending money, and that is to enjoy earning it.
EDGAR WATSON HOWE

No man is born into the world whose work is not born with him; there is always work, and tools to work withal, for those who will.
JAMES RUSSELL LOWELL

Far and away the best prize that life offers is the chance to work hard at work worth doing.
THEODORE ROOSEVELT

A dream does not become reality through magic; it takes sweat, determination, and hard work.
COLIN POWELL

Hard works beats talent if talent doesn't work hard.
TIM NOTKE

The highest reward for man's toil is not what he gets for it but what he becomes by it.
JOHN RUSKIN

I'm a great believer in luck, and I find the harder I work, the more I have of it.
THOMAS JEFFERSON

Doing the best at this moment puts you in the best place for the next moment.
OPRAH WINFREY

Work hard, have fun, make history.
JEFF BEZOS

But though labor is good for man, it may be, and unfortunately often is, carried to excess. Many are wearily asking themselves, "Ah why should life all labor be?"
JOHN LUBBOCK

Life has granted nothing to mankind save through great labor.
HORACE

Without labor, nothing prospers.
SOPHOCLES

If you love your work, you'll be out there every day trying to do it the best you can possibly can, and pretty soon everybody around will catch the passion from you - like a fever.
SAM WALTON

Talent is cheaper than table salt. What separates the talented individual from the successful one is hard work.
STEPHEN KING

If you want work well done, select a busy man: the other kind has no time.
ELBERT HUBBARD

A lot of hard work is hidden behind nice things.
RALPH LAUREN

The only way to do great work is to love what you do.
STEVE JOBS

When you undervalue what you do, the world will undervalue who you are.
OPRAH WINFREY

A day's work is a day's work, neither more nor less, and the man who does it needs a day's sustenance, a night's repose and due leisure, whether he be a painter or ploughman.
GEORGE BERNARD SHAW

Continuity of purpose is one of the most essential ingredients of happiness in the long run, and for most men this comes chiefly through their work.
BERTRAND RUSSELL

The work praises the man.
IRISH PROVERB

Whenever it is possible, a boy should choose some occupation which he should do even if he did not need the money.
WILLIAM LYON PHELPS

To love what you do and feel that it matters – how could anything be more fun?
KATHERINE GRAHAM

Opportunity is missed by most people because it is dressed in overalls, and looks like work.
THOMAS ALVA EDISON

I can't imagine anything more worthwhile than doing what I most love. And they pay me for it.
EDGAR WINTER

Do not hire a man who does your work for money, but him who does it for the love of it.
HENRY DAVID THOREAU

I think the person who takes a job in order to live – that is to say, for the money – has turned himself into a slave.
JOSEPH CAMPBELL

The best preparation for good work tomorrow is to do good work today.

ELBERT HUBBARD

To find out what one is fitted to do, and to secure an opportunity to do it, is the key to happiness.

JOHN DEWEY

If you put all your strength and faith and vigor into a job and try to do the best you can, the money will come.

LAWERENCE WELK

Work is the grand cure of all the maladies and miseries that ever beset mankind – honest work, which you intend getting done.

THOMAS CARLYLE

Labor, if it were not necessary for the existence, would be indispensable for the happiness of man.

SAMUEL JOHNSON

When skill and love work together, expect a masterpiece.

JOHN RUSKIN

There is honor in labor. Work is the medicine of the soul. It is more: it is your very life, without which you would amount to little.

GRENVILLE KLEISER

When a man has equipped himself by thought and study for a bigger job, it usually happens that promotion comes along even before it is expected.

P. G. WINNETT

Labor is rest from the sorrows that greet us; from all the petty vexations that meet us; from the sin-promptings that assail us; from the world-sirens that lure us to ill.

F. S. OSGOOD

We ought not to judge of men's merits by their qualifications, but by the use they make of them.

CHARRON

Nothing worthwhile comes easily. Half effort does not produce half results. It produces no results. Work, continuous work and hard work, is the only way to accomplish results that lasts.

HAMILTON HOLT

People forget how fast you did a job – but they remember how well you did it.

HOWARD W. NEWTON

Men who do things without being told draw the most wages.

EDWIN H. STUART

Work is the greatest remedy available for both mental and physical afflictions.

KORSAREN

We would rather have one man or woman working with us than three merely working for us.

J. DABNEY DAY

A professional is a man who can do his job when he doesn't feel like it. An amateur is a man who can't do his job when he does feel like it.

JAMES AGATE

To know how to do something well is to enjoy it.

PEARL S. BUCK

Work is good, provided you do not forget to live.

BANTU PROVERB

I see no virtues where I smell no sweat.

FRANCIS QUARLES

What is the good life if its chief element, and that which must always be its chief element, is odious? No, the only economy is to arrange so that your daily labour shall be useful joy.

EDWARD CARPENTER

To provide a good living for himself and family is the very first duty of every man.
WILLIAM COBBETT

Now pause with yourselfe, and view the end of all your labours...unspeakable pleasure and infinite commodity.
WILLIAM LAWSON

In order that people may be happy in their work, these three things are needed: They must be fit for it: they must not do too much of it: and they must have a sense of success in it.
JOHN RUSKIN

When men are rightly occupied their amusement grows out of their work as the color-petals out of a fruitful flower.
JOHN RUSKIN

The day is always his who works in it with serenity and great aims.
RALPH WALDO EMERSON

All service ranks the same with God.
ROBERT BROWNING

Whatsoever thy hand findeth to do, do it with thy might.
BIBLE

Begin; to have begun is half of the work. Let the half still remain; again begin this and thou wilt have done all.
AUSONIUS

By the work one knows the workman.
JEAN DE LA FONTAINE

If people knew how hard I have had to work to gain my mastery, it wouldn't seem wonderful at all.
MICHAELANGELO

To the man who himself strives earnestly, God also lends a helpful hand.
AESCHYLUS

If it falls your lot to be a street sweeper, sweep streets as Raphael painted pictures, sweep streets as Michelangelo carved marble, sweep streets as Beethoven composed music, sweep streets as Shakespeare wrote poetry. Seep streets so well that all the hosts of Heaven and earth will have to pause and say, "Here lived a great street sweeper who swept his job well."
MARTIN LUTHER KING, JR.

When love and skill work together, expect a masterpiece.
CHARLES READE

Whatever is worth doing at all, is worth doing well.
EARL OF CHESTERFIELD

Always do more than is required of you.
GEORGE SMITH PATTON

It is quality rather than quantity that counts.
LUCIUS ANNAEUS SENECA

You can only become truly accomplished at something you love. Don't make money your goal. Instead, pursue the things you love doing, and then do them so well that people can't take their eyes off you.
MAYA ANGELOU

The biggest mistake people make in life is not trying to make a living at doing what they enjoy most.
MALCOLM FORBES

Everything considered, work is less boring than amusing oneself.
CHARLES BAUDELAIRE

Labor is man's greatest function. He is nothing, he can do nothing, he can achieve nothing, he can fulfill nothing, without work.
ORVILLE DEWEY

Man must work. That is certain as the sun. But he may work grudgingly or he may work gratefully; he may work as a man, or he may work as a machine. There is no work so rude, that he may not exalt it; no work so impassive, that he may not breathe a soul into it; no work so dull that he may not enliven it.

HENRY GILES

Unless the job means more than the pay it will never pay more.

H. BERTRAM LEWIS

The best mental work is accomplished in the early morning hours when the mind is rested, recuperated and vigorous; hence early rising is advisable.

WALTER MATTHEWS

I never knew an early rising, hard-working, prudent man who complained of bad luck.

JOSEPH ADDISON

ABOUT THE AUTHOR

Born and raised in northeastern Indiana, Larry John Phillips is married with 2 children and 5 grandchildren. He is a semi-retired business owner with a B.S. degree from Purdue University. During his free time, in addition to collecting quotations, Larry enjoys playing golf, gardening and spending time at their lake cottage with family.

During the last 40 years, Larry collected quotations on different topics and formed a habit of reflecting on them as part of his morning routine. Over the years he continued to expand the collection of his favorite quotations and today it consists of over 100 topics and nearly 5,000 quotations. The journey with quotations has had a profound, uplifting, and thought-provoking impact on his life.

Progressive Rising Phoenix Press is an independent publisher. We offer wholesale pricing and multiple binding options with no minimum purchases for schools, libraries, book clubs, and retail vendors. We offer substantial discounts on bulk orders and discounts on individual sales through our online store. Please visit our website at:

www.ProgressiveRisingPhoenix.com

If you enjoyed reading this book, please review it on Amazon, B & N, or Goodreads. Thank you in advance!